The Usborne
Essential
Atlas
of the World

Stephanie Turnbull

Designers: Stephen Moncrieff and Helen Wood
Consultant cartographic editor: Craig Asquith

Cartography by European Map Graphics Ltd
Map design by Laura Fearn
and Keith Newell

Usborne Quicklinks

The Usborne Quicklinks Website is packed with links to all the best websites on the internet. For links to over 50 recommended websites for this book, go to www.usborne-quicklinks.com and enter the keywords "essential atlas".

There you will find links to websites where you can:
- explore interactive maps of the Earth
- discover how satellite images can show the way land and weather can change over time
- take virtual tours of countries around the world
- try quizzes to test your general knowledge of countries across the globe
- find out about some of the world's wildlife and habitats

Internet safety
When using the internet, make sure you follow these internet safety guidelines which are also displayed on the Usborne Quicklinks Website.

- Children should ask their parent's or guardian's permission before using the internet.
- Never give details of your full name, address, telephone number or school, or any other personal information.
- If a website asks you to log in or register by typing your name or email address, children should ask an adult's permission first.

The recommended websites are regularly reviewed and updated, but Usborne Publishing is not responsible and does not accept liability for the availability or content of any website other than its own, or for any exposure to harmful, offensive, or inaccurate material which may appear on the Web. We recommend that children are supervised while on the internet. For more on using the internet safely and securely, see the Net Help area on the Usborne Quicklinks Website.

CONTENTS

MAPS AND ATLASES

A map is an image that represents a particular area of the Earth's surface, usually from above and at a reduced size. A map can show the whole world or just a street. An atlas is a collection of maps, along with useful information about the areas shown.

What maps show

Unlike an aerial photograph, which shows exactly what an area looks like from above, a map can show features of the area in a clearer, simplified way. There can be many kinds of maps of a place, each giving different kinds of information. For example, maps can show the names of places, the position of borders between countries, or the types of crops that grow.

This map was drawn in 1584. Although people at this time knew much less about the shapes and locations of countries, they still created many maps of the world.

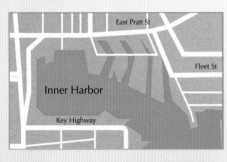

On the left is a simple map of Baltimore Harbor, U.S.A. It just shows the area's main streets.

On this aerial photograph of the same area it's difficult to see the streets.

Internet links

For links to websites where you can find out more about maps and map-making, see physical and political maps of different countries, and find street maps of towns and cities around the world, go to **www.usborne-quicklinks.com**.

Map features

Maps are designed to be clear, so most of them use conventions to help us recognize certain features. Land is often shown as green, and seas, rivers and lakes are usually shown as blue. Symbols can also be used to represent features. The meanings of the symbols are usually explained in a key.

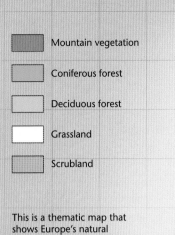

Mountain vegetation

Coniferous forest

Deciduous forest

Grassland

Scrubland

This is a thematic map that shows Europe's natural vegetation. The key above indicates the type of land that the different shading represents.

Kinds of maps

There are many different kinds of maps. Physical maps focus on natural features such as mountains, rivers and lakes. Political maps focus on the division of the Earth's surface into separate states*.

Some maps are thematic. This means that only certain information, such as climate types or population, is represented. You can find out more about thematic maps on pages 14 and 15.

Which way is up?

Although the Earth doesn't have a top and a bottom, north is usually at the top of maps. But it is sometimes more convenient to reposition a map, so north might not necessarily be at the top. Some maps have a compass symbol that indicates where north lies.

Scale

The size of a map in relation to the area it shows is called its scale. Some maps have a scale bar, which is a rule with measurements. It tells you how many miles or km are represented by a certain distance on the map. Other maps show this ratio in numbers. The figure 1:100 may mean,

for example, that 1cm on the map represents 100cm on the Earth's surface. The scale of a map depends on its purpose. A map showing the whole world is on a very small scale, but a town plan is on a much larger scale so that features, such as roads and buildings, can be shown clearly.

1:80,000,000

| 0 | 1,000 | 2,000 | 3,000km |

| 0 | | 1,000 | 2,000 miles |

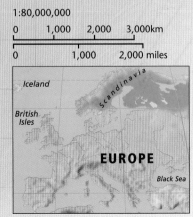

This map of Europe is on a small scale so that it all fits onto one small map.

1:7,000,000

| 0 | 100 | 200 | 300km |

| 0 | | 100 | 200 miles |

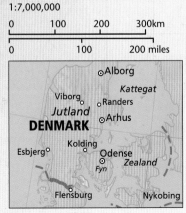

This map of Denmark is on a larger scale to show more detail.

DIVIDING LINES

Map-makers divide up the Earth with imaginary lines that help us measure distances and find where places are. There are two sets of lines, called latitude and longitude.

This Arctic fox lives in northern Canada, very near the Arctic Circle line of latitude.

Latitude lines

Lines of latitude run around the globe. They are parallel to each other and get shorter the closer they are to the two poles. The latitude line that runs around the middle of the Earth is called the Equator. It is the most important line of latitude as all other lines are measured north or south of it.

Longitude lines

Lines of longitude run from the North Pole to the South Pole. All the lines are the same length, and they all meet at the North and South Poles.

The most important line of longitude is the Prime Meridian Line, which runs through Greenwich, in England. All other lines of longitude are measured east or west of this line.

Other lines

The Equator is not the only named latitude line. The Tropic of Cancer is a line north of the Equator, and the Tropic of Capricorn is at the same distance south of the Equator. Between these lines is the hottest, stormiest part of the world. It is called the tropics.

The Arctic Circle is a latitude line far north of the Equator. The area north of this includes the North Pole and is called the Arctic. On the other side of the globe is the Antarctic Circle. The area south of this includes the South Pole and is known as the Antarctic.

Latitude lines   Longitude lines

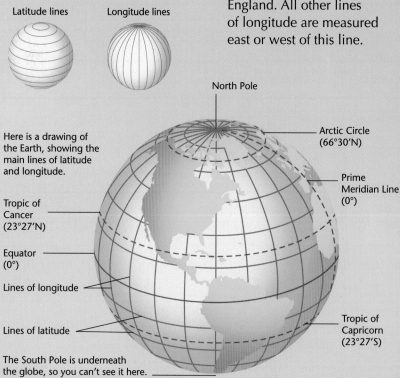

Here is a drawing of the Earth, showing the main lines of latitude and longitude.

North Pole

Arctic Circle (66°30'N)

Prime Meridian Line (0°)

Tropic of Cancer (23°27'N)

Equator (0°)

Lines of longitude

Lines of latitude

Tropic of Capricorn (23°27'S)

The South Pole is underneath the globe, so you can't see it here.

Internet links

For links to websites where you can find out more about maps and map-making and how lines of latitude and longitude are used in GPS, go to **www.usborne-quicklinks.com**

Using the lines

Lines of latitude and longitude are measured in degrees (°). We describe the positions of places according to which lines of latitude and longitude are nearest to them. For example, a place with a location of 50°S and 100°E has a latitude 50 degrees south of the Equator, and a longitude 100 degrees east of the Prime Meridian Line.

Exact locations

The distance between degrees is divided up to give even more precise measurements. Each degree is divided into 60 minutes ('), and each minute is divided into 60 seconds ("). The subdivisions allow us to locate any place on Earth. For example, the city of New York, U.S.A., is at 40°42'51"N and 74°00'23"W.

The steamy rainforests of Malaysia lie near the Equator. Many orangutans, like the one shown here, live in these rainforests.

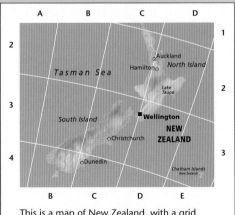

This is a map of New Zealand, with a grid formed by lines of latitude and longitude.

Using a grid

Lines of latitude and longitude form grids on maps. The maps in this book look similar to the one on the left. The vertical columns formed by lines of longitude are marked with letters, and the horizontal rows formed by lines of latitude are numbered.

All the places listed in the map index on page 98 have a letter and a number reference that tell you where to find them on a particular page. For example, on the map on the left, the city of Christchurch would have a grid reference of C3.

LOOKING AT THE EARTH

Modern technology has enabled scientists to make more accurate maps of the world than ever before. Even remote places, such as deserts, ocean floors and mountain ranges, have been mapped in detail using information from satellites that observe the Earth from space.

What is a satellite?

Artificial satellites are machines that orbit, or travel around, the Earth. They observe the Earth using a technique called remote sensing. Instruments on the satellite monitor the Earth without touching it, and send back pictures of its surface. Satellites also monitor moons and other planets.

This satellite monitors the Earth 24 hours a day. It uses powerful radar that pierces through clouds. This means that the satellite can provide images of the Earth in all weather conditions.

Satellite movement

Some satellites orbit the Earth at a height of between 5km (3 miles) and 1,500km (930 miles), providing views of different parts of the planet. Others stay above the same place all the time, moving at the same speed as the Earth rotates to give a constant view of a particular area. These are called geostationary satellites. They travel at a height of around 36,000km (22,370 miles).

Internet links

For links to websites where you can find out more about maps and map-making and see detailed satellite images of the Earth, go to **www.usborne-quicklinks.com**

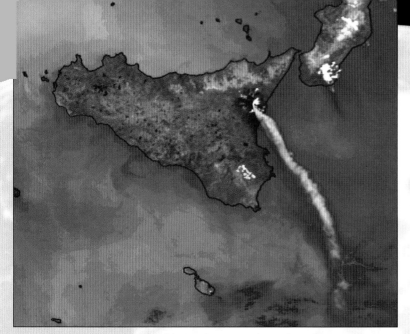

Satellite uses

The information provided by satellites helps scientists to produce accurate maps. Satellite pictures can also be used to help predict and monitor natural hazards such as volcanic eruptions or earthquakes. Some satellites monitor the weather. Satellite images can also show the effects that people have on their environment, for example the destruction of rainforests in South America.

This satellite image of Sicily was taken in July 2001. It shows the volcano Mount Etna erupting. You can see smoke from the volcano on the right of the picture.

Remote sensing

Satellites use a range of remote sensing techniques. One type is radar, which can provide images of the Earth even when it is dark or cloudy. Radar works by reflecting radio waves off a target object. The time it takes for a wave to bounce back indicates how far away the object is.

Powerful cameras provide pictures of the Earth's surface. Often, infrared cameras are used. Different surfaces reflect the infrared rays differently, so infrared images of the Earth are able to show its various types of land surfaces, such as deserts, grasslands and forests.

This satellite image of the Earth shows different types of land. Deserts and other dry regions are red, and areas with lots of vegetation are orange and yellow.

HOW MAPS ARE MADE

The process of making maps is called cartography. Map-makers, or cartographers, compile each map by gathering information about the area and then representing it as an image as accurately as possible.

Internet links

For links to websites where you can find out more about maps and map-making, go to **www.usborne-quicklinks.com**

Creating maps

Many sources are used to create maps. These include satellite images and aerial photographs. Cartographers often visit the area to be mapped, where they take many extra measurements.

In addition, cartographers use statistics, such as population figures, from censuses and other documents. As the maps are being made, many people check them to make sure they are accurate and up-to-date.

Map projections

Cartographers can't draw maps that show the world exactly as it is, because it is impossible to show a curved surface on a flat map without distorting (stretching or squashing) some areas. A representation of the Earth on a map is called a projection. Projections are worked out using complex mathematics.

There are three basic types of projections – cylindrical, conical and azimuthal, but there are also variations on these. They all distort the Earth's surface in some way, either by altering the shapes or sizes of areas of land or the distance between places.

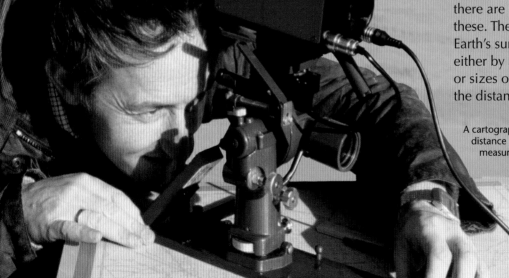

A cartographer uses an electronic distance measurer to check the measurements of an area of land.

Cylindrical projections

A cylindrical projection is similar to what you would get if you wrapped a piece of paper around a globe to form a cylinder and then shone a light inside the globe. The shapes of countries would be projected onto the paper. Near the middle they would be accurate, but farther away they would be distorted.

Cartographers often alter the basic cylindrical projection to make the distortion less obvious in certain areas, but they can never make a map that is completely accurate.

This picture of a piece of paper wrapped around a globe illustrates how a cylindrical projection is made.

Below is a type of cylindrical projection called the Mercator Projection, which was invented in 1596 by a cartographer named Gerardus Mercator. It makes countries the right shape, but makes those near the poles too big.

This cylindrical projection makes countries the right size in relation to each other, but some parts are too long. The projection was created in 1973 by Arno Peters. It is called the Peters Projection.

Conical projections

A conical projection is similar to the image you would get if you wrapped a cone of paper around part of a globe, then shone a light inside the globe. Where the cone touches the globe, the projection will be most accurate.

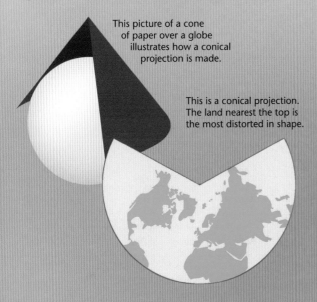

This picture of a cone of paper over a globe illustrates how a conical projection is made.

This is a conical projection. The land nearest the top is the most distorted in shape.

Azimuthal projections

An azimuthal projection is like an image made by holding paper in front of a globe, and shining a light through it. Land projected onto the middle of the paper would be accurate, but areas farther away would be distorted.

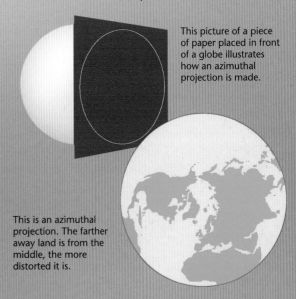

This picture of a piece of paper placed in front of a globe illustrates how an azimuthal projection is made.

This is an azimuthal projection. The farther away land is from the middle, the more distorted it is.

STATES AND BORDERS

The world's main land masses, which are called continents, are divided into independent states and dependent territories. The different areas are separated by borders.

What is a state?

A state is an area of land that has its own government* and is fully independent. Independent states are also known as countries.

Some large countries, such as the U.S.A., are split into several regions. Each region has its own government, which is responsible for the affairs of that region. In the U.S.A. these regions are also known as states.

Changing states

States don't always stay the same. They can divide or merge. For example, Germany was split into two states after the Second World War, and was then reunited as one state in 1990. Sometimes an area becomes independent and a new state is formed. For example, Croatia and Slovenia were once part of Yugoslavia, but are now separate states.

The picture above shows people sitting on the Berlin Wall. The wall formed a border between East and West Berlin when East and West Germany were separate states. It has now been pulled down.

What is a territory?

A dependent territory is an area of land that has a very limited government or no government at all. Instead, the land is owned and governed by a separate, independent state. For example, French Guiana in South America is a dependent territory of France.

*Governments, 83

Border disputes

Sometimes states disagree about where the border between them should be. This can lead to long conflicts, such as the war between Eritrea and Ethiopia. Eritrea was once part of Ethiopia but became an independent state in 1993. The two countries are still disputing the position of the border between them. Thousands of people have been killed in the conflict.

Borders often follow natural features such as rivers or mountain ranges. The Danube River separates several countries. Above, it is shown separating Serbia (left) and Romania (right).

Internet links

For links to websites where you can find flags, facts, maps, and try quizzes to test your knowledge of different countries around the world, go to **www.usborne-quicklinks.com**

Some borders are marked by barriers. Guards check that anyone crossing from one state to another is permitted to do so. This barrier marks the border between Belarus and Poland.

THEMATIC MAPS

Maps that represent information on particular themes, like the ones on these pages, are known as thematic maps. They help you to identify patterns and make comparisons between the features of different areas.

Earth's resources

The Earth contains all kinds of useful resources. Rocks and minerals can be used as building materials, and fuels such as coal, oil and gas contain energy that can be turned into heat and electricity.

Countries with large amounts of natural resources can become very rich. For example, Saudi Arabia, in western Asia, has large oil and gas reserves, which it exports all over the world.

This is an oil field, where oil is extracted from the ground using pumps. It is then piped to refineries and turned into products such as motor fuel.

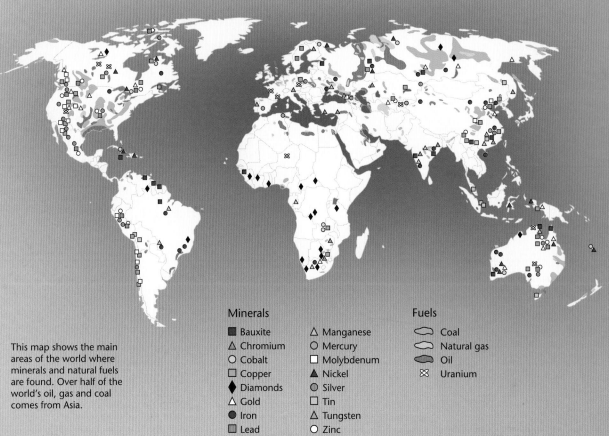

This map shows the main areas of the world where minerals and natural fuels are found. Over half of the world's oil, gas and coal comes from Asia.

Minerals

- ■ Bauxite
- △ Chromium
- ○ Cobalt
- □ Copper
- ◆ Diamonds
- △ Gold
- ● Iron
- ▨ Lead
- △ Manganese
- ○ Mercury
- □ Molybdenum
- ▲ Nickel
- ◍ Silver
- □ Tin
- △ Tungsten
- ○ Zinc

Fuels

- ⬭ Coal
- ⬭ Natural gas
- ⬭ Oil
- ⊠ Uranium

Different climates

The long-term or typical pattern of weather in a particular area is known as its climate. Climates vary across the world and depend largely on each area's latitude. The hottest parts of the world are those closest to the Equator.

Climate is also affected by other factors, such as wind and the height of the land. Oceans influence climate too – places near the sea normally have a milder, wetter climate than areas farther inland.

On this map, land is divided into five climate types. Dry areas are generally hot, but temperatures there can fall very low too. Some dry places, such as the Gobi Desert in eastern Asia, are extremely cold in winter.

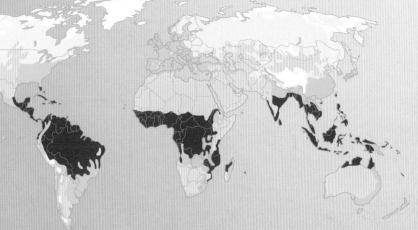

☐ Polar
☐ Cold
☐ Temperate
☐ Dry
■ Tropical

World population

There are more than six billion people in the world, and the population is still growing. Experts think it may reach more than nine billion by 2050. The number of people living in a given area is known as its population density. Europe and Asia are the most densely populated continents in the world. About a third of the world's population lives in China and India alone.

Internet link

For links to websites where you can find out more about maps and map-making and the population of the world, go to **www.usborne-quicklinks.com**

This map shows the average population density by country. The shading indicates the number of people per sq km (0.386 sq miles).

■ Over 500 people
▦ 200–500 people
☐ 100–200 people
☐ 50–100 people
☐ 10–50 people
☐ Fewer than 10 people

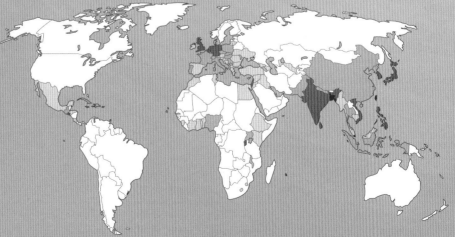

HOW TO USE THE MAPS

The maps in this atlas cover the whole world and are grouped by continent. At the beginning of each section there is a political map showing the whole continent. The rest of the maps are larger scale maps showing more detailed views of the region.

Political maps

The shading on the political maps in this book is there to help you see clearly the different states, or countries, that make up each continent. The main purpose of these maps is to show country borders and capital cities. Alongside them there are facts and figures about the continents and their features.

This is a section of the political map of South America. You can see the whole map on pages 30–31.

Environmental maps

The majority of the maps in this book are environmental maps, like the one on the right. The shading on these maps shows different types of land, or environments, such as desert, mountain or wetland.

The main key on the opposite page shows what the different shading means. It also shows the symbols used to represent towns, cities and other features. There is a smaller key on each environmental map repeating the most important information from this key.

Finding places

To find a particular place or feature on the environmental maps, look up its name in the index on pages 98–111. Its page number and grid reference is given next to the name. You can find out how to use the grid on page 7.

The map on the right is part of the environmental map of the U.S.A. The numbered labels at the top explain some important features of these maps.

❶ The letters and numbers in the border help you to find a place you have looked up in the index.

❷ Lines of latitude and longitude are shown as thin blue lines.

❸ The names of countries are shown in large, bold type with capital letters.

❹ The thick purple lines are country boundaries.

❺ The thinner purple lines are boundaries of internal regions within a country.

Main key

Land cover:
- Boreal forest
- Temperate forest
- Tropical forest
- Temperate grassland
- Savanna
- Semi-desert and scrub
- Hot desert
- Wetland
- Mountain (Only high mountains are marked.)
- Tundra
- Ice
- Cultivation
- Urban

Cities and towns:
- ■ National capital
- ● Internal capital
- ⊙ Major city or town
- ○ Other town

Boundaries:
- International boundary
- International boundary through water
- Internal boundary
- Internal boundary through water

Water features:
- Sea
- Lake or reservoir
- Seasonal lake
- Dry lake/salt pan
- River
- Seasonal river
- Waterfall/dam

Other features:
- ▲ 2,490m (7,988ft) Height above or below sea level (Only a selection of elevation points are given. Places below sea level have a minus sign in front of the height.)
- ⁛ Ruin or other place of interest
- ᴨᴨᴨ Ancient wall

Scale:
This tells you the size of the map in relation to the area it represents. For example:

1:10,900,000

| 0 | 200 | 400km |

| 0 | 100 | 200 | 300 miles |

GREENLAND
(Denmark)

ICELAND

NORW

ALASKA
(U.S.A.)

Arctic Circle

C A N A D A

DENMA

UNITED
KINGDOM

IRELAND

NETH

BELG.

LU

SW

FRANCE

UNITED STATES
OF AMERICA

Azores
(Portugal)

PORTUGAL

SPAIN

TUNI

MOROCCO

Canary Islands
(Spain)

ALGERI

Tropic of Cancer

WESTERN SAHARA
(Morocco)

Hawaiian
Islands
(U.S.A.)

20°
N

THE BAHAMAS

MAURITANIA

MALI

NIG

MEXICO

CUBA

DOMINICAN
REPUBLIC

HAITI

CAPE VERDE

SENEGAL

THE GAMBIA
GUINEA-BISSAU

BURKINA
FASO

BENIN

BELIZE

GUATEMALA

HONDURAS

JAMAICA

DOMINICA

GUINEA

TOGO

NIGE

EL SALVADOR

NICARAGUA

Caribbean Sea

SIERRA LEONE

IVORY
COAST

GHANA

COSTA RICA

TRINIDAD AND TOBAGO

LIBERIA

PANAMA

VENEZUELA

GUYANA

SURINAME

EQUATOR
GUIN

P A C I F I C

COLOMBIA

FRENCH GUIANA
(France)

SAO TOME AND
PRINCIPE

O C E A N

Galapagos Islands
(Ecuador)

ECUADOR

A T L A N T I C

Equator

KIRIBATI

PERU

BRAZIL

O C E A N

Cook
Islands
(New Zealand)

French
Polynesia
(France)

BOLIVIA

20°
S

Tropic of Capricorn

Pitcairn
Islands
(U.K.)

PARAGUAY

1:72,700,000

CHILE

URUGUAY

0   1,000   2,000   3,000   4,000   5,000km

ARGENTINA

0   1,000   2,000   3,000 miles

Falkland Islands
(U.K.)

South Georgia
(U.K.)

40°

Antarctic Circle

Weddell
Sea

ARCTIC OCEAN

20° E   40°   60°   80°   100°   120°   140°   160°   180°

Svalbard
(Norway)

Arctic Circle   80°

RUSSIA   60°

WEDEN FINLAND
          ESTONIA
LATVIA
RUSSIA LITHUANIA
RMANY   BELARUS
POLAND
CZECH REP.
S.. SLOVAKIA UKRAINE
.. HUNGARY MOLDOVA
O.. ROMANIA
..B.H. SERB. BULGARIA
MONT. KOS.
Y.. MAC. GEORGIA
ALB.
          GREECE TURKEY

KAZAKHSTAN

Black Sea   Caspian   UZBEKISTAN   KYRGYZSTAN
             Sea
ARM.   TAJIKISTAN
AZER. TURKMENISTAN

MONGOLIA

NORTH
KOREA
SOUTH
KOREA   **JAPAN**   40°

CYPRUS SYRIA
LEB. ISRAEL IRAQ   **IRAN**   AFGHANISTAN
Mediterranean Sea JORDAN   **CHINA**
LIBYA   KUWAIT   PAKISTAN

PACIFIC

OCEAN

Tropic of Cancer

EGYPT   BAHRAIN   NEPAL   BHUTAN   20°
SAUDI QATAR   N
ARABIA U.A.E. OMAN   BANGLA-
                        DESH   BURMA
            INDIA   (MYANMAR) LAOS
CHAD   THAILAND VIETNAM   **PHILIPPINES**   Northern
SUDAN   ERITREA YEMEN   CAMBODIA   Mariana
         DJIBOUTI   Islands
CENTRAL   SRI LANKA   (U.S.A.)   **MARSHALL**
AFRICAN ETHIOPIA   **ISLANDS**
REPUBLIC   SOMALIA   BRUNEI
MEROON
BON UGANDA KENYA   MALDIVES   **MALAYSIA**   **PALAU**   **FEDERATED STATES**
NGO CONGO RWANDA   SINGAPORE   **OF MICRONESIA**   Equator   0°
(DEMOCRATIC BURUNDI
REPUBLIC) TANZANIA   SEYCHELLES   **INDONESIA**   **PAPUA**   NAURU   KIRIBATI
                                                        NEW GUINEA
ANGOLA COMOROS   **INDIAN**   EAST TIMOR   SOLOMON   TUVALU
        ZAMBIA MALAWI   **ISLANDS**
                      OCEAN   Coral Sea   SAMOA
AMIBIA ZIMBABWE   Islands   VANUATU
        MADAGASCAR MAURITIUS   Territory   FIJI TONGA   20°
MIBIA BOTSWANA MOZAMBIQUE Reunion   (Australia) New   S
                             (France)   Caledonia
                SWAZILAND   (France)   Tropic of Capricorn
         LESOTHO
SOUTH AFRICA   **AUSTRALIA**

Kerguelen Islands
     (France)   40°

                                                                    NEW
                                                                    ZEALAND

SOUTHERN OCEAN   60°

                                       Antarctic Circle

                The shading on this map is there to help
                you see the different countries clearly.

ANTARCTICA   80°

0° E   40°   60°   80°   100°   120°   140°   160°   180°

Beaufort Sea

Victoria Island

Queen Elizabeth Islands

Ellesmere Island

Baffin Bay

Baffin Island

Greenland

Greenland Sea

Iceland

Arctic Circle

Alaska
Mount McKinley
▲
6,194m
(20,321ft)

Yukon

60°

Hudson Bay

Labrador Sea

British Isles

North Sea

Aleutian Islands

Gulf of Alaska

Rocky Mountains

Great Plains

NORTH AMERICA

Great Lakes

Appalachian Mountains

Newfoundland

Azores

Atlas Mountains

40°

Mississippi

Tropic of Cancer

Canary Islands

20° N

Hawaiian Islands

Gulf of Mexico

Cuba

Greater Antilles

West Indies

Lesser Antilles

Caribbean Sea

Cape Verde Islands

Guiana Highlands

Equator

PACIFIC

Polynesia

Galapagos Islands

Amazon Basin

Amazon

Selvas

ATLANTIC

OCEAN

OCEAN

SOUTH AMERICA

Andes

Tahiti

20° S

Tropic of Capricorn

Easter Island

Atacama Desert

Aconcagua
▲
6,959m
(22,831ft)

Pampas

40°

1:72,700,000
0 1,000 2,000 3,000 4,000 5,000km

0 1,000 2,000 3,000 miles

Patagonia

Falkland Islands

South Georgia

60°

Cape Horn

Antarctic Circle

Antarctic Peninsula

Weddell Sea

80°

ARCTIC OCEAN

Svalbard
North Cape
Barents Sea

Scandinavia

North European Plain

EUROPE

Danube

Black Sea

Mediterranean Sea

Novaya
Zemlya

Ob

Ural Mountains

Volga

Mount
Elbrus
5,642m
(18,510ft)

Zagros Mountains

Kara Sea

Severnaya
Zemlya

Laptev Sea

New Siberia
Islands

East Siberian Sea

Arctic Circle

80°

60°

Verkhoyansk Range

Siberia

Yenisey

Aral
Sea

Caspian
Sea

ASIA

Altai Mountains

Lake
Baikal

Gobi
Desert

Sea
of
Okhotsk

Kamchatka
Peninsula

Hokkaido

Honshu

Sea
of
Japan

40°

S a h a r a

Red Sea

Arabian
Peninsula

Himalayas

Ganges

Mount Everest
8,850m
(29,035ft)

Huang
He (Yellow)

Chang Jiang (Yangtze)

Yellow
Sea

Taiwan

East
China
Sea

Chang Jiang

Tropic of Cancer

20°
N

S a h e l

AFRICA

Ethiopian
Highlands

Lake
Victoria

Congo
Basin

Kilimanjaro
5,895m
(19,340ft)

Rift Valley

Arabian
Sea

Deccan
Plateau

Sri Lanka

Seychelles

Bay
of
Bengal

Mekong

South
China
Sea

Sumatra

Borneo

Greater Sunda Islands

Java

Lesser Sunda Islands

Philippine
Islands

Celebes
Sea

Micronesia

New Guinea
Mount Wilhelm
4,509m
(14,793ft)

Arafura
Sea

PACIFIC

OCEAN

Melanesia

Solomon
Islands

Equator

Congo

Namib Desert

Comoro
Islands

INDIAN

OCEAN

Madagascar

Mauritius

Reunion

Kalahari
Desert

Drakensberg

Cape of Good Hope

Great Sandy
Desert

Coral
Sea

Great Barrier Reef

New
Caledonia

Fiji
Islands

20°
S

Tropic of Capricorn

AUSTRALASIA AND OCEANIA

Great Victoria
Desert

Great Dividing Range

Tasman
Sea

North
Island

40°

Kerguelen
Islands

Tasmania

South
Island

SOUTHERN OCEAN

60°

Antarctic Circle

See page 17 for key.

ANTARCTICA

80°

20° E   40°   60°   80°   100°   120°   140°   160°   180°

NORTH AMERICA

The name "North America" can be used to mean different things. In this atlas, North America includes Greenland, Canada, the U.S.A., the Caribbean, and the countries of Central America, the narrow strip of land between the U.S.A. and South America. This continent contains over 20 countries, ranging from Canada, the world's second largest state, to tiny islands such as Grenada and Saint Lucia.

These are columns of rock called hoodoos in Bryce Canyon National Park, U.S.A.

Arctic Circle

ARCTIC OCEAN

Bering Sea

Yukon

Beaufort Sea

Victoria Island

ALASKA
(U.S.A.)

⊙ Anchorage

CANADA

Vancouver ⊙

Columbia

Missouri

PACIFIC

OCEAN

Hawaiian Islands
(U.S.A.)

UNITED STATES

Colorado

Los Angeles ⊙

Rio Grande

Tropic of Cancer

MEXICO

Mexico City

The shading on this map is there to help you see clearly the different countries that make up the continent.

Internet links

For links to websites where you can find out more about the countries in North America, go to www.usborne-quicklinks.com

GREENLAND
(Denmark)

Ellesmere
Island

Queen
Elizabeth
Islands

Baffin
Island

Nuuk

Arctic Circle

Hudson
Bay

Newfoundland

St. Lawrence

Montreal
Ottawa

Great
Lakes

ATLANTIC

Chicago

New York

OCEAN

Washington D.C.

OF AMERICA

Mississippi

Bermuda
(U.K.)

Tropic of Cancer

Houston

THE
BAHAMAS
Nassau

Gulf of
Mexico

Havana

CUBA

Port-au-
Prince

DOMINICAN
REP.

Guadeloupe
(France)

Puerto
Rico
(U.S.A.)

DOMINICA
Martinique (France)

Santo
Domingo

BARBADOS

Kingston

HAITI

JAMAICA

Port-of-Spain

TRINIDAD
AND TOBAGO

BELIZE

Belmopan

Caribbean Sea

GUATEMALA
Guatemala City

HONDURAS

Tegucigalpa

San Salvador
EL SALVADOR

NICARAGUA
Managua

San Jose

Panama City

COSTA RICA

PANAMA

Facts

Total land area 24,709,000 sq km (9,540,000 sq miles)

Total population 528 million

Biggest city Mexico City, Mexico

Biggest country Canada 9,984,670 sq km (3,855,103 sq miles)

Smallest country Saint Kitts and Nevis 261 sq km (101 sq miles)

Highest mountain Mount McKinley, Alaska, U.S.A. 6,194m (20,321ft)

Longest river Mississippi/Missouri, U.S.A. 6,019km (3,741 miles)

Biggest lake Lake Superior, between the U.S.A. and Canada 82,414 sq km (31,820 sq miles)

Highest waterfall Yosemite Falls, on the Yosemite Creek, California, U.S.A. 739m (2,425ft)

Biggest desert Great Basin Desert, U.S.A. 518,000 sq km (200,000 sq miles)

Biggest island Greenland 2,166,086 sq km (836,330 sq miles)

Main mineral deposits Silver, gold, copper, lead, zinc, graphite, molybdenum, nickel

Main fuel deposits Oil, coal, natural gas, uranium

The bald eagle is the national bird of the U.S.A. It is not really bald, but has white feathers on its head.

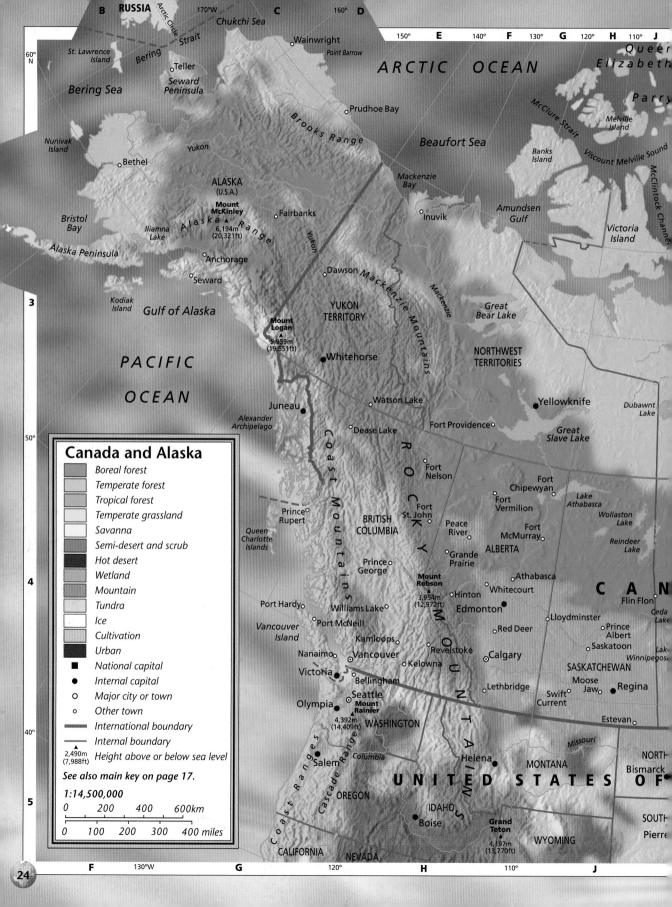

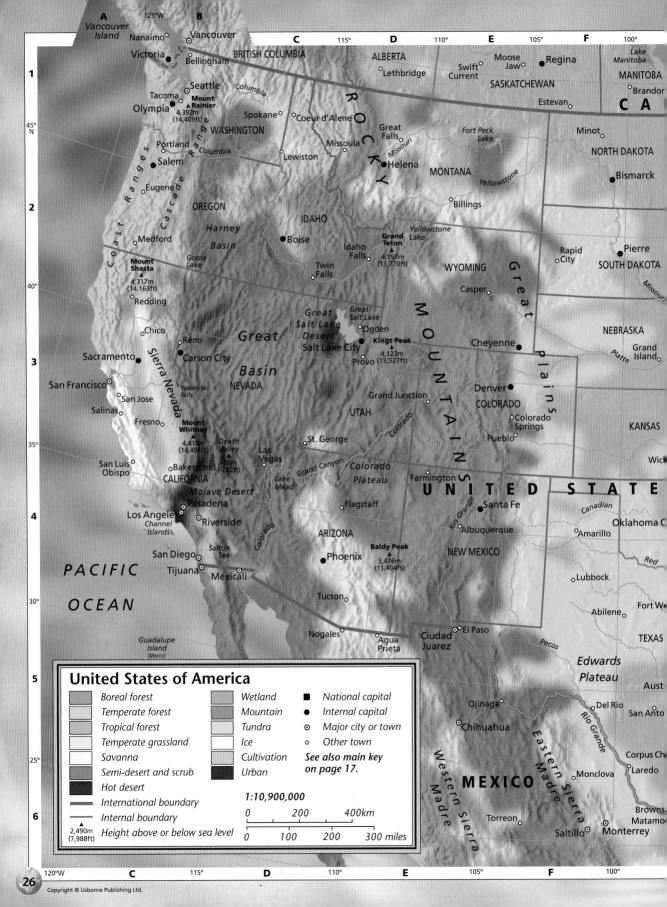

United States of America — map

Grid references (top): A 125°W · B · C 115° · D 110° · E 105° · F 100°
Grid references (bottom): 120°W · C · 115° · D · 110° · E · 105° · F · 100°
Row markers (left): 1 · 45°N · 2 · 40° · 3 · 35° · 4 · 30° · 5 · 25° · 6

CANADA

BRITISH COLUMBIA · ALBERTA · SASKATCHEWAN · MANITOBA

Vancouver Island · Nanaimo · Vancouver · Victoria · Bellingham · Seattle · Tacoma · Olympia · Mount Rainier 4,392m (14,409ft) · Spokane · Coeur d'Alene · Lethbridge · Swift Current · Moose Jaw · Regina · Estevan · Lake Manitoba · Brandon

Columbia · WASHINGTON · Portland · Salem · Lewiston · Missoula · Great Falls · Missouri · Fort Peck Lake · Minot · NORTH DAKOTA

Coast Ranges · Cascade Range · Columbia · OREGON · Eugene · Medford · Harney Basin · Goose Lake · IDAHO · Boise · Idaho Falls · Twin Falls · Helena · MONTANA · Yellowstone · Billings · Bismarck

Mount Shasta 4,317m (14,163ft) · Redding · Chico · Reno · Carson City · Great Salt Lake Desert · Great Salt Lake · Ogden · Salt Lake City · Kings Peak 4,123m (13,527ft) · Provo · Grand Teton 4,197m (13,770ft) · Yellowstone Lake · WYOMING · Casper · Rapid City · Pierre · SOUTH DAKOTA · Missouri

Sacramento · San Francisco · San Jose · Salinas · Fresno · Sierra Nevada · Yosemite Falls · Great Basin · NEVADA · Cheyenne · Denver · COLORADO · Colorado Springs · Pueblo · NEBRASKA · Grand Island · Platte · KANSAS · Wich...

Mount Whitney 4,418m (14,494ft) · Death Valley −86m (−282ft) · Las Vegas · St. George · UTAH · Grand Junction · Colorado · Grand Canyon · Colorado Plateau · Farmington · UNITED STATES

San Luis Obispo · Bakersfield · CALIFORNIA · Mojave Desert · Pasadena · Los Angeles · Channel Islands · Riverside · Salton Sea · San Diego · Tijuana · Mexicali · Lake Mead · Flagstaff · ARIZONA · Phoenix · Baldy Peak 3,476m (11,404ft) · Colorado · Rio Grande · Santa Fe · Albuquerque · NEW MEXICO · Canadian · Amarillo · Oklahoma C... · Lubbock · Red

PACIFIC OCEAN · Guadalupe Island (Mexico) · Nogales · Agua Prieta · Ciudad Juarez · El Paso · Pecos · Abilene · Fort W... · TEXAS · Edwards Plateau · Aust...

MEXICO · Ojinaga · Chihuahua · Western Sierra Madre · Eastern Sierra Madre · Rio Grande · Del Rio · San Anto... · Corpus Ch... · Laredo · Monclova · Torreon · Saltillo · Monterrey · Browns... · Matamo...

United States of America

Boreal forest
Temperate forest
Tropical forest
Temperate grassland
Savanna
Semi-desert and scrub
Hot desert
■ International boundary
▲ Internal boundary
2,490m (7,988ft) Height above or below sea level

Wetland
Mountain
Tundra
Ice
Cultivation
Urban

■ National capital
● Internal capital
⊙ Major city or town
○ Other town

See also main key on page 17.

1:10,900,000

0 — 200 — 400km
0 — 100 — 200 — 300 miles

UNITED STATES OF AMERICA
CALIFORNIA
ARIZONA
NEW MEXICO
OKLAHOMA
ARKANSAS
MISSISSIPPI
TEXAS
LOUISIANA
San Diego
Tijuana
Mexicali
Phoenix
Tucson
Nogales
Agua Prieta
Ciudad Juarez
El Paso
Lubbock
Abilene
Fort Worth
Dallas
Texarkana
Little Rock
Tupelo
Shreveport
Jackson
Hattiesburg
Waco
Austin
Houston
San Antonio
Galveston
Baton Rouge
New Orleans
Mississippi Delta
Mississippi
Red
Pecos
Edwards Plateau
Rio Grande
Guadalupe Island (Mexico)
Cedros Island
Point Eugenia
Lower California
Gulf of California
Hermosillo
Ciudad Obregon
Western Sierra Madre
Ojinaga
Chihuahua
Plateau of Mexico
Eastern Sierra Madre
Laredo
Corpus Christi
Monclova
Brownsville
Matamoros
Monterrey
Saltillo
Torreon
Los Mochis
Culiacan
Tropic of Cancer
La Paz
Cape San Lucas
Durango
4,054m (13,300ft)
Ciudad Victoria
Gulf of Mexico
Mazatlan
MEXICO
Matehuala
San Luis Potosi
Tampico
Aguascalientes
Leon
Puerto Vallarta
Guadalajara
Celaya
Merida
Yucatan Peninsula
Revillagigedo Islands (Mexico)
Colima
Morelia
Uruapan
Teotihuacan
Mexico City
Puebla
Veracruz
Bay of Campeche
Campeche
Orizaba 5,610m (18,405ft)
Tehuacan
Ciudad del Carmen
Coatzacoalcos
Villahermosa
Southern Sierra Madre
Oaxaca
Isthmus of Tehuantepec
Acapulco
Juchitan
Gulf of Tehuantepec
Belmopan
Tikal
BELIZE
Tuxtla Gutierrez
Tajumulco 4,220m (13,845ft)
GUATEMALA
Quetzaltenango
Tapachula
Guatemala City
San Salvador
EL SALVADOR
PACIFIC OCEAN
Equator
Galapagos Islands (Ecuador)
Puerto Ayora
ATLANTIC OCEAN
Virgin Islands (U.K.)
San Juan
Puerto Rico (U.S.A.)
Virgin Islands (U.S.A.)
Anguilla (U.K.)
St. Martin (France and Netherlands)
Leeward Islands
ANTIGUA AND BARBUDA
St. John's
Basseterre
ST. KITTS AND NEVIS
Montserrat (U.K.)
Guadeloupe (France)
Basse-Terre
Windward Islands
1:7,300,000
0 100 200km
0 50 100 miles
Roseau
DOMINICA
Martinique (France)
Fort-de-France
Caribbean Sea
Lesser Antilles
Castries
ST. LUCIA
Kingstown
BARBADOS
ST. VINCENT AND THE GRENADINES
Bridgetown
St. George's
GRENADA
Tobago
Margarita Island
Porlamar
Port-of-Spain
TRINIDAD AND TOBAGO
Cumana
VENEZUELA
Trinidad
120°W 115° 110° 105° 100° 95° 90°
65°W 60°
30° N 25° 20° 15° 10° 5° N 0°
A B C D E F
L M N

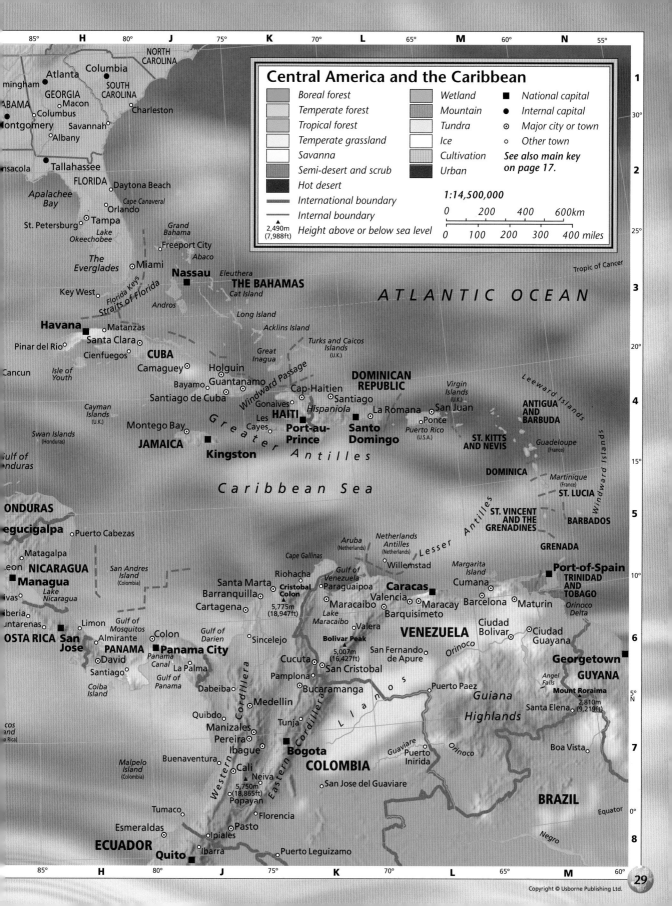

SOUTH AMERICA

Triangle-shaped South America is made up of only 12 independent countries, along with French Guiana, which belongs to France. A huge part of this continent is taken up with the Amazon rainforest, which contains over a third of the world's trees. South America also has dusty deserts, towering mountains and, in Venezuela, the world's highest waterfall – Angel Falls.

This is a guanaco. Guanacos are members of the camel family that live in South America. Guanaco hair is used to make textiles.

Caribbean Sea

Caracas

VENEZUELA

Medellin○   Bogota

COLOMBIA

Orinoco

Equator

Quito

ECUADOR

Galapagos
Islands
(Ecuador)

Guayaquil○

Man

PERU

Lima

BOLIVIA

La Paz

Sucr

Tropic of Capricorn

CHILE

PACIFIC

OCEAN

Santiago   ○Mendoza

ARGENTI

Cape Horn

Drake Passa

The shading on this map is there to help you see clearly the different countries that make up the continent.

This is a red-eyed tree frog. These frogs live in rainforests in South and Central America.

Georgetown
Paramaribo
YANA   Cayenne
URINAME   FRENCH
GUIANA
(France)

azon   Equator

B R A Z I L

Recife

Brasilia

Parana

Belo Horizonte

RAGUAY   Sao Paulo   Rio de Janeiro

Asuncion   Tropic of Capricorn

Porto Alegre

ATLANTIC

RUGUAY
Montevideo
OCEAN
enos Aires

alkland Islands
(U.K.)

Facts

Total land area 17,840,000 sq km (6,888,062 sq miles)

Total population 382 million

Biggest city Sao Paulo, Brazil

Biggest country Brazil 8,547,400 sq km (3,287,612 sq miles)

Smallest country Suriname 163,270 sq km (63,252 sq miles)

Highest mountain Aconcagua, Argentina 6,962m (22,841ft)

Longest river Amazon, mainly in Brazil 6,437km (4,000 miles)

Biggest lake Lake Maracaibo, Venezuela 13,210 sq km (5,100 sq miles)

Highest waterfall Angel Falls, on the Churun River, Venezuela 979m (3,212ft)

Biggest desert Patagonian Desert, Argentina 673,000 sq km (260,000 sq miles)

Biggest island Tierra del Fuego 46,360 sq km (17,900 sq miles)

Main mineral deposits Copper, tin, molybdenum, bauxite, emeralds

Main fuel deposits Oil, coal

Internet links

For links to websites where you can find out more about the countries in South America, go to **www.usborne-quicklinks.com**

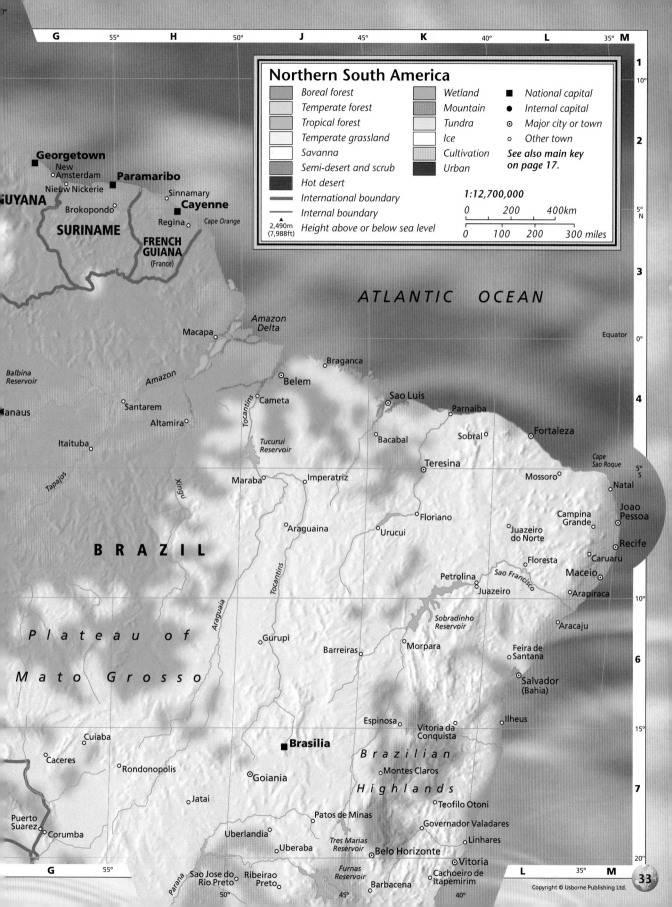

Northern South America

Key:
- Boreal forest
- Temperate forest
- Tropical forest
- Temperate grassland
- Savanna
- Semi-desert and scrub
- Hot desert
- Wetland
- Mountain
- Tundra
- Ice
- Cultivation
- Urban
- International boundary
- Internal boundary

2,490m (7,988ft) Height above or below sea level

- ■ National capital
- ● Internal capital
- ⊙ Major city or town
- ○ Other town

See also main key on page 17.

1:12,700,000

0   200   400km

0   100   200   300 miles

ATLANTIC OCEAN

Georgetown
New Amsterdam
Nieuw Nickerie
GUYANA
Brokopondo
SURINAME
Paramaribo
Sinnamary
Cayenne
Regina
Cape Orange
FRENCH GUIANA (France)

Macapa
Amazon Delta
Braganca
Belem
Balbina Reservoir
Amazon
Santarem
Manaus
Altamira
Cameta
Tucurui Reservoir
Sao Luis
Parnaiba
Bacabal
Sobral
Fortaleza
Cape Sao Roque
Teresina
Mossoro
Natal
Itaituba
Maraba
Imperatriz
Floriano
Juazeiro do Norte
Campina Grande
Joao Pessoa
Recife
Tapajos
Xingu
Araguaina
Urucui
Floresta
Caruaru
Maceio
BRAZIL
Tocantins
Petrolina
Juazeiro
Sao Francisco
Arapiraca
Sobradinho Reservoir
Aracaju
Plateau of
Gurupi
Barreiras
Morpara
Feira de Santana
Araguaia
Salvador (Bahia)
Mato Grosso
Espinosa
Vitoria da Conquista
Ilheus
Cuiaba
Brasilia
Brazilian
Caceres
Rondonopolis
Goiania
Montes Claros
Highlands
Jatai
Teofilo Otoni
Governador Valadares
Puerto Suarez
Corumba
Patos de Minas
Linhares
Uberlandia
Uberaba
Tres Marias Reservoir
Belo Horizonte
Parana
Sao Jose do Rio Preto
Ribeirao Preto
Furnas Reservoir
Vitoria
Cachoeiro de Itapemirim
Barbacena

Equator

L

K

J

H

G

F

E

D 70°W

BRAZIL

Brazilian Highlands

Plateau of Mato Grosso

BOLIVIA

PARAGUAY

PERU

URUGUAY

CHILE

Gran Chaco

Atacama Desert

Andes

Tropic of Capricorn

Sobradinho Reservoir
Morpara
Feira de Santana
Ilheus
Vitória da Conquista
Teófilo Otoni
Linhares
Espinosa
Montes Claros
Governador Valadares
Cachoeiro de Itapemirim
Campos
Barreiras
Belo Horizonte
Vitória
Bartacena
Juiz de Fora
Macae
Rio de Janeiro
Nova Iguacu
Mount AguIhas Negras 2,787m (9,144ft)
Patos de Minas
Tres Marias Reservoir
Furnas Reservoir
Pocós de Caldas
São Paulo
Brasilia
Goiania
Uberaba
Uberlandia
Ribeirao Preto
Araraquara
Campinas
Curitiba
Paranagua
Florianopolis
Itajai
Gurupi
Jatai
São Jose do Rio Preto
Presidente Prudente
Marilia
Itapetininga
Guarapuava
Criciuma
Caxias do Sul
Porto Alegre
Rondonopolis
Campo Grande
Londrina
Cascavel
Foz do Iguacu
Passo Fundo
Santa Maria
Rio Grande
Patos Lagoon
Pelotas
Mirim Lake
Cuiaba
Caceres
Dourados
Ponta Pora
Iguacu Falls
Ciudad del Este
Eldorado
Bage
Melo
Minas
Tocantins
Araguaia
Paraná
Corumba
Puerto Suarez
Pedro Juan Caballero
Concepcion
Posadas
Uruguaiana
Rivera
Tacuarembo
Durazno
Rio Branco
Riberalta
Cobija
Trinidad
Magdalena
San Jose de Chiquitos
Concepcion
Santa Cruz
Paraguay
PARAGUAY
Asuncion
Villarrica
Encarnacion
Formosa
Reconquista
Concordia
Salto
Paysandu
Gualeguaychu
San Nicolas de los Arroyos
Buenos
Rurrenabaque
Puerto Maldonado
Cochabamba
Charagua
Camiri
Tartagal
Corrientes
Santiago del Estero
Santa Fe
Venado Tuerto
Rosario
Chacabuco
Juliaca
Puno
La Paz
Mount Illimani 6,402m (21,004ft)
Oruro
Challapata
Potosi
Uyuni
Tupiza
Sucre
Tarija
San Salvador de Jujuy
San Miguel de Tucuman
Salado
San Francisco
Villa Maria
Rufino
Pilcomayo
Rio Cuarto
Merlo
Lake Titicaca
Lake Poopo
Ollague
Calama
San Pedro de Atacama
Salta
Catamarca
La Rioja
Cordoba
San Juan
San Luis
Villa Mercedes
Mendoza
Tacna
Arica
Pica
Iquique
Antofagasta
Aconcagua 6,908m (22,831ft)
Mount Ojos del Salado 6,959m (22,664ft)
Taltal
Chanaral
Copiapo
Vallenar
Coquimbo
Ovalle
Illapel
San Salvador
Valparaiso
Santiago
Rancagua
Nicaragua
Tropic of Capricorn

34

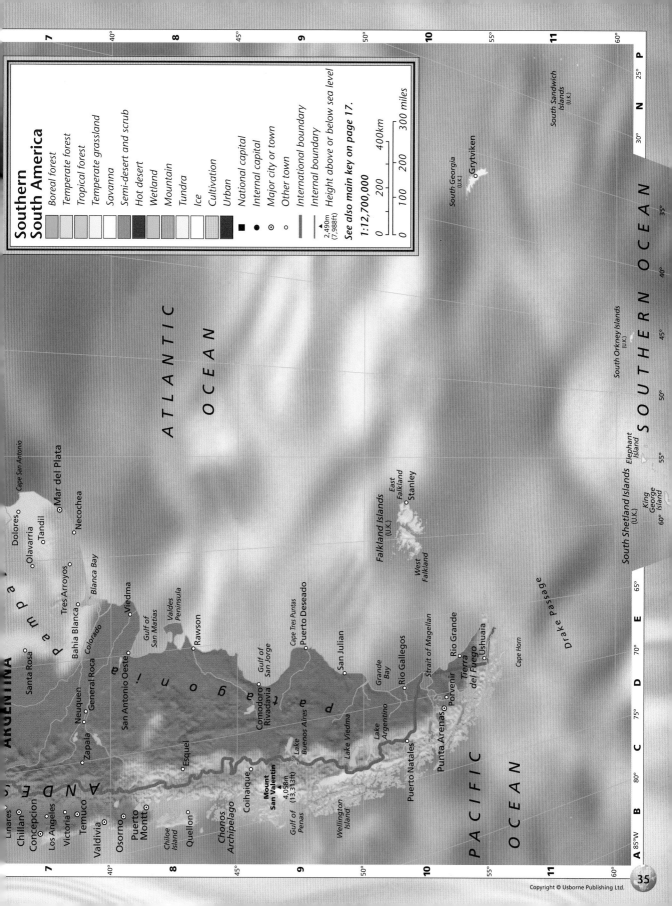

AUSTRALASIA AND OCEANIA

Australasia is made up of Australia, New Zealand and Papua New Guinea. Oceania is a collection of over 20,000 islands stretching out into the Pacific Ocean.

International Date Line

Northern Mariana Islands (U.S.A.)

Guam (U.S.A.)

MARSHALL ISLANDS

■ Melekeok

Palikir ■

■ Majuro

PALAU

FEDERATED STATES OF MICRONESIA

■ Bairiki

Equator

■ Yaren

NAURU

KIRIBATI

INDIAN

PAPUA NEW GUINEA

New Guinea

SOLOMON ISLANDS

TUVALU
Funafuti ■

OCEAN

Arafura Sea

Port ■ Moresby

Honiara ■

■ SAMOA

Wallis and Futuna (France)

Ap

Coral Sea Islands Territory (Australia)

VANUATU

FIJI

Coral Sea

New Caledonia (France)

Port Vila ■

■ Suva

TONGA

○ Noumea

Nukualofa ■

Tropic of Capricorn

AUSTRALIA

Brisbane ○

Darling

Perth ○

Adelaide ○

Murray

○ Sydney
■ **Canberra**

NEW ZEALAND

Auckland ○

Melbourne ○

North Island

Tasmania

Tasman Sea

■ Wellington

○ Christchurch

South Island

International Date Line

This small island is part of Papua New Guinea.

The shading on this map is there to help you see clearly the different countries that make up the continent.

PACIFIC OCEAN

Line Islands

Equator

okelau
(New Zealand)

merican
amoa
(U.S.A.)

Marquesas
Islands

Niue
(New Zealand)

Society
Islands

French
Polynesia
(France)

Cook Islands
(New Zealand)

Pitcairn Islands
(U.K.)

Tropic of Capricorn

Facts

Total land area 9,008,458 sq km (3,478,185 sq miles)
Total population 32 million
Biggest city Sydney, Australia
Biggest country Australia 7,686,850 sq km (2,967,909 sq miles)
Smallest country Nauru 21 sq km (8 sq miles)

Highest mountain Mount Wilhelm, Papua New Guinea 4,509m (14,793ft)
Longest river Murray/Darling River, Australia 3,718km (2,310 miles)
Biggest lake Lake Eyre, Australia 9,500 sq km (3,668 sq miles)
Highest waterfall Sutherland Falls, on the Arthur River, New Zealand 580m (1,904ft)
Biggest desert Great Victoria Desert, Australia 424,400 sq km (163,862 sq miles)
Biggest island New Guinea 786,000 sq km (303,500 sq miles) (Australia is counted as a continental land mass and not as an island.)

Main mineral deposits Iron, nickel, precious stones, lead, bauxite
Main fuel deposits Oil, coal, uranium

The Moorish idol fish is found in shallow waters throughout the Pacific. It has a long, distinctive dorsal fin.

Internet links

For links to websites where you can find out more about Australia and New Zealand, go to **www.usborne-quicklinks.com**

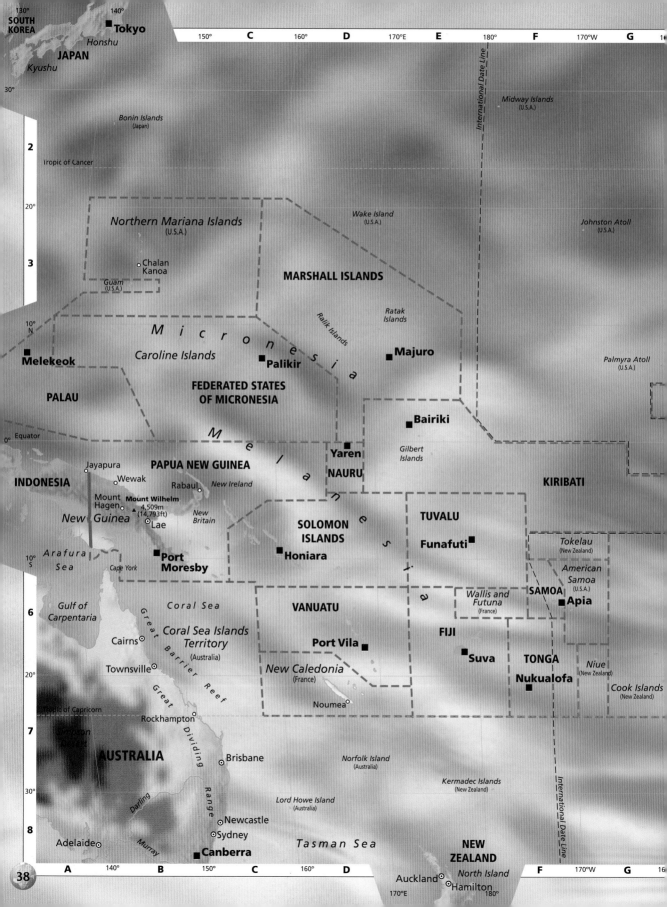

SOUTH
KOREA

130°   140°   150°   **C**   160°   **D**   170°E   **E**   180°   **F**   170°W   **G**

■ **Tokyo**
Honshu
JAPAN
Kyushu

30°

*Bonin Islands
(Japan)*

*Midway Islands
(U.S.A.)*

2

20°

Tropic of Cancer

*Wake Island
(U.S.A.)*

*Johnston Atoll
(U.S.A.)*

*Northern Mariana Islands
(U.S.A.)*

3

MARSHALL ISLANDS

○ **Chalan
Kanoa**

*Guam
(U.S.A.)*

10°
N

M i c r o n e s i a

Caroline Islands

*Ralik
Islands*

*Ratak
Islands*

□ **Majuro**

*Palmyra Atoll
(U.S.A.)*

■ **Melekeok**

□ **Palikir**

PALAU

**FEDERATED STATES
OF MICRONESIA**

0°   *Equator*

M e l a n e s i a

■ **Bairiki**

*Gilbert
Islands*

Jayapura ○
PAPUA NEW GUINEA
INDONESIA
Wewak ○
Rabaul ○
New Ireland

■ **Yaren**
NAURU

KIRIBATI

*Mount
Hagen* ○
Mount Wilhelm
4,509m
(14,793ft) ▲
○ *Lae*
New Guinea
*New
Britain*

TUVALU

**SOLOMON
ISLANDS**
■ **Honiara**

■ **Funafuti**

*Tokelau
(New Zealand)*

*American
Samoa
(U.S.A.)*

□ **Port
Moresby**

10°
S
*Arafura
Sea*

Cape York

SAMOA ■ **Apia**

*Gulf of
Carpentaria*

Coral Sea

VANUATU

*Wallis and
Futuna
(France)*

6

Cairns ○

*Coral Sea Islands
Territory*
(Australia)

FIJI

■ **Port Vila**

■ **Suva**

Townsville ○

20°

*New Caledonia
(France)*

TONGA
■ **Nukualofa**

*Niue
(New Zealand)*

*Cook Islands
(New Zealand)*

Noumea ○

Tropic of Capricorn
Rockhampton ○

7

*Simpson
Desert*

*Great
Dividing*

AUSTRALIA

Brisbane ○

*Norfolk Island
(Australia)*

*Kermadec Islands
(New Zealand)*

30°

Darling

Range

*Lord Howe Island
(Australia)*

Newcastle ○

8

Adelaide ○

Murray

○ *Sydney*

■ **Canberra**

Tasman Sea

**NEW
ZEALAND**

38   **A**   140°   **B**   150°   **C**   160°   **D**

Auckland ○   *North Island*
170°E   ○ *Hamilton*   180°

F   170°W   **G**

Great Barrier Reef

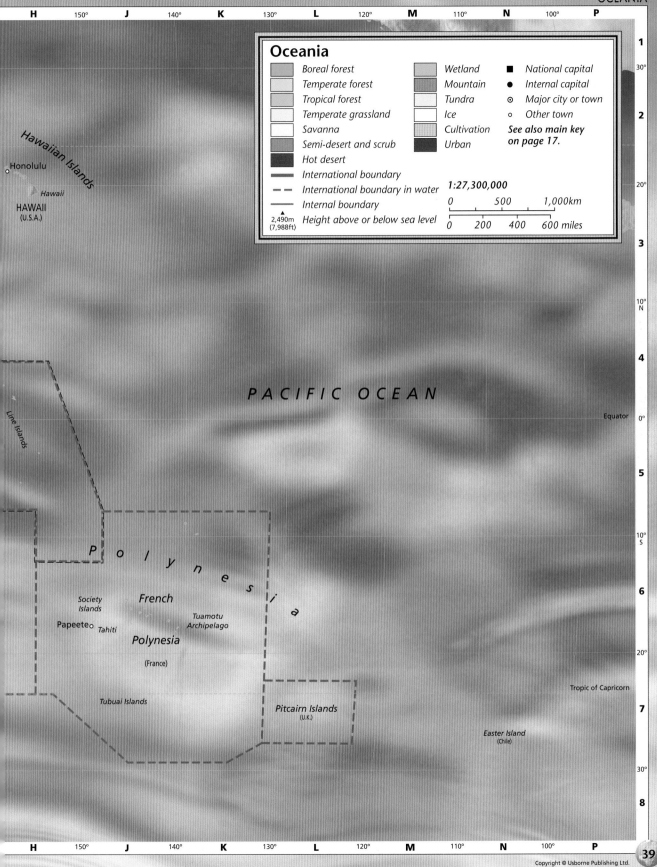

Oceania

Boreal forest		Wetland	■	National capital
Temperate forest		Mountain	●	Internal capital
Tropical forest		Tundra	⊙	Major city or town
Temperate grassland		Ice	○	Other town
Savanna		Cultivation		
Semi-desert and scrub		Urban		
Hot desert				

See also main key on page 17.

International boundary
International boundary in water
Internal boundary
▲ 2,490m (7,988ft) Height above or below sea level

1:27,300,000

0   500   1,000km
0   200   400   600 miles

PACIFIC OCEAN

Honolulu
Hawaii
HAWAII (U.S.A.)
Hawaiian Islands

Line Islands

Equator

P o l y n e s i a

Society Islands
Papeete○ Tahiti
French Polynesia (France)
Tuamotu Archipelago

Tubuai Islands

Pitcairn Islands (U.K.)

Easter Island (Chile)

Tropic of Capricorn

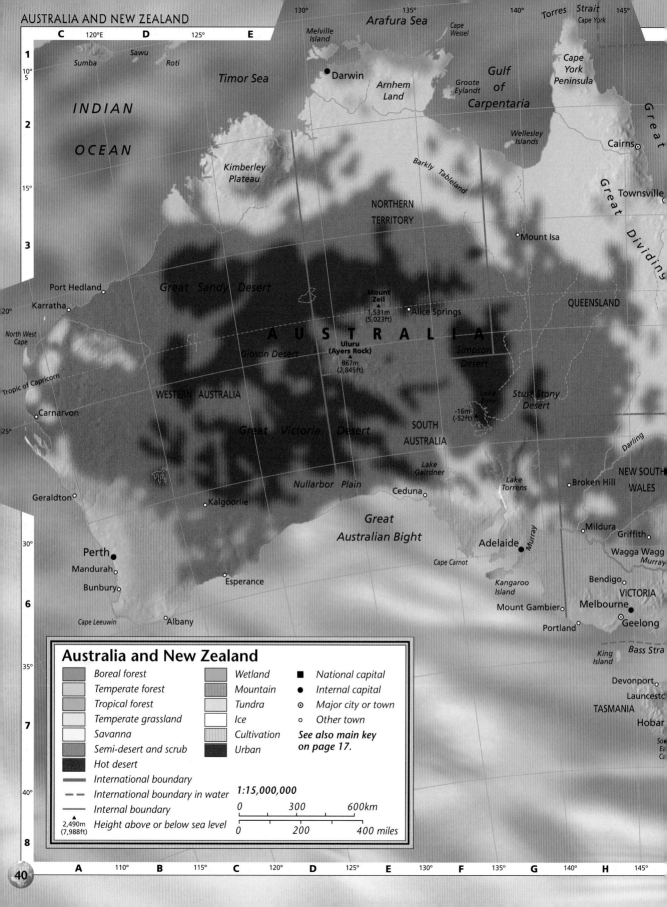

C 120°E D 125° E

Arafura Sea

Torres Strait
Cape York

1
10°S
Sumba
Sawu
Roti
Melville
Island
Cape
Wessel

Timor Sea
Darwin
Arnhem
Land
Gulf
of
Carpentaria
Cape
York
Peninsula

INDIAN

2
Groote
Eylandt
Wellesley
Islands
Cairns

OCEAN
Kimberley
Plateau
Barkly Tableland
Great
Dividing

15°
NORTHERN
TERRITORY
Townsville

3
Mount Isa

Port Hedland
Great Sandy Desert
Mount
Zeil
1,531m
(5,023ft)
Alice Springs
QUEENSLAND

Karratha
20°

North West
Cape
Gibson Desert
Uluru
(Ayers Rock)
867m
(2,845ft)
Simpson
Desert

Tropic of Capricorn
Carnarvon
WESTERN AUSTRALIA
-16m
(-52ft)
Lake
Eyre
Sturt Stony
Desert

25°
Great Victoria Desert
SOUTH
AUSTRALIA
Darling

Geraldton
Nullarbor Plain
Lake
Gairdner
Ceduna
Lake
Torrens
Broken Hill
NEW SOUTH
WALES

Kalgoorlie
Mildura
Griffith

30°
Great
Australian Bight
Adelaide
Murray
Wagga Wagga
Murray

Perth
Mandurah
Esperance
Cape Carnot
Kangaroo
Island
Bendigo
VICTORIA

Bunbury
Mount Gambier
Melbourne

6
Cape Leeuwin
Albany
Portland
Geelong

King
Island
Bass Stra

35°
Devonport
Launcesto

TASMANIA
Hobar

7

Australia and New Zealand

Boreal forest	Wetland	■	National capital
Temperate forest	Mountain	●	Internal capital
Tropical forest	Tundra	⊙	Major city or town
Temperate grassland	Ice	○	Other town
Savanna	Cultivation		
Semi-desert and scrub	Urban		
Hot desert			

See also main key
on page 17.

International boundary

International boundary in water

Internal boundary

▲ 2,490m
(7,988ft) Height above or below sea level

1:15,000,000

0   300   600km

0   200   400 miles

8

A 110° B 115° C 120° D 125° E 130° F 135° G 140° H 145°

SOLOMON ISLANDS

Rennell Island

Santa Cruz Islands

TUVALU

Coral Sea

10° S — **1**

Banks Islands

Coral Sea Islands Territory
(Australia)

VANUATU

Espiritu Santo

2

○ Luganville

Malakula

FIJI

Barrier Reef

15° —

○ Mackay

Chesterfield Islands

Efate ■ **Port Vila**

Vanua Levu

Lautoka ○

○ ckhampton

New Caledonia
(France)

Viti Levu ■ **Suva**

○ Gladstone

○ Bundaberg

20° —

Range

Fraser Island

Noumea ○

Loyalty Islands

○ Gympie

4

○ Toowoomba ● **Brisbane**

Tropic of Capricorn

● Gold Coast

PACIFIC OCEAN

○ Moree

Great Dividing Range

○ Grafton

25° —

Norfolk Island
(Australia)

○ Dubbo

Lord Howe Island
(Australia)

○ Port Macquarie

5

○ Newcastle

● Sydney
○ Wollongong

Kermadec Islands
(New Zealand)

30° —

■ **Canberra**
AUSTRALIAN CAPITAL
Mount TERRITORY
sciuszko

North Cape

29m
313ft)

6

Tasman Sea

○ Whangarei

flinders island

○ Auckland

North Island

35° —

○ Hamilton

East Cape

New Plymouth ○

○ Rotorua
Lake Taupo

Cape Farewell

○ Napier

7

Nelson ○

South Island

Cook Strait

■ **Wellington**

Aoraki
(Mount Cook)

NEW ZEALAND

○ **Christchurch**

Sutherland Falls

3,754m
(12,316ft)

40° —

Cape Providence

○ **Dunedin**

8

Invercargill ○

Chatham Islands
(New Zealand)

Stewart Island

South West Cape

ASIA

Asia is the largest continent and has over 40 countries, including Russia, the biggest country in the world. As well as large land masses, it has thousands of islands and inlets, giving it over 160,000km (100,000 miles) of coastline. Asia also contains the Himalayas, the world's highest mountain range. Turkey and Russia are part in Europe and part in Asia, but both are shown in full on this map.

Internet links

For links to websites where you can find out more about the countries in Asia, go to
www.usborne-quicklinks.com

The shading on this map is there to help you see clearly the different countries that make up the continent.

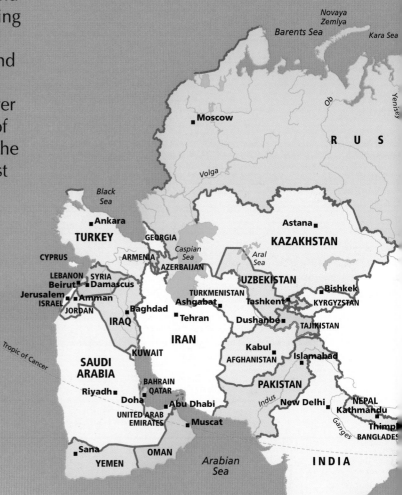

ARCTIC OCEAN

Franz Josef Land

Novaya Zemlya

Barents Sea

Kara Sea

Ob

Yenisey

Moscow

R U S

Volga

Black Sea

Ankara

TURKEY

GEORGIA

Caspian Sea

Astana

KAZAKHSTAN

Aral Sea

CYPRUS

ARMENIA

AZERBAIJAN

UZBEKISTAN

Bishkek

LEBANON

SYRIA

TURKMENISTAN

Tashkent

KYRGYZSTAN

Beirut

Damascus

Ashgabat

Jerusalem

Amman

Dushanbe

TAJIKISTAN

ISRAEL

JORDAN

Baghdad

Tehran

IRAQ

IRAN

Kabul

Islamabad

KUWAIT

AFGHANISTAN

Tropic of Cancer

SAUDI ARABIA

BAHRAIN

QATAR

PAKISTAN

Riyadh

Doha

Indus

New Delhi

NEPAL

Abu Dhabi

Kathmandu

UNITED ARAB EMIRATES

Muscat

Thimp

Ganges

BANGLADES

Sana

OMAN

Arabian Sea

INDIA

YEMEN

Socotra (Yemen)

Bay of Bengal

INDIAN OCEAN

Equator

Sri Jayewardenepura Kotte

SRI LANKA

Colombo

MALDIVES

Male

A type of Chinese sailing boat called a junk in the port at Singapore

42

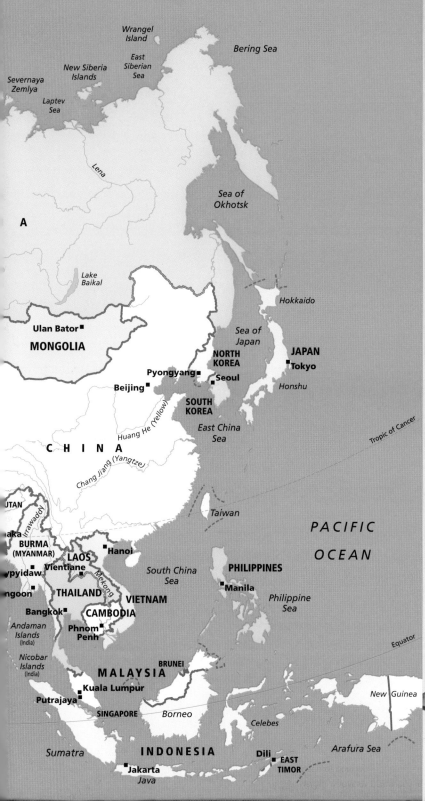

Wrangel
Island

Bering Sea

*New Siberia
Islands*

*East
Siberian
Sea*

*Severnaya
Zemlya*

*Laptev
Sea*

Lena

A

*Sea of
Okhotsk*

*Lake
Baikal*

Hokkaido

Ulan Bator■

MONGOLIA

*Sea of
Japan*

**NORTH
KOREA**

JAPAN
■Tokyo

Pyongyang■

■Seoul

Beijing■

**SOUTH
KOREA**

Honshu

C H I N A

Huang He (Yellow)

*East China
Sea*

Tropic of Cancer

Chang Jiang (Yangtze)

Taiwan

**PACIFIC

OCEAN**

UTAN

(Irrawaddy)

aka

**BURMA
(MYANMAR)**

■Hanoi

LAOS

■Vientiane

ypyidaw■

*South China
Sea*

PHILIPPINES

ngoon■

THAILAND

Mekong

VIETNAM

■Manila

*Philippine
Sea*

Bangkok■

CAMBODIA

*Andaman
Islands*
(India)

Phnom
Penh■

*Nicobar
Islands*
(India)

BRUNEI

Equator

M A L A Y S I A

■Kuala Lumpur

New Guinea

Putrajaya■

SINGAPORE

Borneo

Celebes

Sumatra

I N D O N E S I A

Dili
■

■
**EAST
TIMOR**

Arafura Sea

■Jakarta

Java

Facts

Total land area 44,537,920 sq km
(17,196,090 sq miles)
Total population 3.8 billion (including
all of Russia)
Biggest city Tokyo, Japan
Biggest country Russia *Total area:
17,075,200 sq km (6,592,735 sq miles)
Area of Asiatic Russia: 12,780,800 sq km
(4,934,667 sq miles)*
Smallest country Maldives *300 sq km
(116 sq miles)*

Highest mountain Mount Everest,
Nepal/China border *8,850m (29,035ft)*
Longest river Chang Jiang (Yangtze),
China *6,380km (3,964 miles)*
Biggest lake Caspian Sea, western Asia
370,999 sq km (143,243 sq miles)
Highest waterfall Jog Falls, on the
Sharavati River, India *253m (830ft)*
Biggest desert Arabian Desert, in and
around Saudi Arabia *2,230,000 sq km
(900,000 sq miles)*
Biggest island Borneo *751,100 sq km
(290,000 sq miles)*

Main mineral deposits Zinc, mica, tin,
chromium, iron, nickel
Main fuel deposits Oil, coal, uranium,
natural gas

These are lotus flowers, Asian water
lilies known for their beauty. In China
they are associated with purity and
for Buddhists they are sacred.

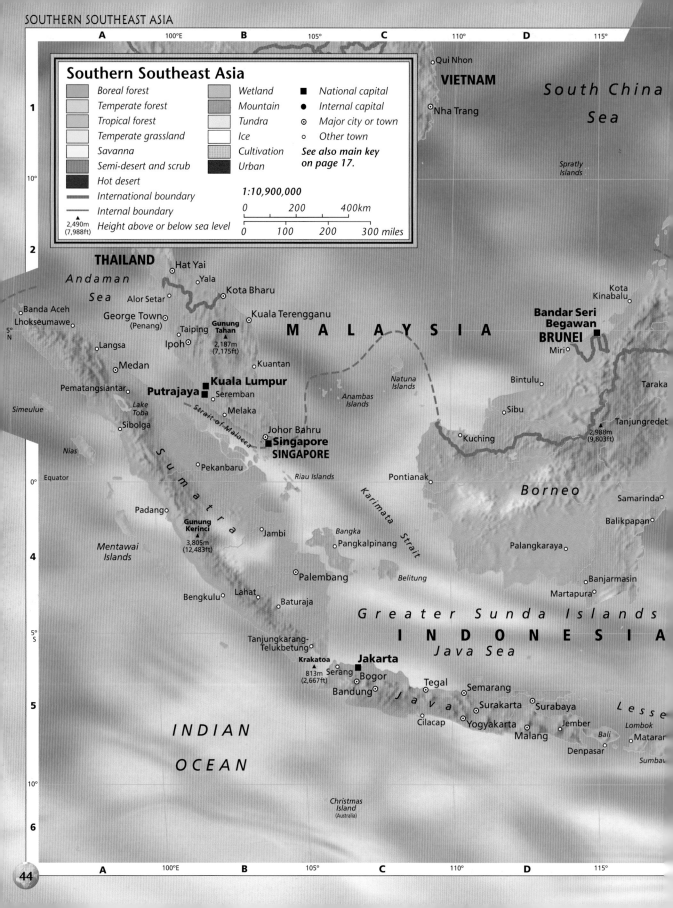

Southern Southeast Asia

	Boreal forest
	Temperate forest
	Tropical forest
	Temperate grassland
	Savanna
	Semi-desert and scrub
	Hot desert
———	International boundary
———	Internal boundary
▲ 2,490m (7,988ft)	Height above or below sea level

	Wetland
	Mountain
	Tundra
	Ice
	Cultivation
	Urban

■	National capital
●	Internal capital
⊙	Major city or town
○	Other town

See also main key on page 17.

1:10,900,000

0   200   400km

0   100   200   300 miles

VIETNAM

Qui Nhon

Nha Trang

South China Sea

Spratly Islands

THAILAND

Andaman Sea

Hat Yai
Yala
Kota Bharu
Alor Setar
Kuala Terengganu

MALAYSIA

Kota Kinabalu

Bandar Seri Begawan
BRUNEI
Miri

Banda Aceh
Lhokseumawe
George Town (Penang)
Taiping
Ipoh
Gunung Tahan ▲ 2,187m (7,175ft)
Kuantan

Natuna Islands

Bintulu

Taraka

Langsa
Medan

Kuala Lumpur
Putrajaya ■ Seremban
Melaka

Anambas Islands

Sibu

Tanjungredet ▲ 2,988m (9,803ft)

Pematangsiantar

Johor Bahru
Singapore
SINGAPORE

Kuching

Simeulue

Lake Toba
Sibolga

Strait of Malacca

Pontianak

Borneo

Samarinda

Nias

Pekanbaru

Riau Islands

Balikpapan

Equator

Sumatra

Padango

Gunung Kerinci ▲ 3,805m (12,483ft)

Jambi

Bangka

Karimata Strait

Palangkaraya

Mentawai Islands

Pangkalpinang

Banjarmasin
Martapura

Palembang

Belitung

Bengkulu
Lahat
Baturaja

Greater Sunda Islands

I N D O N E S I A

Java Sea

Tanjungkarang-Telukbetung

Krakatoa ▲ 813m (2,667ft)
Serang
Jakarta ■ Bogor
Bandung

Java

Tegal
Semarang
Surakarta
Surabaya

Lesser

Cilacap
Yogyakarta
Jember
Malang
Denpasar

Lombok
Bali
Matarar

Sumbav

INDIAN OCEAN

Christmas Island (Australia)

120° Cabanatuan
125°
Luzon
Olongapo
Quezon City
Manila ■

Lucena
Naga
Calapan
Legaspi
Mindoro

PHILIPPINES

Masbate
Masbate
Roxas
Calbayog
Samar
Tacloban

*Calamian
Group*
Panay

Philippine

Taytay
Iloilo
Bacolod
Cebu
Sea

Negros
Puerto Princesa
Dumaguete
Bohol
Surigao

Butuan
alawan
Cagayan de Oro

Pagadian
Iligan
Mindanao
Davao

Sulu Sea
Zamboanga

Jolo
General Santos

andakan
*Sulu
Archipelago*

wau

Celebes Sea
*Talaud
Islands*

*Sangihe
Islands*

Morotai

Manado
Halmahera

Ternate

*Molucca
Sea*

Palu
Peleng
Obi

Celebes
*Sula
Islands*
Ceram Sea
Ceram

Palopo
Buru
Ambon

Parepare
Kendari

Watampone
Buton

Ujung Pandang
Banda Sea

Flores Sea

unda Islands
Wetar

Flores
Ende
Dili ■

Sumba
Sawu Sea
Timor
EAST TIMOR

Sawu
Kupang

Roti
Timor Sea

Makassar Strait

PACIFIC

OCEAN

PALAU

5°
N

3

Equator 0°

Biak

Sorong

Misool
Yapen

Fakfak

Maoke Range
Jayapura
Puncak Jaya
5,030m
(16,502ft)
*New
Guinea*

5°
S

*Aru
Islands*

*Tanimbar
Islands*
Dolak

Arafura Sea
Torres Strait

10°

AUSTRALIA

6

Darwin NORTHERN TERRITORY

120°
F
125°
G
130°
H
135°
J
140°

Inset map

J 140°E
K
145°
L
150°
M Equator 155° N
0°
0°

*Admiralty
Islands*
**PACIFIC
OCEAN**

4
Jayapura
Bismarck Sea
New Ireland
4
1

Wewak
Rabaul

Mount Wilhelm
4,509m
(14,793ft) ▲
Madang
New Britain

5°
S
Mount Hagen
Lae
5°
S

New Guinea
PAPUA NEW GUINEA

5
Kerema
Solomon Sea
5

*Gulf of
Papua*
*D'Entrecasteaux
Islands*

10°
**Port
Moresby** ■
10°

Torres Strait
Cape York
1:16,400,000

6
*Cape York
Peninsula*
0
400km
6
2

AUSTRALIA
0
200 miles

J 140°E
K
145°
L
150°
M
155°
N

Brahmaputra
Lhasa

H i m a l a y a s

Mount Everest
8,850m
(29,035ft)
NEPAL
Thimphu
Darjeeling
BHUTAN
Biratnagar
Darbhanga
Rangpur
Bhagalpur
Ganges
Rajshahi
Sylhet
BANGLADESH
Dhaka
Asansol
Khulna
Jamshedpur
Kolkata
(Calcutta)
Chittagong

INDIA

Dibrugarh
Jorhat
Brahmaputra
Guwahati
Shillong

Imphal

Aizawl

Myitkyina

Lashio

Monywa
Mandalay

Mount Victoria
3,053m
(10,016ft)

Sittwe

Mouths of the Ganges

Bay of Bengal

BURMA
(MYANMAR)

Taunggyi

Naypyidaw
Pye
Sandoway
Irrawaddy
Henzada
Pegu
Pathein
Thaton
Rangoon
Moulmein
Mouths of the
Irrawaddy

I N D I A N

O C E A N

Andaman
Islands
(India)

Andaman
Sea

Port Blair

Little
Andaman

Tavoy

Mergui

Mergui
Archipelago

Ten Degree Channel

Prachuap
Khiri Khan

Nicobar Islands
(India)

Chumphon

Banda Aceh

Lhokseumawe

Sumatra

Langsa

INDONESIA

Mekong
Chang Jiang (Yangtze)
Salween

Chengdu
Wanxian
Enshi
Gongga Shan
7,556m
(24,790ft)
Leshan
Chongqing
Neijiang
Luzhou
Xichang
Yibin
C H I
Zhaotong
Zunyi
Huaihu
Panzhihua
Guiyang
Anshun
Kunming
Chang Jiang (Yangtze)
Liuzhou

Dali
Baoshan

Kaiyuan
Nannin
Simao
Gejiu
Ha Giang
Red
Lao Cai
Phongsali
Thai Nguyen
Qinzhou
Son La
Hanoi
Hai Phong

Mekong
Louangphrabang
Thanh Hoa
Gulf of
Tonkin

LAOS
Vinh

Chiang Mai
Vientiane
Sanya

Salween
Udon Thani
Phitsanulok
Savannakhet
Khon
Kaen
Hue
Da Nanc
Nakhon Sawan
Ubon
Ratchathani
THAILAND
Pakxe
Nakhon Ratchasima
Attapu
VIETNAM
Bangkok
Stoeng Treng
Qui Nhon
Angkor
Tonle Sap
Pattaya
Batdambang
CAMBODIA
Buon Me
Thuot
Kampong
Chhnang
Kampong
Cham
Da Lat
Nha
Tran
Krong
Kaoh Kong
Phnom
Penh
Bien Hoa
Kampong Saom
Mekong
Ho Chi Minh City
(Saigon)
Long Xuyen
Can Tho
Gulf of Thailand
Bac Lieu
Con Son

Nakhon Si
Thammarat

Hat Yai
Yala
Kota Bharu
Alor Setar
Kuala Terengganu
George Town
(Penang)
Gunung
Tahan
Taiping
Ipoh
2,187m
(7,175ft)
MALAYSIA
Natuna
Islands
(Indonesia)

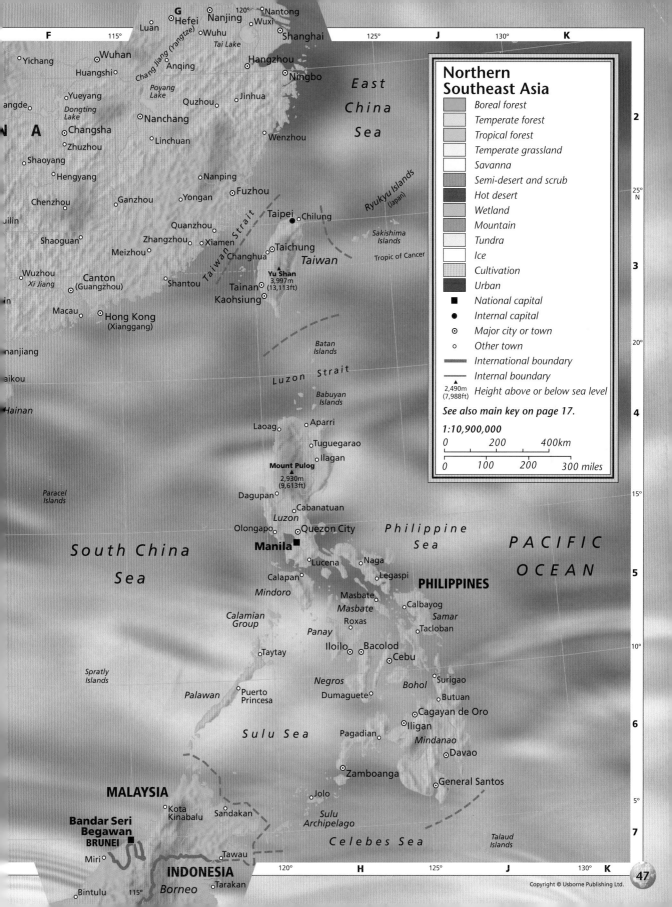

Yichang   Wuhan
Huangshi
angde   Yueyang   Dongting Lake   Luan   Hefei   Nanjing   Wuxi   Shanghai
Chang Jiang (Yangtze)   Wuhu   Anqing   Hangzhou
Poyang Lake   Ningbo   Tai Lake
Changsha   Nanchang   Quzhou   Jinhua   **East China Sea**

Zhuzhou   Linchuan   Wenzhou   2
Shaoyang
Chenzhou   Hengyang   Nanping   25° N
uilin   Ganzhou   Fuzhou   **Northern Southeast Asia**
Shaoguan   Zhangzhou   Yongan
in   Meizhou   Quanzhou   Taipei Chilung   Ryukyu Islands (Japan)
Wuzhou   Xiamen   Changhua   Sakishima Islands
Xi Jiang   Canton (Guangzhou)   Shantou   Taichung   Taiwan   Tropic of Cancer   3
Zhangzhou   Yu Shan 3,997m (13,113ft)   Tainan
Macau   Hong Kong (Xianggang)   Kaohsiung

nanjiang   Batan Islands   20°
aikou   Luzon Strait
Hainan   Babuyan Islands   4
Laoag   Aparri
Paracel Islands   Tuguegarao   Ilagan
Mount Pulog 2,930m (9,613ft)
Dagupan   15°
South China Sea   Cabanatuan
Luzon
Olongapo   Quezon City   **Philippine Sea**   **PACIFIC OCEAN**
Manila   Lucena   Naga
Calapan   Legaspi   **PHILIPPINES**   5
Mindoro   Masbate
Calamian Group   Masbate   Calbayog
Roxas   Samar
Panay   Tacloban
Spratly Islands   Taytay   Iloilo   Bacolod   Cebu   10°
Negros   Bohol   Surigao
Palawan   Puerto Princesa   Dumaguete   Butuan
Cagayan de Oro
Sulu Sea   Iligan   6
Pagadian   Mindanao
Davao
Zamboanga   General Santos
MALAYSIA   Jolo
Kota Kinabalu   Sandakan   Sulu Archipelago   Talaud Islands   5°
Bandar Seri Begawan   Sulu   **Celebes Sea**
BRUNEI   7
Miri   Tawau
INDONESIA
Bintulu   115°   Borneo   Tarakan   120°   H   125°   J   130°   K

Legend

	Boreal forest
	Temperate forest
	Tropical forest
	Temperate grassland
	Savanna
	Semi-desert and scrub
	Hot desert
	Wetland
	Mountain
	Tundra
	Ice
	Cultivation
	Urban
■	National capital
●	Internal capital
⊙	Major city or town
○	Other town
—	International boundary
—	Internal boundary
▲ 2,490m (7,988ft)	Height above or below sea level

See also main key on page 17.

1:10,900,000

0   200   400km
0   100   200   300 miles

A 80°E B 85° C 90° D 95° E 100° F 105° G 110°

KAZAKHSTAN

Karamay

2 Almaty
Yining
Kuytun
Shihezi
Altay

Bulgan

■ **Ulan Bator**

Dzungarian Basin

Altai Mountains

KYRGYZSTAN

Urumqi

MONGOLIA

▲ **Pik Pobedy**
7,439m
(24,406ft)
Aksu

T i e n   S h a n

Turpan

40°
N
Korla
Bosten Lake
-154m
(-505ft)

Turpan Depression

Hami

Erenhc

G o b i   D e s e r t

3 *Tarim Basin*
Lop Lake

Mogao Caves

Baotou
Hohhot

Yumen

Hotan

Taklimakan Desert

Altun Mountains

5,547m
(18,199ft)

The Great Wall of China

Wuhai

Yinchuan

Taiyu

Kunlun Mountains

35°

Qaidam Basin

Golmud

Qinghai Lake

Xining

Lanzhou

C H I N A

Huang He (Yellow)

4

Baoji

Mount Li
(Terracotta Ar

Plateau of Tibet

Siling Lake

30°

Yushu

Shiyan

Xian

Xiangfa

TIBET

Nam Lake

Brahmaputra

Salween

Mekong

Chang Jiang (Yangtze)

Chengdu

Yichang

H i m a l a y a s

NEPAL

■ **Kathmandu**

Lhasa

Gongga Shan
7,556m
(24,790ft)

Leshan

Chongqing

Changde

5

▲ **Mount Everest**
8,850m
(29,035ft)

Darjeeling

Luzhou

Darbhanga

Patna

Biratnagar

■ **Thimphu**
BHUTAN

Brahmaputra

Dibrugarh

Xichang

Chang Jiang (Yangtze)

Zunyi

Huaihua

Hengy

Ganges

Bhagalpur

Rangpur

Guwahati

Shillong

Panzhihua

Guiyang

INDIA

Ranchi

Asansol

Rajshahi

Sylhet

Imphal

Myitkyina

Dali

Tropic of Cancer

BANGLADESH

Dhaka ■

Aizawl

Kunming

Guilin

6

Kolkata
(Calcutta)

Khulna

Liuzhou

Chittagong

Red

Gejiu

Wuzhou

Cuttack

Mouths of the Ganges

Monywa

Lashio

Mandalay

Simao

Lao Cai

Nanning

Yulin

20°

Bay of Bengal

Mount Victoria
3,053m
(10,016ft)

Sittwe

**BURMA
(MYANMAR)**

Taunggyi

Phongsali

Son La

Thai
Nguyen

Zhanjiar

Hanoi

I N D I A N

Naypyidaw ■

Sandoway

Pye

Salween

Mekong

Louangphrabang

Hai
Phong

Gulf of Tonkin

Haikou

7

O C E A N

Irrawaddy

Chiang
Mai

Thanh Hoa

LAOS

VIETNAM

Hainan

Henzada

Pathein

Pegu

Rangoon

THAILAND

Vientiane

Udon Thani

Vinh

Sanya

C 90°E D *Mouths of the Irrawaddy*

Moulmein

95°

100° F 105° G 110°

48

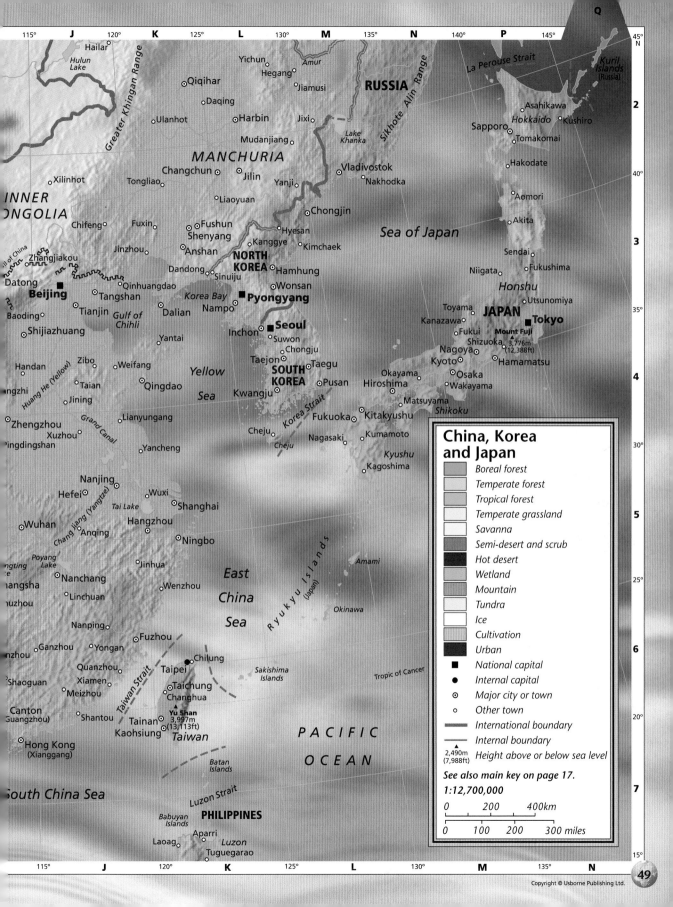

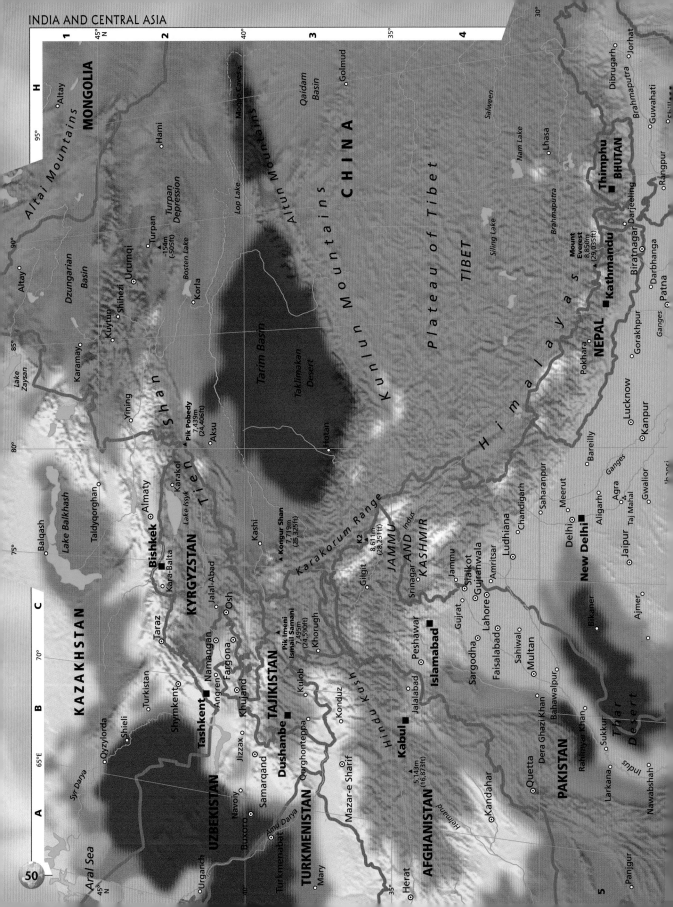

MONGOLIA

Altay

Altai Mountains

Hami

Mount Gavesh

CHINA

Qaidam Basin

Golmud

Altun Mountains

Turpan Depression

Urumqi

Shihezi

Kuytun

Turpan

-154m (-505ft)

Bosten Lake

Lop Lake

TIBET

Salween

Nam Lake

Lhasa

Brahmaputra

Plateau of Tibet

Siling Lake

Thimphu

BHUTAN

Darjeeling

Dibrugarh

Jorhat

Brahmaputra

Guwahati

Altay

Dzungarian Basin

Karamay

Korla

Kunlun Mountains

H i m a l a y a s

Mount Everest 8,850m (29,035ft)

Kathmandu

Rangpur

Lake Zaysan

Yining

Shan

Tarim Basin

Taklimakan Desert

Brahmaputra

NEPAL

Pokhara

Biratnagar

Darbhanga

Patna

Lake Balkhash

Taldyqorghan

Karakol

Tien

Aksu

▲ Pik Pobedy 7,439m (24,406ft)

Hotan

Gorakhpur

Ganges

Balqash

Almaty

Lake Issyk

Kashi

Lucknow

Kanpur

Bareilly

Ganges

Qyzylorda

Shieli

Bishkek

KYRGYZSTAN

Kara-Balta

Jalal-Abad

▲ Kongur Shan 7,719m (25,325ft)

Karakorum Range

Indus

Saharanpur

Meerut

Aligarh

Agra

Gwalior

Taj Mahal

KAZAKHSTAN

Taraz

Osh

K2 8,611m (28,251ft)

Gilgit

JAMMU AND KASHMIR

Srinagar

Chandigarh

Delhi

New Delhi

Jaipur

Ajmer

Shymkent

Turkistan

Namangan

Fargona

Khujand

Khorugh

Jammu

Ludhiana

Amritsar

Sialkot

Gujranwala

Bikaner

Tashkent

Angren

Jizzax

Pik imeni Ismail Samani 7,495m (24,590ft)

Kulob

Konduz

Peshawar

Gujrat

Lahore

Sahiwalo

Multan

UZBEKISTAN

TAJIKISTAN

Dushanbe

Qurghonteppa

Hindu Kush

Islamabad

Jalalabad

Kabul

Sargodha

Faisalabad

Thar Desert

Bahawalpur

Navoiy

Buxoro

Samarqand

Mazar-e Sharif

5,143m (16,873ft)

Dera Ghazi Khan

Rahimyar Khan

Sukkur

Urganch

Amu Darya

Turkmenabat

Quetta

PAKISTAN

Larkana

Indus

Aral Sea

Syr Darya

TURKMENISTAN

Mary

Helmand

AFGHANISTAN

Kandahar

Nawabshah

Panjgur

Herat

50

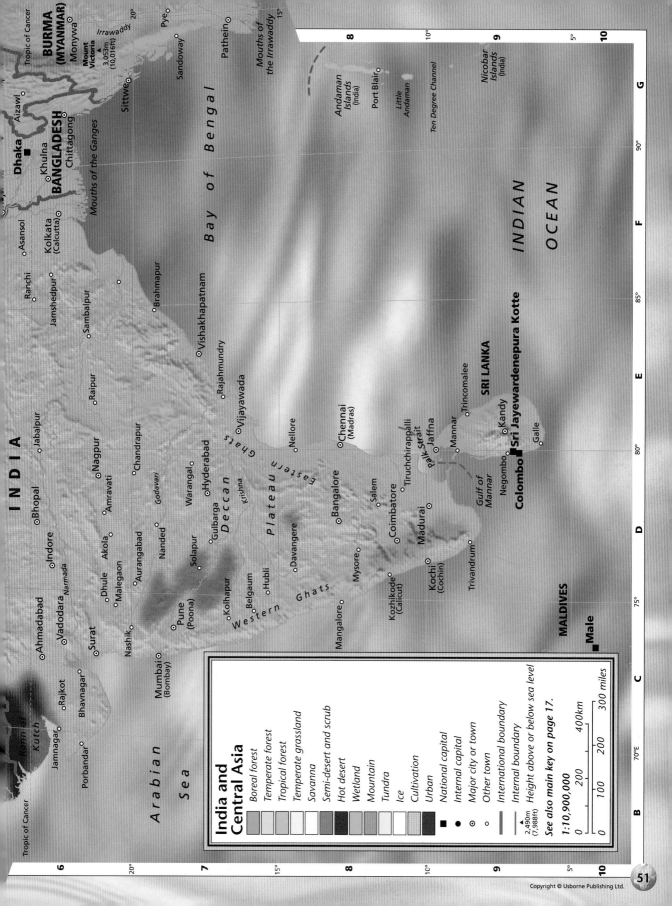

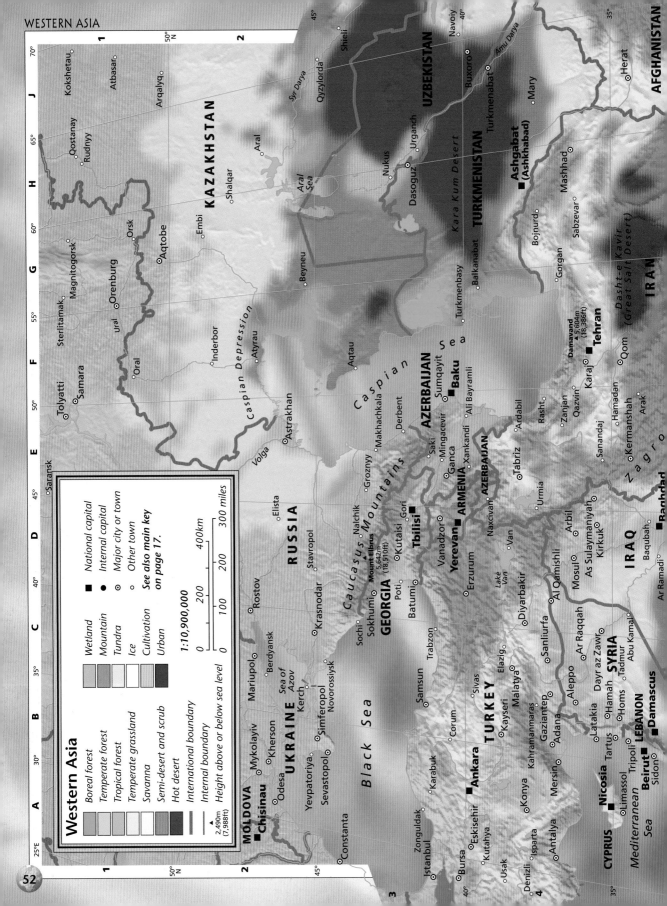

Western Asia

Boreal forest	■ National capital
Temperate forest	● Internal capital
Tropical forest	⊙ Major city or town
Temperate grassland	○ Other town
Savanna	**See also main key on page 17.**
Semi-desert and scrub	
Hot desert	

International boundary

Internal boundary

Height above or below sea level

1:10,900,000

0   100   200   300 miles

0   200   400km

▲ 2,490m (7,988ft)

Map labels

1   50°N   2

70°   65°   60°   55°   50°   45°   40°   35°   30°   25°E

Kokshetau
Atbasar
Qostanay
Rudnyy
Arqalyq
Magnitogorsk
Orsk
Orenburg
Aqtobe
Embi
Sterlitamak
Ural
Oral
Inderbor
Atyrau
Tolyatti
Samara
Beyneu
Saransk
Elista
Rostov
Stavropol
Krasnodar
Novorossiysk
Mariupol
Berdyansk
Kerch
Simferopol
Sevastopol
Yevpatoriya
Odesa
Kherson
Mykolayiv
Chisinau
Zonguldak
Istanbul
Bursa
Eskisehir
Kutahya
Usak
Denizli
Isparta
Antalya
Konya
Mersin
Adana
Kahramanmaras
Gaziantep
Kayseri
Sivas
Corum
Samsun
Trabzon
Sochi
Sokhumi
Batumi
Poti
Kutaisi
Tbilisi
Vanadzor
Yerevan
Erzurum
Diyarbakir
Elazig
Malatya
Sanliurfa
Ar Raqqah
Aleppo
Hamah
Homs
Latakia
Tartus
Tripoli
Beirut
Sidon
Damascus
Nicosia
Limassol
Tadmur
Dayr az Zawr
Abu Kamal
Mosul
Al Qamishli
Arbil
Kirkuk
As Sulaymaniyah
Baqubah
Ar Ramadi
Baghdad
Van
Lake Van
Urmia
Tabriz
Ardabil
Rasht
Zanjan
Qazvin
Karaj
Tehran
Qom
Arak
Hamadan
Sanandaj
Kermanshah
Xankandi
Naxcivan
Ganca
Mingacevir
Saki
Ali Bayramli
Baku
Sumqayit
Makhachkala
Derbent
Groznyy
Nalchik
Mount Elbrus 5,642m (18,510ft)
Gori
Aqtau
Shalqar
Aral
Aral Sea
Nukus
Dasoguz
Urganch
Shieli
Navoiy
Buxoro
Mary
Turkmenabat
Ashgabat (Ashkhabad)
Balkanabat
Turkmenbasy
Gorgan
Bojnurd
Sabzevar
Mashhad
Herat
Damavand ▲5,604m (18,386ft)

Country labels

RUSSIA
KAZAKHSTAN
UKRAINE
MOLDOVA
GEORGIA
ARMENIA
AZERBAIJAN
TURKEY
CYPRUS
SYRIA
LEBANON
IRAQ
IRAN
UZBEKISTAN
TURKMENISTAN
AFGHANISTAN

Physical features

Black Sea
Sea of Azov
Mediterranean Sea
Caucasus Mountains
Caspian Sea
Caspian Depression
Kara Kum Desert
Dasht-e Kavir (Great Salt Desert)
Zagros
Volga
Ural
Sur Darya
Amu Darya

PAKISTAN

Helmand

30°

Zabol

Zahedan

Iranshahr

Panjgur

Turbat

25°

Kerman

Sirjan

Bandar-e Abbas

Gulf of Oman

Tropic of Cancer

Masirah Island

Sur

Strait of Hormuz

OMAN

Suhar

Muscat

Persepolis

Shiraz

Busheher

Ahvaz

Tigris

Euphrates

Abadan

Basra

Al Amarah

An Nasiriyah

Kuwait City

KUWAIT

Ad Dammam

Al Mubarrez

Haradh

Persian Gulf
(The Gulf)

Manama

BAHRAIN

Doha

QATAR

Abu Dhabi

UNITED ARAB
EMIRATES

Sharjah

Dubai

Al Ayn

OMAN

Arabian Sea

INDIAN

OCEAN

60°

H

G

55°

F

Socotra
(Yemen)

Cape Guardafui

Salalah

Rub al Khali
(Empty Quarter)

Arabian
Peninsula

SAUDI ARABIA

Riyadh

Buraydah

Hail

Medina

Mecca

At Taif

Jedda

Najran

Abha

3,133m
(10,279ft)

Asir

Farasan
Islands

Sadah

Marib

Sana

Dhamar

Ibb

Taizz

YEMEN

Hadhramaut

Al Mukalla

Aden

Gulf of Aden

SOMALIA

Berbera

Hargeysa

45°

Dire Dawa

Djibouti

DJIBOUTI

Dikhil

Bab al Mandab

Assab

Al Hudaydah

4,620m
(15,157ft)

Ras Dashen

Gonder

Bahir Dar

Lake Tana

Blue Nile

Ethiopian
Highlands

ETHIOPIA

Mekele

-116m
(-381ft) Kobar
Sink

Dese

Massawa

Asmara

Keren

ERITREA

Karora

Teseney

Kassala

Gedaref

Wad Medani

SUDAN

Atbarah

Port Sudan

Nubian Desert

Nile

Lake
Nasser

Aswan
Aswan High Dam
Tropic of Cancer

EGYPT

Luxor

Valley of
the Kings

Qena

Sohag

Asyut

El Minya

Beni Suef

Pyramids of Giza

Cairo

Ismailia

El Mansura

Port Said

Suez

Suez Canal

Delta

Jerusalem

Amman

Gaza

Beer Sheva

ISRAEL

JORDAN

Petra

Maan

Al Aqabah

Elat

Sinai

Mount
Sinai
2,285m
(7,497ft)

Sharm el Sheikh

Hurghada

Tabuk

Arabian
Desert

Hejaz

Red Sea

Syrian Desert

An Najaf

Mountains

Yazd

Dese

Dahlak
Archipelago

3,760m
(12,336ft)

7

20°

8

15°

9

7

20°

8

15°

9

6

30°

25°

35°E

40°

45°

50°

53

Copyright © Usborne Publishing Ltd.

ARCTIC

A
B
C
D
E

1

2

80°
20°
40°
60°
80°

60°

Svalbard
(Norway)

Franz Josef
Land

Norwegian
Sea

Arctic Circle

UNITED
KINGDOM
● **London**

North
Sea

NORWAY
■ **Oslo**

Paris ●

BELGIUM
NETHERLANDS

LUXEMBOURG

FRANCE

DENMARK

SWEDEN

GERMANY

■ **Berlin**

Baltic
Sea

■ **Stockholm**

FINLAND

● Murmansk

North Cape

Barents
Sea

Novaya
Zemlya

Kara
Sea

CZECH
REPUBLIC

AUSTRIA

POLAND

LITHUANIA

■ **Warsaw**

SLOVAKIA

■ **Budapest**

HUNGARY

■ **Vilnius**

LATVIA

ESTONIA

■ **Minsk**

BELARUS

■ **Helsinki**

Lake
Ladoga

St. Petersburg ●

Lake
Onega

Cherepovets ○

● Arkhangelsk

● Vorkuta

Norilsk ○

Kola
Peninsula

3

ROMANIA

MOLDOVA

■ **Chisinau**

■ **Kiev** ○

UKRAINE

Lviv ○

■ **Moscow**

Ryazan ○

Nizhniy Novgorod ○

Volga

Kazan ○

Perm ○

Ukhta ○

Novyy Urengoy ○

Ob

West Siberian
Plain

Surgut ○

Yenisey

Kharkiv ○

Odesa ○

Dnipropetrovsk ○

Voronezh ○

Samara ○

Yekaterinburg ○

Ob

Irtysh

Simferopol ○

Rostov ○

Volgograd ○

Krasnodar ○

Volga

Oral ○

Orenburg ○

Chelyabinsk ○

Omsk ○

Tomsk ○

Krasnoyars

R U S S

40°
N

Black
Sea

■ **Ankara**

TURKEY

Adana ○

Mount Elbrus
▲
5,642m
(18,510ft)

Astrakhan ○

Aqtobe ○

Atyrau ○

KAZAKHSTAN

■ **Astana**

Pavlodar ○

Novosibirsk ○

Barnaul ○

Abaka

GEORGIA

■ **Tbilisi**

ARMENIA

■ **Yerevan**

AZERBAIJAN

■ **Baku**

Caspian Sea

Aqtau ○

Aral
Sea

Qaraghandy ○

Oskemen ○

Kyzyl ○

Aleppo ○

SYRIA

Mosul ○

Tabriz ○

Nukus ○

Qyzylorda ○

Balqash ○

Lake
Balkhash

Altay ○

Alta

Damavand
▲
5,604m
(18,386ft)

Dasoguz ○

TURKMENISTAN

UZBEKISTAN

Shymkent ○

4

■ **Baghdad**

IRAQ

■ **Tehran**

Ahvaz ○

Esfahan ○

Mashhad ○

Ashgabat
(Ashkhabad) ■

Turkmenabat ○

■ **Tashkent**

Samarqand ○

■ **Dushanbe**

TAJIKISTAN

■ **Bishkek**

KYRGYZSTAN

Osh ○

Almaty ○

Tien Shan

Aksu ○

Urumqi ○

Kuwait City ●

KUWAIT

IRAN

Shiraz ○

Herat ○

Mazar-e Sharif ○

AFGHANISTAN

SAUDI
ARABIA

■ **Riyadh**

■ **Manama**

QATAR

■ **Doha**

Bandar-e
Abbas ○

Persian Gulf
(The Gulf)

Zahedan ○

Kandahar ○

■ **Kabul**

■ **Islamabad**

Srinagar ○

K2
▲
8,611m
(28,251ft)

PAKISTAN

Indus

Lahore ○

INDIA

Plateau of Tibet

■ **Abu Dhabi**

C
60°E
D
80°
E

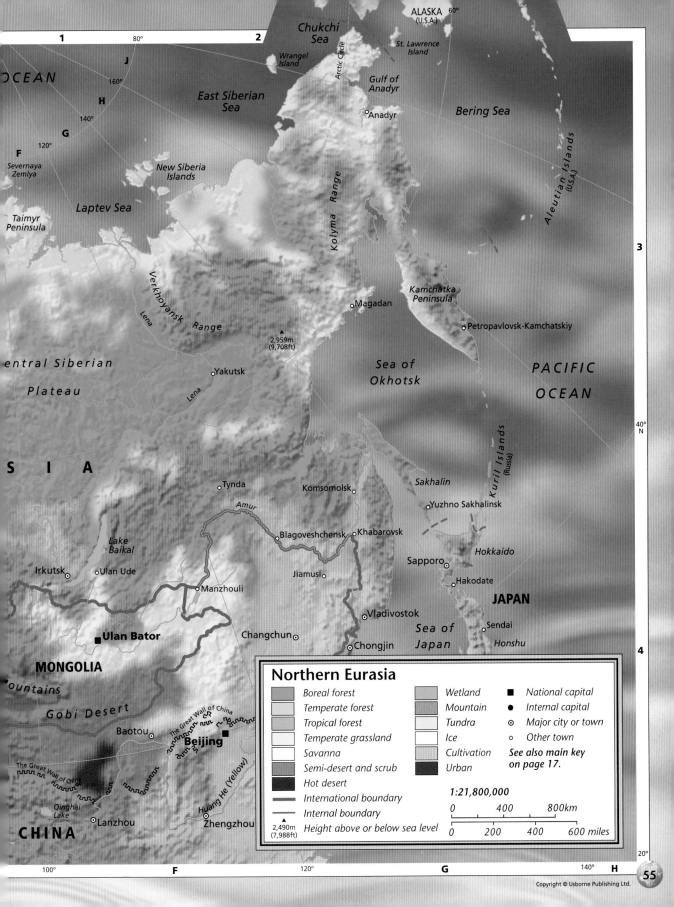

ALASKA 60°
(U.S.A.)

OCEAN

Chukchi
Sea

St. Lawrence
Island

Wrangel
Island

East Siberian
Sea

Gulf of
Anadyr

Bering Sea

° Anadyr

Aleutian Islands
(U.S.A.)

New Siberia
Islands

Severnaya
Zemlya

Laptev Sea

Taimyr
Peninsula

Kolyma Range

Kamchatka
Peninsula

PACIFIC

OCEAN

Verkhoyansk Range

Magadan

Petropavlovsk-Kamchatskiy

Lena

2,959m
(9,708ft)

entral Siberian

Plateau

° Yakutsk

Lena

Sea of
Okhotsk

40°
N

S I A

Tynda

Komsomolsk

Sakhalin

Kuril Islands
(Russia)

Amur

Yuzhno Sakhalinsk

Lake
Baikal

Blagoveshchensk

Khabarovsk

Hokkaido

Irkutsk

Ulan Ude

Jiamusi

Sapporo

Manzhouli

Hakodate

JAPAN

Vladivostok

Sendai

Ulan Bator

Changchun

Sea of
Japan

Honshu

MONGOLIA

Chongjin

ountains

Gobi Desert

The Great Wall of China

Baotou

Beijing

The Great Wall of China

Huang He (Yellow)

Qinghai
Lake

Lanzhou

CHINA

Zhengzhou

Northern Eurasia

Boreal forest	Wetland
Temperate forest	Mountain
Tropical forest	Tundra
Temperate grassland	Ice
Savanna	Cultivation
Semi-desert and scrub	Urban
Hot desert	

■ National capital
● Internal capital
⊙ Major city or town
○ Other town

*See also main key
on page 17.*

International boundary
Internal boundary

2,490m
(7,988ft) Height above or below sea level

1:21,800,000

0   400   800km

0   200   400   600 miles

20°

100°   F   120°   G   140°   H

EUROPE

Europe is a small continent, packed with over 40 countries and more than 700 million people. It has no deserts, but its geography ranges from high mountain ranges to icy tundra, rocky islands and lush farmland. With dozens of islands and peninsulas, many of Europe's countries are largely surrounded by sea.

The shading on this map is there to help you see clearly the different countries that make up the continent.

Internet links

For links to websites where you can find out more about the countries in Europe, go to www.usborne-quicklinks.com

Arctic Circle

ARCTIC OCEAN

Reykjavik
ICELAND

Norwegian
Sea

Faroe Islands
(Denmark)

SWEDEN

Shetland
Islands

NORWAY

Orkney
Islands

Oslo

Stockholm

North
Sea

DENMARK
Copenhagen

Baltic
Sea

IRELAND
Dublin

UNITED
KINGDOM

The
Hague
Amsterdam

NETHERLANDS

Berlin

POLAN

London

Brussels

BELGIUM

GERMANY

Paris

LUXEMBOURG
Luxembourg

Prague

CZECH
REPUBLIC

Rhine

Vienna

Bratislava

LIECHTENSTEIN

Bern
Vaduz

AUSTRIA

Budapest

Bay
of
Biscay

FRANCE

SWITZERLAND

SLOVENIA
Ljubljana

HUNGAR

Zagreb
CROATIA

ATLANTIC

OCEAN

MONACO

SAN MARINO

BOSNIA AND
HERZEGOVINA
Sarajevo

ANDORRA

Andorra
la Vella

ITALY

MONTENEGR

PORTUGAL

Corsica

Podgorica

Lisbon

Madrid

Rome
VATICAN CITY

ALBAN

SPAIN

Balearic
Islands

Sardinia

Tira

Mediterranean Sea

Sicily

MALTA
Valletta

56

Barents Sea

⊙ Murmansk

Arctic Circle

⊙ Arkhangelsk

FINLAND

elsinki

RUSSIA

■ St. Petersburg

■ Tallinn
ESTONIA

Nizhniy Novgorod ⊙   Kazan ⊙

Riga■ **LATVIA**

■ **Moscow**

LITHUANIA
■ Vilnius

SSIA

■ **Minsk**

BELARUS

Volga

Warsaw

■ **Kiev**

Volgograd ⊙

Dnieper

UKRAINE

OVAKIA

MOLDOVA

■ **Chisinau**

ROMANIA

Black Sea

elgrade

■ **Bucharest**

Danube

RBIA

Pristina BULGARIA

OSOVO ■ Sofia

■ Skopje

ACEDONIA

TURKEY

REECE

■ Athens

Crete

Russia and Turkey lie partly in Europe
and partly in Asia. This map shows the
European parts. You can see full maps
of the countries in the Asia section of
the atlas, starting on page 42.

Facts

Total land area 10,205,720 sq km
(3,940,428 sq miles) (including
European Russia)
Total population 731 million
(including all of Russia)
Biggest city Paris, France
Biggest country Russia *Total area:
17,075,200 sq km (6,592,735 sq
miles) Area of European Russia:
4,294,400 sq km (1,658,068 sq
miles)*
Smallest country Vatican City *0.44
sq km (0.17 sq miles)*

Highest mountain Elbrus, Russia
5,642m (18,510ft)
Longest river Volga *3,692km
(2,294 miles)*
Biggest lake Lake Ladoga, Russia
17,700 sq km (6,834 sq miles)
Highest waterfall Utigard, on the
Jostedal Glacier, Norway *818m
(2,685ft)*
Biggest desert No deserts in Europe
Biggest island Great Britain *229,870
sq km (88,753 sq miles)*

Main mineral deposits Bauxite, zinc,
iron, potash, fluorspar
Main fuel deposits Oil, coal, natural
gas, peat, uranium

A dairy cow in Devon,
in the south of England

57

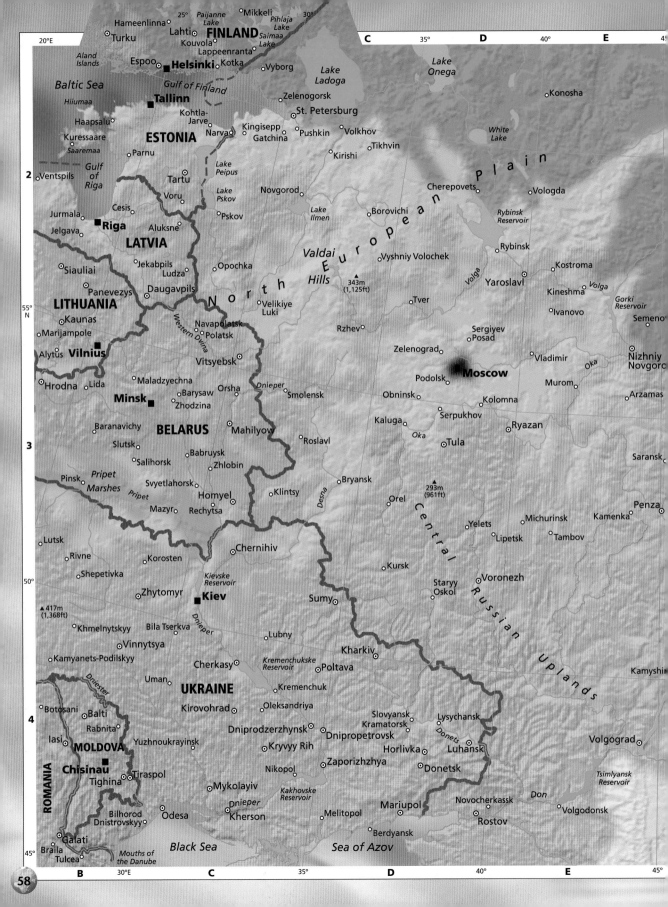

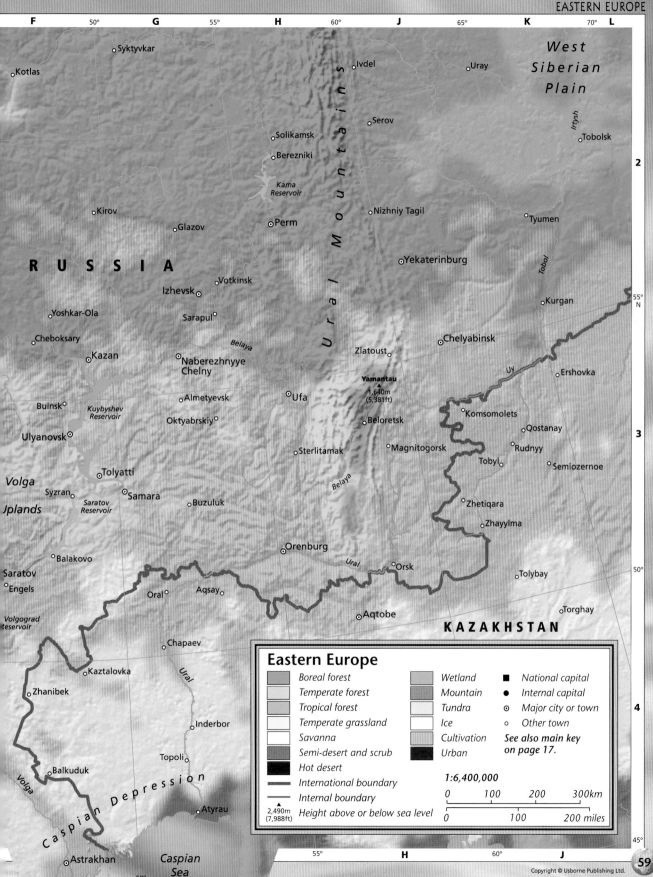

West
Siberian
Plain

F · 50° · G · 55° · H · 60° · J · 65° · K · 70° · L

Kotlas
Syktyvkar
Ivdel
Uray

2

Serov
Solikamsk
Berezniki
Tobolsk

Kama
Reservoir

Kirov
Nizhniy Tagil
Glazov
Perm
Tyumen

Yekaterinburg

R U S S I A

55°
N

Izhevsk
Votkinsk
Yoshkar-Ola
Sarapul
Kurgan

Cheboksary
Belaya
Zlatoust
Chelyabinsk

Ural Mountains

Kazan
Naberezhnyye
Chelny
Yamantau
1,640m
(5,381ft)
Ershovka
Uy

Buinsk
Kuybyshev
Reservoir
Almetyevsk
Ufa
Beloretsk
Komsomolets

Ulyanovsk
Oktyabrskiy
Qostanay
Rudnyy

3

Sterlitamak
Magnitogorsk
Tobyl
Semiozernoe

Volga
Tolyatti
Belaya

Jplands
Syzran
Samara
Saratov
Reservoir
Buzuluk
Zhetiqara

Zhayylma

Balakovo
Orenburg

Saratov
Ural
Orsk
Tolybay

50°

Engels
Oral
Aqsay

Volgograd
Reservoir
Aqtobe
Torghay

K A Z A K H S T A N

Chapaev

Kaztalovka
Ural

Zhanibek

Inderbor

4

Topoli

Balkuduk

Volga
Caspian Depression
Atyrau

Astrakhan
Caspian
Sea

45°

50° · 55° · H · 60° · J

Eastern Europe

▦ Boreal forest	▦ Wetland	■ National capital
▦ Temperate forest	▦ Mountain	● Internal capital
▦ Tropical forest	▦ Tundra	⊙ Major city or town
▦ Temperate grassland	▦ Ice	○ Other town
▦ Savanna	▦ Cultivation	**See also main key**
▦ Semi-desert and scrub	▦ Urban	**on page 17.**
▦ Hot desert		

International boundary
Internal boundary

▲ 2,490m
(7,988ft)
Height above or below sea level

1:6,400,000

0   100   200   300km

0   100   200 miles

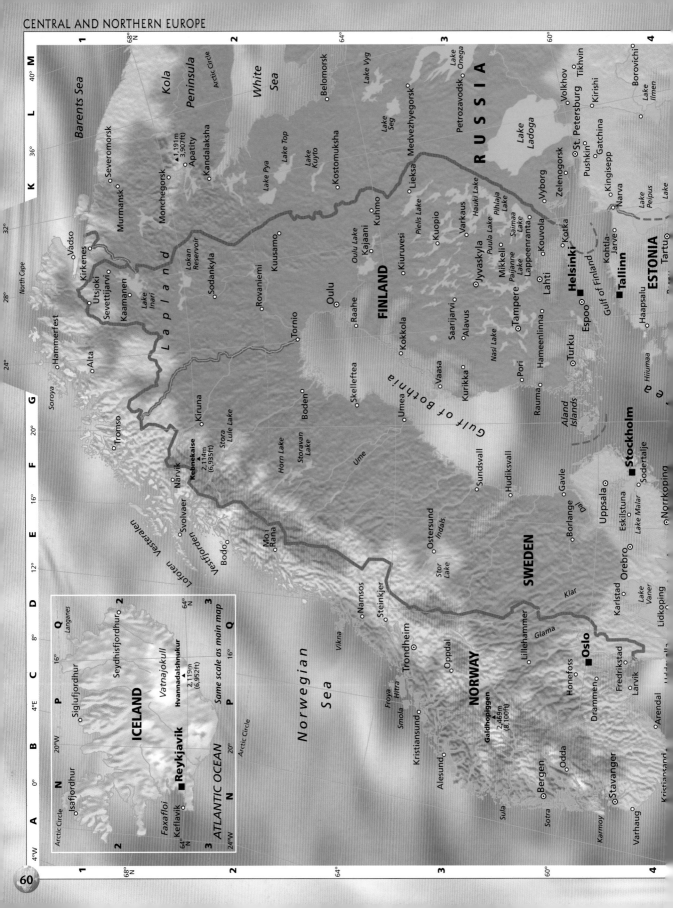

Top coordinates: 1 | 68°N | 2 | 64° | 3 | 60° | 4

Top latitude markers: 40° M | 36° K | 32° | 28° | 24° G | 20° F | 16° E | 12° D | 8° C | 4°E B | 0° A | 4°W

Barents Sea

Kola Peninsula

Arctic Circle

White Sea

RUSSIA

Severomorsk
Murmansk
Monchegorsk
▲1,191m
3,907ft
Apatity
Kandalaksha

Lake Top
Lake Vyg
Belomorsk

Lake Pya
Lake Kuyto
Kostomuksha

Lake Seg

Lake Onega
Medvezhyegorsk
Petrozavodsk

Lake Ladoga

Volkhov
Tikhvin
St. Petersburg
Pushkin
Gatchina
Kirishi
Borovichi

Lake Ilmen

Zelenogorsk
Vyborg
Kingisepp
Narva

Lake Peipus
Lake

Vadso
Kirkenes
Utsjoki
Sevettijarvi
Kaamanen

Lieksa
Kuhmo

Pielis Lake
Hauki Lake
Pihlaja Lake
Saimaa Lake
Lappeenranta

Kouvola
Kotka

Helsinki
Espoo

Gulf of Finland

Kohtla-Jarve
Tallinn

ESTONIA
Tartu

Hammerfest
Alta
Soroya

Tromso

Lake Inari

Lokan Reservoir
Sodankyla

Kuusamo

Oulu Lake
Kajaani
Varkaus
Kiuruvesi
Kuopio
Jyvaskyla
Mikkeli
Pajanne Lake

Lahti
Hameenlinna

Haapsalu
Hiiumaa

Lapland

Rovaniemi

Raahe
Oulu

FINLAND

Saarijarvi
Alavus

Nasi Lake
Tampere

Turku

North Cape

Sevettijarvi

Tornio

Skelleftea

Kokkola

Vaasa
Kurikka

Pori
Rauma

Aland Islands

Stockholm
Sodertalje

Kebnekaise
▲2,114m
(6,935ft)
Narvik
Svolvaer

Lofoten

Vesteralen

Kiruna

Stora Lule Lake
Boden

Horn Lake
Storavan Lake

Ume

Umea

Gulf of Bothnia

Gavle
Uppsala
Eskilstuna
Lake Malar

Norrkoping

Bodo
Moi Rana

Sundsvall
Hudiksvall

Borlange
Dal

Vatfjorden

Ostersund
Indals

Stor Lake

SWEDEN

Orebro
Lake Vaner
Lidkoping

Norwegian Sea

Namsos
Steinkjer

Trondheim
Oppdal

Vikna

Froya
Hitra
Smola

Lillehammer
Glama

Karlstad
Klar

Kristiansund

Galdhopiggen
▲2,469m
(8,100ft)

NORWAY

Honefoss
Drammen
Oslo
Fredrikstad
Larvik

Alesund

Bergen
Odda
Sula
Sotra

Stavanger
Arendal

Varhaug
Karmoy
Kristiansand

Inset map — Iceland:

A | B | C | D | (top: N P Q)

4°W | 0° | 4°E B | 20°W | 16° | 8° C | 64°N D | 16° Q | 3

Arctic Circle

Langanes

Isafjordhur
Siglufjordhur
Seydhisfjordhur

ICELAND

Vatnajokull
Hvannadalshnukur
▲2,119m
(6,952ft)

Faxafloi
Keflavik
Reykjavik

ATLANTIC OCEAN

Arctic Circle

Same scale as main map

64°N
24°W

Bottom coordinates: 1 | 68°N | 2 | 64° | 3 | 60° | 4

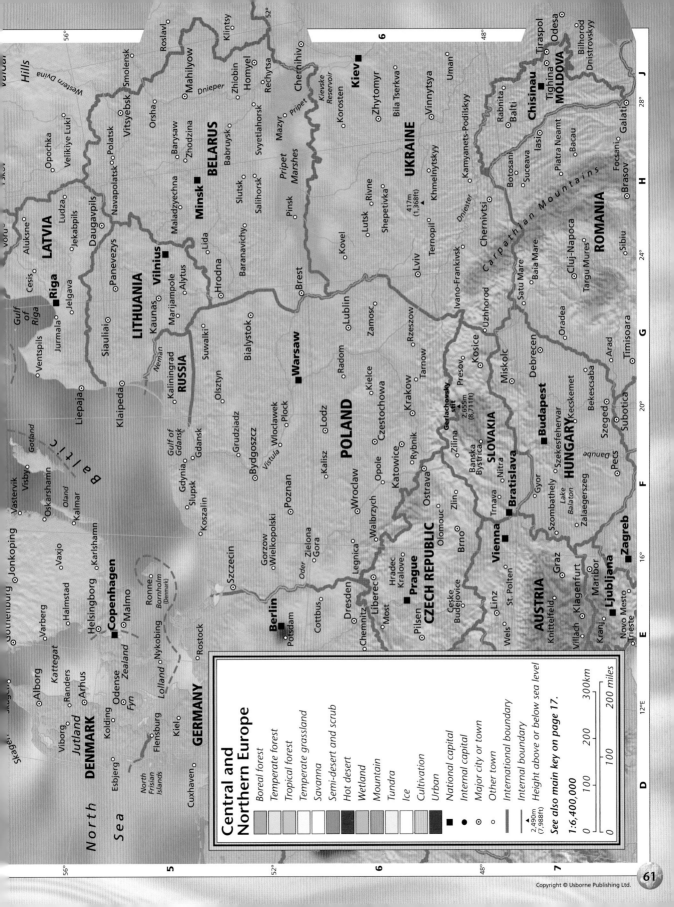

Central and Northern Europe

Boreal forest
Temperate forest
Tropical forest
Temperate grassland
Savanna
Semi-desert and scrub
Hot desert
Wetland
Mountain
Tundra
Ice
Cultivation
Urban

■ National capital
● Internal capital
⊙ Major city or town
○ Other town
— International boundary
— Internal boundary
▲ 2,490m (7,988ft) Height above or below sea level

See also main key on page 17.

1:6,400,000

0   100   200   300km
0   100   200 miles

Countries and labels

DENMARK
GERMANY
LATVIA
LITHUANIA
RUSSIA
POLAND
BELARUS
UKRAINE
CZECH REPUBLIC
SLOVAKIA
AUSTRIA
HUNGARY
ROMANIA
MOLDOVA

Baltic Sea
North Sea
Gulf of Riga
Gulf of Gdansk
Carpathian Mountains
Pripet Marshes
Kievske Reservoir

National capitals
Copenhagen
Berlin
Riga
Vilnius
Minsk
Warsaw
Kiev
Prague
Bratislava
Vienna
Budapest
Ljubljana
Zagreb
Chisinau

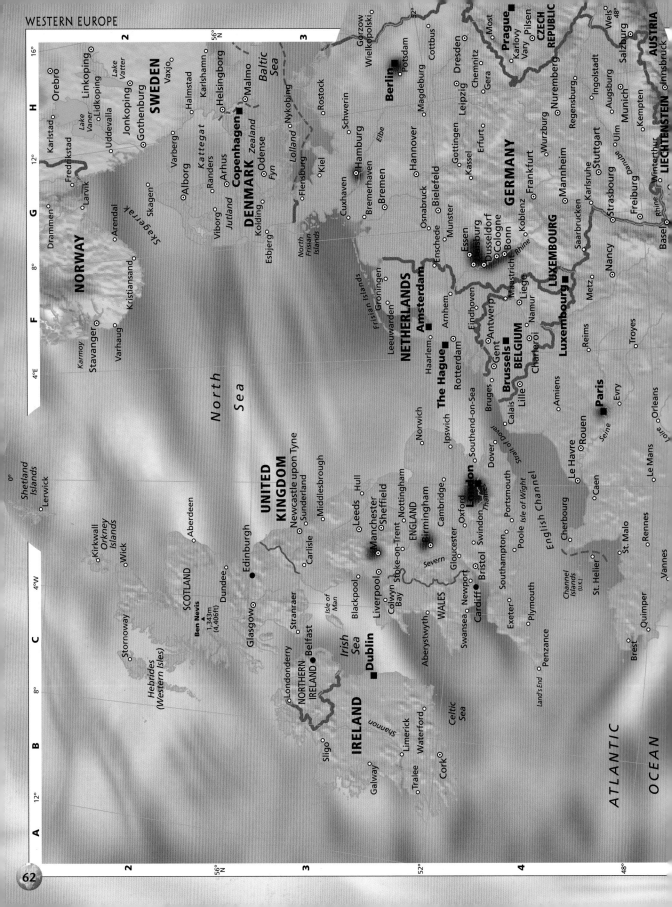

ATLANTIC

OCEAN

IRELAND

Galway
Sligo
Tralee
Cork
Limerick
Waterford
Celtic
Sea
Shannon

NORTHERN
IRELAND
Belfast
Londonderry
Dublin

Stranraer
Glasgow
Hebrides
(Western Isles)
Stornoway
SCOTLAND
Ben Nevis
1,343m
(4,406ft)
Dundee
Edinburgh

Kirkwall
Orkney
Islands
Wick
Aberdeen
Shetland
Islands
Lerwick

Isle of
Man
Irish
Sea

Blackpool
Liverpool
Colwyn
Bay
Aberystwyth
WALES
Swansea
Newport
Cardiff
Land's End
Penzance
Brest
Quimper
Vannes

Manchester
Stoke-on-Trent
Sheffield
Leeds
Hull
Nottingham
Birmingham
ENGLAND
Gloucester
Severn
Bristol
Swindon
Exeter
Plymouth
Channel
Islands
(U.K.)
St. Helier
St. Malo
Rennes
Le Mans

Carlisle
Middlesbrough
Newcastle upon Tyne
Sunderland

UNITED
KINGDOM

Leeds
Cambridge
Oxford
London
Thames
Southampton
Portsmouth
Poole
Isle of Wight
English Channel
Cherbourg
Caen
Le Havre
Rouen
Seine
Paris
Evry

Norwich
Ipswich
Southend-on-Sea
Dover
Strait of Dover
Calais
Boulogne
Amiens
Reims
Troyes
Orleans
Loire

NORTH
Sea

NORWAY

Stavanger
Karmoy
Varhaug
Kristiansand
Arendal
Larvik
Drammen

SWEDEN

Orebro
Karlstad
Fredrikstad
Uddevalla
Linkoping
Lidkoping
Vaxjo
Jonkoping
Gothenburg
Lake
Vatter
Lake
Vaner
Varberg
Halmstad
Helsingborg
Malmo
Karlshamn
Helsingborg

Baltic
Sea

Rostock
Nykobing
Lolland
Zealand
Copenhagen
DENMARK
Odense
Fyn
Kolding
Randers
Arhus
Viborg
Alborg
Skagen
Skagerrak
Kattegat
Jutland
Esbjerg

North
Frisian
Islands
Kiel
Flensburg
Cuxhaven
Bremerhaven
Bremen
Hamburg
Schwerin
Elbe
Berlin
Potsdam
Cottbus
Gorzow
Wielkopolski
Dresden
Chemnitz
Gera
Leipzig
Magdeburg
Hannover
Gottingen
Kassel
Erfurt
Wurzburg
Frankfurt
GERMANY
Nuremberg
Regensburg
Ingolstadt
Augsburg
Munich
Kempten
AUSTRIA
Innsbruck
Salzburg
LIECHTENSTEIN
Winterthur
Basel
Freiburg
Rhine
Danube
Strasbourg
Nancy
Metz
LUXEMBOURG
Luxembourg
Saarbrucken
Karlsruhe
Stuttgart
Mannheim
Koblenz
Bonn
Cologne
Dusseldorf
Essen
Duisburg
Munster
Osnabruck
Bielefeld
Enschede
Groningen
Leeuwarden
Frisian Islands
NETHERLANDS
Amsterdam
Haarlem
The Hague
Rotterdam
Arnhem
Eindhoven
Maastricht
Liege
Namur
Charleroi
BELGIUM
Brussels
Gent
Antwerp
Bruges
Lille
Most
Pilsen
Karlovy
Vary
Prague
CZECH
REPUBLIC
Wels

North
Frisian
Islands

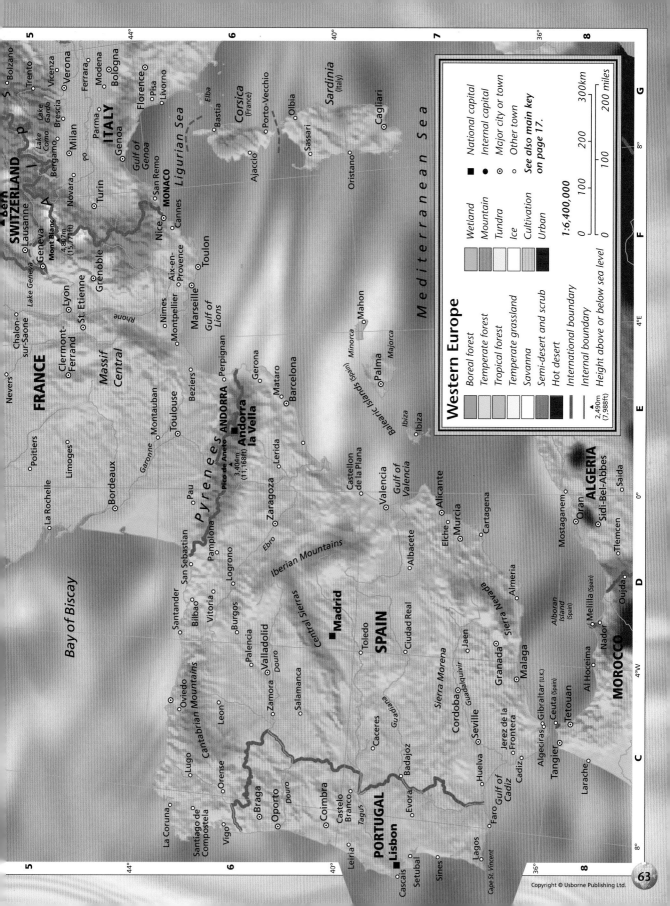

A 0° B 4°E C 8° D 12° E 16°

Cherbourg
Le Havre
Caen
Rouen
Amiens
Charleroi
Namur
BELGIUM
Koblenz
Frankfurt
Erfurt
Gera
Dresden
Chemnitz
Wroclaw
Walbrzych
Op

LUXEMBOURG
Luxembourg
Most
Liberec
Hradec Kralove
Karlovy Vary
Pilsen
Prague
CZECH REPUBLIC

Paris
Reims
Metz
Saarbrucken
Mannheim
Wurzburg
Nuremberg
Karlovy Vary
Olomouc
Brno
Zlir

Evry
GERMANY
Regensburg

Le Mans
Orleans
Troyes
Nancy
Karlsruhe
Stuttgart
Ingolstadt
Danube
Augsburg
Ceske Budejovice
Linz
Vienna
Trna

Angers
Tours
Strasbourg
Rhine
Ulm
Munich
Wels
St. Polten
Bratislav

Poitiers
Nevers
Dijon
Freiburg
Kempten
Salzburg
Gyor

FRANCE
Besancon
Basel
Zurich
Winterthur
Innsbruck
AUSTRIA
Knittelfeld
Szombathely
Chalon-sur-Saone
Biel
Lucerne
Vaduz
LIECHTENSTEIN
Grossglockner 3,798m (12,461ft)
Graz
La Balat

Limoges
Geneva
BERN
SWITZERLAND
Lausanne
Lake Geneva
A L P S
Villach
Klagenfurt
Zalaegersz

Clermont-Ferrand
Lyon
Mont Blanc 4,807m (15,771ft)
Bolzano
Kranj
SLOVENIA
Ljubljana
Maribor

Massif Central
Grenoble
Novara
Lake Como
Trento
Bergamo
Lake Garda
Brescia
Vicenza
Novo Mesto
Trieste
Zagreb
CROATIA

Garonne
Milan
Turin
Po
Verona
Venice
Rijeka
Karlovac
Slavon Br

Montauban
Parma
Modena
Ferrara
Bologna
Pula
Banja Luka
BOSNIA AND HERZEGOVIN
Zen

Toulouse
Rhone
Genoa
Gulf of Genoa
Ravenna
Rimini
Zadar
Dinaric Alps

Montpellier
Nimes
Aix-en-Provence
Nice
San Remo
MONACO
Cannes
ITALY
Livorno
Pisa
Florence
SAN MARINO
Ancona
Split
Mos

Beziers
Andorra la Vella
Gulf of Lions
Marseille
Toulon
Ligurian Sea
Perugia
Apennines
Adriatic Sea

Bastia
Elba
Terni
Pescara

Ajaccio
Corsica (France)
VATICAN CITY
Rome
Foggia
Bari

Porto-Vecchio
Olbia
Naples
Pompeii
Salerno
Taranto

Sassari
Sardinia (Italy)
Tyrrhenian Sea
Cosenza
Catanzar

Oristano
Lipari Islands

Cagliari
Mediterranean Sea

Trapani
Palermo
Messina

Sicily
Mount Etna 3,323m (10,902ft)
Catania

Annaba
Menzel Bourguiba
Bizerte
Carthage
Agrigento
Ragusa
Syracuse

Guelma
Tunis
Pantelleria (Italy)

Souk Ahras
Nabeul
MALTA
Valletta

TUNISIA
Sousse
Monastir
Pelagian Islands (Italy)

Tebessa
Kairouan

Kasserine
El Jem
Biskra

Southern Europe

	Boreal forest
	Temperate forest
	Tropical forest
	Temperate grassland
	Savanna
	Semi-desert and scrub
	Hot desert
	Wetland
	Mountain
	Tundra
	Ice
	Cultivation
	Urban
■	National capital
●	Internal capital
⊙	Major city or town
○	Other town
	International boundary
	Internal boundary
▲ 2,490m (7,988ft)	Height above or below sea level

See also main key on page 17.

1:6,400,000

0   100   200   300km

0   100   200 miles

B 4°E C 8° D 12° E 16°

AFRICA

Africa is the second-biggest continent and has 53 countries altogether. More than a quarter of them are landlocked, with no access to the sea except through other countries. Africa is home to the world's longest river, the Nile, and its largest desert, the Sahara. It also has vast amounts of natural resources, such as gold, copper and diamonds. Many of them have not yet begun to be used.

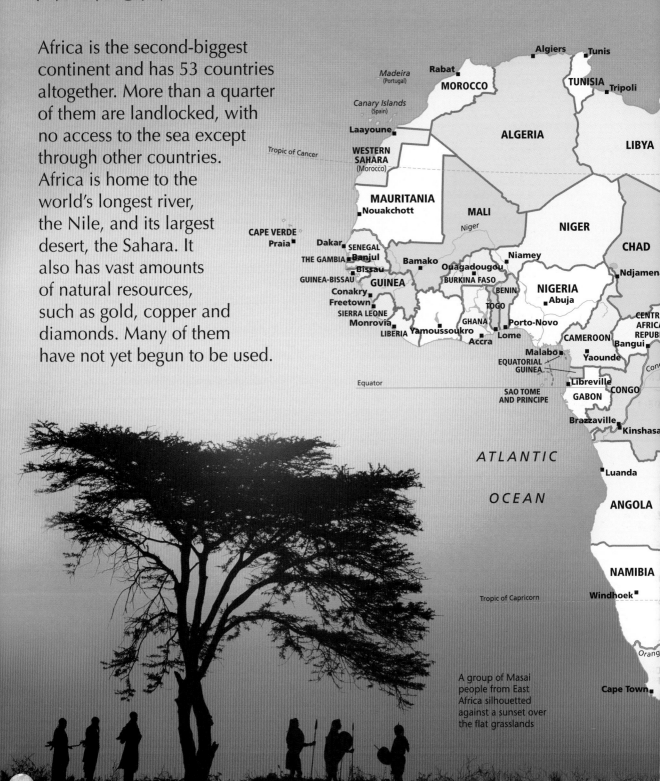

Madeira
(Portugal)

Canary Islands
(Spain)

Tropic of Cancer

Algiers
Tunis
Rabat
MOROCCO
TUNISIA
Tripoli
Laayoune
ALGERIA
LIBYA
WESTERN
SAHARA
(Morocco)
MAURITANIA
Nouakchott
MALI
NIGER
CHAD
Niger
CAPE VERDE
Praia
Dakar
SENEGAL
THE GAMBIA
Banjul
Bamako
Niamey
Ndjamena
Bissau
Ouagadougou
GUINEA-BISSAU
GUINEA
BURKINA FASO
NIGERIA
Conakry
BENIN
Abuja
Freetown
TOGO
SIERRA LEONE
GHANA
Porto-Novo
CENTRAL
Monrovia
Yamoussoukro
Lome
CAMEROON
AFRICAN
LIBERIA
Accra
Bangui
REPUBLIC
Malabo
Yaounde
EQUATORIAL
GUINEA
Libreville
Equator
Cong
SAO TOME
GABON
CONGO
AND PRINCIPE
Brazzaville
Kinshasa

ATLANTIC

OCEAN

Luanda

ANGOLA

NAMIBIA

Tropic of Capricorn
Windhoek

Orang

A group of Masai people from East Africa silhouetted against a sunset over the flat grasslands

Cape Town

The shading on this map is there to help you see clearly the different countries that make up the continent.

Cairo■

EGYPT

Tropic of Cancer

Nile

Khartoum■

ERITREA
Asmara■

SUDAN

DJIBOUTI■ Djibouti■

Addis Ababa■

SOMALIA

ETHIOPIA

ONGO

UGANDA
Kampala■

KENYA

Mogadishu■

Equator

DEM.

Kigali■
RWANDA■
BURUNDI
Bujumbura■

Nairobi■

REP.)

Dodoma■

Victoria■
SEYCHELLES

TANZANIA ■Dar es Salaam

INDIAN

MALAWI

Moroni■
COMOROS

OCEAN

ZAMBIA
Lusaka■

Lilongwe■

Zambezi

Harare■
ZIMBABWE

MOZAMBIQUE

Antananarivo■

TSWANA

MADAGASCAR

MAURITIUS
■Port Louis

Reunion
(France)

Tropic of Capricorn

orone■
Pretoria■
(Tshwane) Maputo■

Mbabane■ SWAZILAND
Lobamba■

emfontein■
■Maseru
LESOTHO

OUTH
FRICA

Internet links

For links to websites where you can find out more about the countries in Africa, go to **www.usborne-quicklinks.com**

Facts

Total land area 30,221,532 sq km (11,668,594 sq miles)

Total population 922 million

Biggest city Cairo, Egypt

Biggest country Sudan 2,505,810 sq km (967,493 sq miles)

Smallest country Seychelles 455 sq km (176 sq miles)

Highest mountain Kilimanjaro, Tanzania 5,895m (19,341ft)

Longest river Nile, running from to Burundi to Egypt 6,671km (4,145 miles)

Biggest lake Lake Victoria, between Tanzania, Kenya and Uganda 68,800 sq km (26,564 sq miles)

Highest waterfall Tugela Falls, on the Tugela River, South Africa 610m (2,000ft)

Biggest desert Sahara, North Africa 9,100,000 sq km (3,500,000 sq miles)

Biggest island Madagascar 587,040 sq km (226,656 sq miles)

Main mineral deposits Gold, copper, diamonds, iron ore, manganese, bauxite

Main fuel deposits Coal, uranium, natural gas

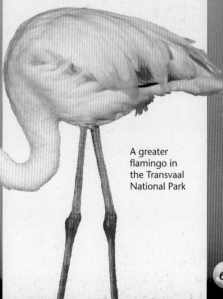

A greater flamingo in the Transvaal National Park

Annaba
Bizerte
Menzel
Carthage
Bourguiba
Tunis
Sicily
(Italy)
Catania
Syracuse
20°
GREECE **Ather**

A 0° B 5°E

Saida
Djelfa
Batna
Tebessa
Kairouan
Sousse
Monastir
El Jem
MALTA
Pelagian Islands
(Italy)
Valletta

Atlas Mountains
Biskra
Gafsa
Sfax
Kerkenah Islands
Pantelleria
(Italy)

2
El Oued
Tozeur
Gabes
Gulf of Gabes
Jerba
Ghardaia
Touggourt
Chott el Jerid

M e d i t e r r a n e a

Ouargla
Tataouine
TUNISIA
Tripoli
Al Khums
Cyrene
Darnah
Leptis Magna
Misratah
Al Bayda

30°N
Gharyan
Benghazi
Tubruq

Tademait Plateau
Ghadamis
Surt
Gulf of Sidra
Ajdabiya

Great Eastern Erg

3
ALGERIA

Sabha
LIBYA

25°
Illizi
Murzuq
Libya

Ghat

Ahaggar Mountains
Mount Tahat
2,918m
(9,573ft)
Tropic of Cancer
Al Jaw

4
Tamanrasset

Djado Plateau
Tibesti Mountains

20°
Emi Koussi
3,415m
(11,204ft)

MALI S A H A R A

5
Agadez
Faya-Largeau

NIGER
Bodele Depression
Ennedi Plateau

Tahoua
15°
CHAD

Mao
Dosso
Maradi
Zinder
S A H E L
Abeche
Sokoto
Mount M
Birnin-Kebbi
Katsina
Lake Chad
3,08
(10,13
Gusau
Kano
Ndjamena
Kandi
Zaria
Potiskum
Maiduguri
Mongo
Nya
Kaduna
NIGERIA
Am Timan
Kainji Reservoir

7
Saki
Minna
Jos
Kumo
Maroua
Birao
Niger
Bida
Abuja
CAMEROON
Bongor

68
B 5°E C 10° D 15° E 20° F

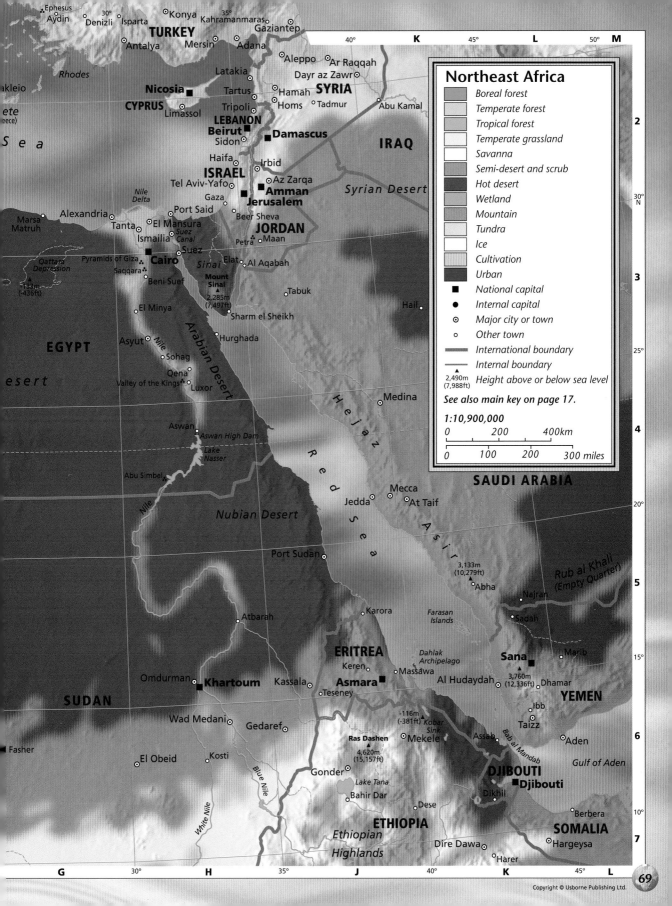

Northeast Africa

Key
- Boreal forest
- Temperate forest
- Tropical forest
- Temperate grassland
- Savanna
- Semi-desert and scrub
- Hot desert
- Wetland
- Mountain
- Tundra
- Ice
- Cultivation
- Urban

■ National capital
● Internal capital
⊙ Major city or town
○ Other town
— International boundary
— Internal boundary
▲ 2,490m (7,988ft) Height above or below sea level

See also main key on page 17.

1:10,900,000

0   200   400km
0   100   200   300 miles

TURKEY
Ephesus
Aydin
30°
Denizli
Isparta
Konya
35°
Kahramanmaras
Gaziantep
40°
K
45°
L
50°
M

Antalya
Mersin
Adana
Aleppo
Ar Raqqah
Dayr az Zawr
Rhodes
Latakia
Hamah
Homs
Tadmur
Abu Kamal
SYRIA
IRAQ

Nicosia
CYPRUS
Limassol
Tartus
Tripoli

LEBANON
Beirut
Sidon
Damascus

kleio
(eece)
Sea

Haifa
Irbid
Az Zarqa
Syrian Desert

ISRAEL
Tel Aviv-Yafo
Gaza
Amman
Jerusalem
Beer Sheva

Nile Delta
Alexandria
Tanta
El Mansura
Port Said
Ismailia
Suez Canal

Marsa Matruh
Suez
Petra
Maan
JORDAN

Qattara Depression
-133m (-436ft)
Pyramids of Giza
Saqqara
Cairo
Beni Suef
Sinai
Elat
Al Aqabah
Tabuk

Mount Sinai
2,285m (7,497ft)
Hail

EGYPT
El Minya
Sharm el Sheikh

Asyut
Nile
Sohag
Hurghada

Arabian Desert
Qena
Valley of the Kings
Luxor

esert

Medina

Aswan
Aswan High Dam
Lake Nasser
Hejaz
Red Sea

Abu Simbel

Mecca
At Taif
Jedda

SAUDI ARABIA

Nubian Desert
Asir

Port Sudan
3,133m (10,279ft)
Abha

Rub al Khali (Empty Quarter)

Najran
Sadah

Atbarah
Karora
Farasan Islands

Omdurman
Khartoum
Kassala
ERITREA
Keren
Dahlak Archipelago
Massawa
Sana
3,760m (12,336ft)
Marib

Asmara
Teseney
Al Hudaydah
Dhamar
YEMEN

SUDAN
Ibb
Taizz

Wad Medani
Gedaref
-116m (-381ft)
Kobar Sink
Mekele
Assab
Aden

Fasher
Gulf of Aden

El Obeid
Kosti
Ras Dashen
4,620m (15,157ft)
Bab al Mandab
Dikhil
Berbera

Gonder
Lake Tana
Dese
DJIBOUTI
Djibouti
SOMALIA

Blue Nile
Bahir Dar

ETHIOPIA
Ethiopian Highlands
Dire Dawa
Hargeysa
Harer

White Nile

G
30°
H
35°
J
40°
K
45°
L

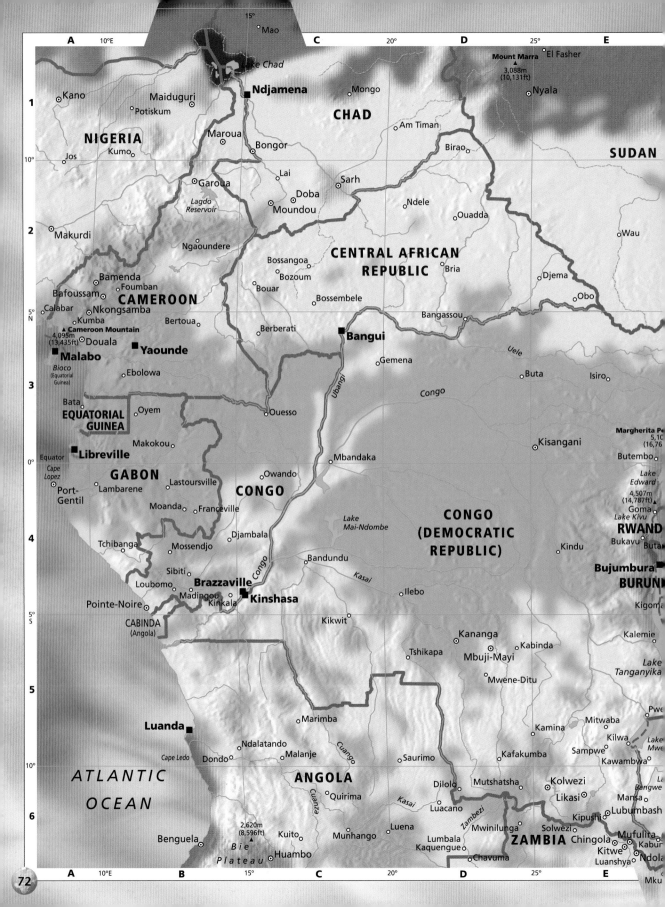

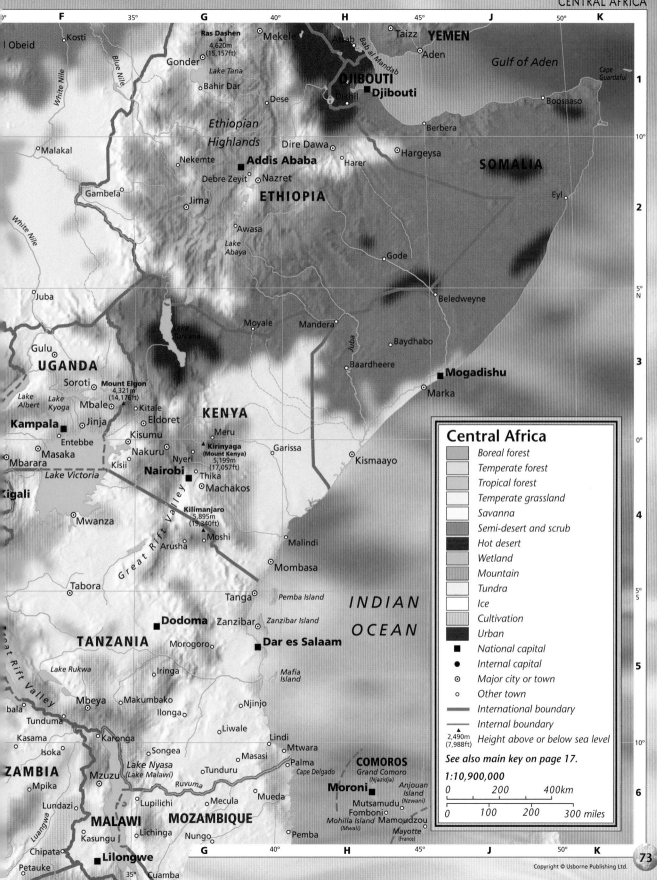

| | F | | 35° | | G | | 40° | | H | | 45° | | J | | 50° | | K | |

l Obeid   Kosti

Ras Dashen
4,620m
(15,157ft)   Mekele

Blue Nile
White Nile
Gonder

Lake Tana

Bahir Dar

Dese

Assab
Bab al Mandab   Taizz   YEMEN

Aden

Gulf of Aden

Cape
Guardafui

DJIBOUTI
Dikhil   Djibouti

Boosaaso

Berbera

Ethiopian
Highlands

Dire Dawa   Hargeysa

SOMALIA

Malakal

Nekemte   Addis Ababa   Harer

Eyl

Gambela

Debre Zeyit   Nazret

Jima   ETHIOPIA

White Nile

Awasa

Lake
Abaya

Gode

Juba

Moyale   Mandera

Baydhabo

Juba

Beledweyne

Gulu

UGANDA   Baardheere

Soroti   Mount Elgon
4,321m
(14,176ft)   Mogadishu

Lake
Albert   Lake
Kyoga   Mbale   Kitale   Marka

Kampala   Jinja   Eldoret   KENYA

Entebbe   Kisumu   Meru   Garissa

Masaka   Nakuru   Kirinyaga
(Mount Kenya)
5,199m
(17,057ft)   Kismaayo

Mbarara   Nyeri

Kisii   Nairobi   Thika

Lake Victoria   Machakos

Kigali   Kilimanjaro
5,895m
(19,340ft)

Mwanza   Arusha   Moshi   Malindi

Great Rift Valley   Mombasa

Tabora   INDIAN

Tanga   Pemba Island   OCEAN

Dodoma   Zanzibar   Zanzibar Island

TANZANIA   Morogoro

Mafia
Island

Lake Rukwa   Iringa

bala   Mbeya   Makumbako   Njinjo

Tunduma   Ilonga

Kasama   Karonga   Liwale

Isoka   Songea   Lindi

Masasi   Mtwara

ZAMBIA   Mzuzu   Lake Nyasa
(Lake Malawi)   Tunduru   Palma   Cape Delgado   COMOROS
Grand Comoro
(Njazidja)

Mpika   Ruvuma   Moroni   Anjouan
Island
(Nzwani)

Lundazi   Lupilichi   Mecula   Mueda   Mutsamudu

Chipata   MALAWI   MOZAMBIQUE   Fomboni   Mamoudzou
Mohilla Island
(Mwali)

Kasungu   Lichinga   Nungo   Mayotte
(France)

Lilongwe

Petauke   Pemba

Cuamba

Copyright © Usborne Publishing Ltd.

Central Africa

- Boreal forest
- Temperate forest
- Tropical forest
- Temperate grassland
- Savanna
- Semi-desert and scrub
- Hot desert
- Wetland
- Mountain
- Tundra
- Ice
- Cultivation
- Urban
- ■ National capital
- ● Internal capital
- ⊙ Major city or town
- ○ Other town
- ── International boundary
- ── Internal boundary
- ▲ 2,490m
(7,988ft)   Height above or below sea level

See also main key on page 17.

1:10,900,000

0   200   400km

0   100   200   300 miles

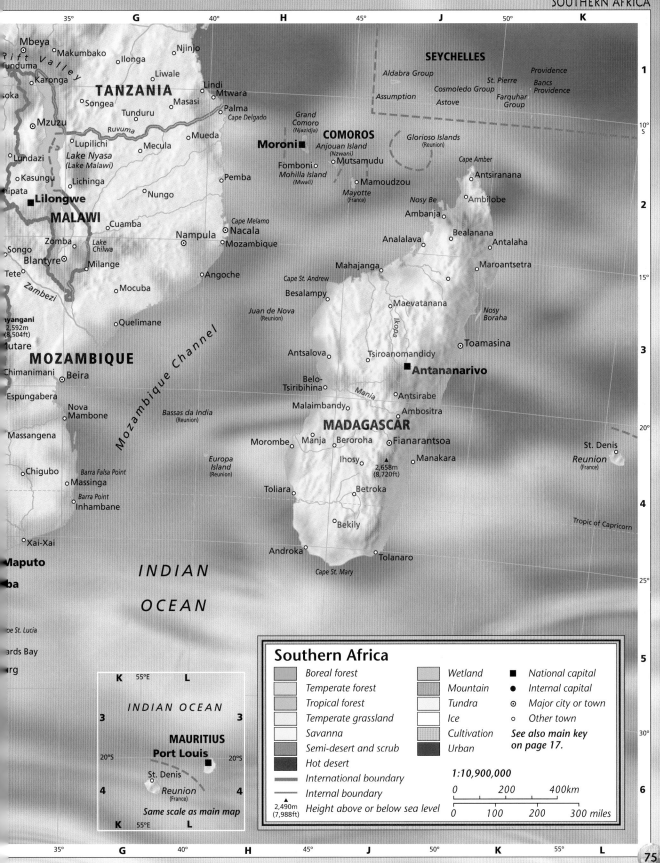

Mbeya
Makumbako
Ilonga
Njinjo
unduma
Karonga
Liwale
Lindi
Mtwara
TANZANIA
oka
Mzuzu
Songea
Masasi
Palma
Tunduru
Cape Delgado
Grand
Comoro
(Njazidja)
SEYCHELLES
Aldabra Group
Providence
St. Pierre
Bancs
Cosmoledo Group
Providence
Assumption
Astove
Farquhar
Group

Lundazi
Lupilichi
Mecula
Mueda
COMOROS
Moroni ■
Anjouan Island
(Nzwani)
Glorioso Islands
(Reunion)
Cape Amber
hipata
Kasungu
Lichinga
Lake Nyasa
(Lake Malawi)
Nungo
Fomboni
Mutsamudu
Antsiranana
Lilongwe ■
Nampula
Cape Melamo
Nacala
Mohilla Island
(Mwali)
Mamoudzou
Mayotte
(France)
Ambilobe
MALAWI
Cuamba
Mozambique
Nosy Be
Ambanja
Zomba
Lake
Chilwa
Analalava
Bealanana
Songo
Blantyre
Milange
Angoche
Cape St. Andrew
Besalampy
Mahajanga
Antalaha
Tete
Zambezi
Maevatanana
Maroantsetra
yangani
2,592m
(8,504ft)
Mocuba
Juan de Nova
(Reunion)
Ikopa
Nosy
Boraha
utare
Quelimane
Antsalova
Tsiroanomandidy
Toamasina

MOZAMBIQUE
Chimanimani
Beira
Belo-
Tsiribihina
Mania
Antananarivo ■
Espungabera
Malaimbandy
Antsirabe
Ambositra

Massangena
Nova
Mambone
Bassas da India
(Reunion)
Morombe
Manja
Beroroha
MADAGASCAR
Fianarantsoa
St. Denis
Reunion
(France)

Chigubo
Barra Falsa Point
Massinga
Europa
Island
(Reunion)
Ihosy
2,658m
(8,720ft)
Manakara
Barra Point
Inhambane
Toliara
Betroka

Xai-Xai
Bekily
Tropic of Capricorn

Maputo
Androka
Tolanaro
ba
Cape St. Mary

INDIAN

OCEAN

oe St. Lucia

ards Bay

rg

INDIAN OCEAN

MAURITIUS
Port Louis

St. Denis

Reunion
(France)

Same scale as main map

Southern Africa

Boreal forest	Wetland	■ National capital
Temperate forest	Mountain	● Internal capital
Tropical forest	Tundra	⊙ Major city or town
Temperate grassland	Ice	○ Other town
Savanna	Cultivation	
Semi-desert and scrub	Urban	See also main key on page 17.
Hot desert		
International boundary		
Internal boundary		1:10,900,000
2,490m (7,988ft) Height above or below sea level		0 200 400km
		0 100 200 300 miles

THE ARCTIC

The Arctic is not a continent. It is
a region north of the Arctic Circle
line of latitude, around the North
Pole. The Arctic consists of the Arctic
Ocean, islands such as Greenland
and the most northerly parts of
mainland Europe, North America and
Asia. The Arctic region is covered in
ice and snow almost all year round.

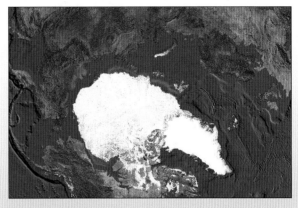

The large white area in this satellite image is ice covering
the Arctic Ocean and Greenland. At the top left of the image
is the edge of Russia and at the top right is part of Europe.

These Inuit people
are wearing thick,
animal-skin coats,
boots and gloves
to keep warm.

Internet link

For a link to a website where you can discover more
about the Arctic, go to **www.usborne-quicklinks.com**

Facts

Size of Arctic Ocean 14,056,000
sq km (5,426,000 sq miles)
Highest point Gunnbjorns
Mountain, Greenland *3,700m
(12,139ft)*
Lowest point Fram Basin, Arctic
Ocean *-4,665m (-15,305ft)*
Lowest recorded temperature
-67.8°C (-90°F)

Main mineral deposits
Diamonds, gold
Main fuel deposits
Oil, natural gas

Seals living in Arctic regions
have a thick layer of fat under
their skin to keep them warm
in the freezing weather.

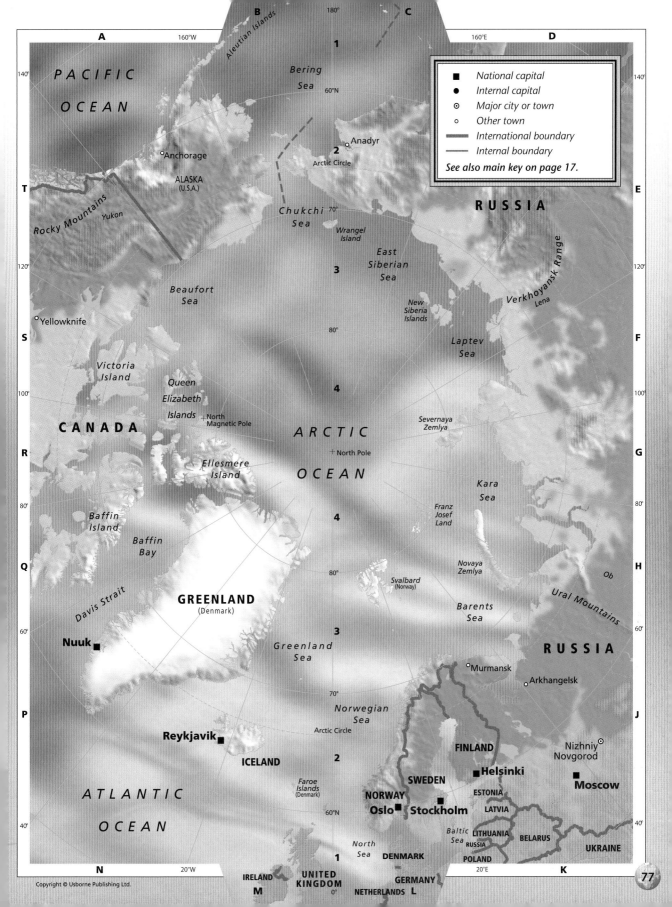

A   160°W   B   Aleutian Islands   180°   C   160°E   D

140°

PACIFIC OCEAN

1

Bering Sea

60°N

°Anchorage

2 °Anadyr

Arctic Circle

ALASKA
(U.S.A.)

T

Rocky Mountains   *Yukon*

70°

Chukchi Sea

Wrangel Island

RUSSIA

E

120°

Beaufort Sea

3

East Siberian Sea

New Siberia Islands

Verkhoyansk Range   *Lena*

120°

°Yellowknife

80°

S

Victoria Island

Queen Elizabeth Islands

North Magnetic Pole

4

A R C T I C

Severnaya Zemlya

Laptev Sea

F

100°

C A N A D A

R

Ellesmere Island

North Pole

O C E A N

Kara Sea

Franz Josef Land

G

80°

80°

Baffin Island

4

80°

Novaya Zemlya

Ob

80°

Q

Baffin Bay

GREENLAND
(Denmark)

Svalbard
(Norway)

Barents Sea

Ural Mountains

H

60°

Davis Strait

3

Greenland Sea

RUSSIA

60°

70°

°Murmansk

°Arkhangelsk

P

Nuuk ■

Norwegian Sea

Arctic Circle

J

Reykjavik ■

2

ICELAND

60°N

Faroe Islands
(Denmark)

FINLAND

Helsinki ■

SWEDEN

Nizhniy° Novgorod

Moscow ■

40°

ATLANTIC

NORWAY

Oslo ■ **Stockholm** ■

ESTONIA

LATVIA

40°

OCEAN

North Sea

1

DENMARK

Baltic Sea

LITHUANIA

RUSSIA

BELARUS

UKRAINE

POLAND

N   20°W   **IRELAND**   **UNITED KINGDOM**   0°   M   **GERMANY**   **NETHERLANDS** L   20°E   K

Key

■ National capital
● Internal capital
⊙ Major city or town
○ Other town
━━ International boundary
━━ Internal boundary

See also main key on page 17.

ANTARCTICA

Antarctica is a huge, frozen continent within the Antarctic Circle. It is almost completely covered by an enormous ice sheet, which is more than 3km (2 miles) deep in some places. Nobody lives permanently in Antarctica, though many scientists visit to study the area. No plants grow in the ice, and the only land animals are tiny mites. But many animals, including penguins, seals, whales and fish, live in the seas around Antarctica.

This ship takes tourists on Antarctic expeditions. Visitors can see animals such as these gentoo penguins, which come onto land to breed.

Internet link

For links to websites where you can find out more about Antarctica, go to **www.usborne-quicklinks.com**

Facts

Total land area 14,000,000 sq km (5,405,442 sq miles), of which 13,720,000 sq km (5,297,333 sq miles) are covered in ice
Highest point Vinson Massif *5,140m (16,863ft)*
Lowest point Bentley Subglacial Trench *-2,555m (-8,382ft)*
Lowest recorded temperature -89.2°C (-128.6°F)

Main mineral deposits Iron ore, chromium, copper, gold, nickel, platinum

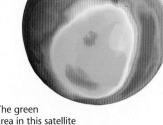

The green area in this satellite photograph is a hole in the ozone layer over Antarctica. The hole is caused by atmospheric pollution.

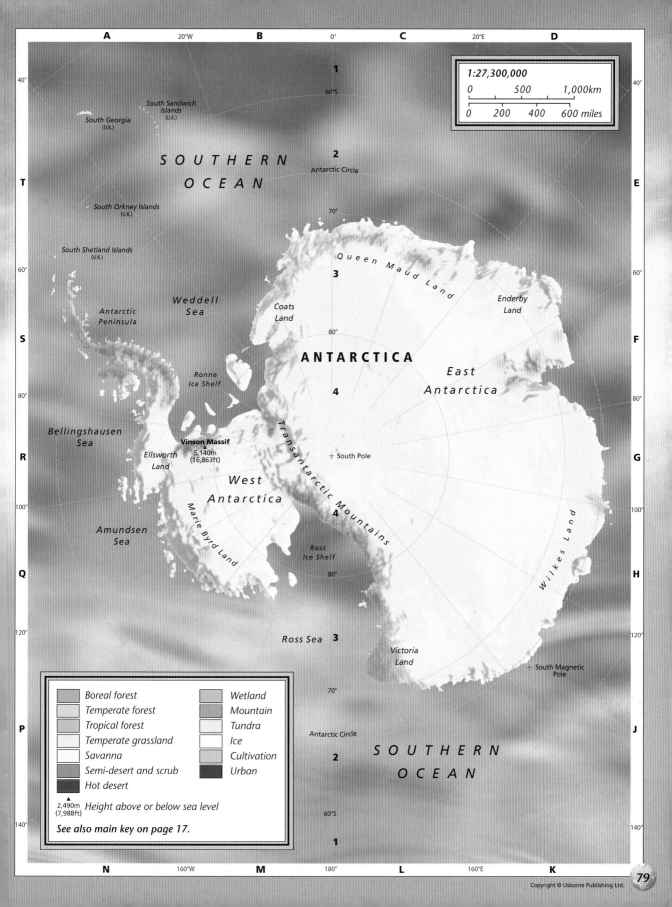

A   20°W   **B**   0°   **C**   20°E   **D**

40°

1

60°S

South Sandwich
Islands
(U.K.)

South Georgia
(U.K.)

40°

S O U T H E R N
O C E A N

2

Antarctic Circle

T

South Orkney Islands
(U.K.)

70°

E

South Shetland Islands
(U.K.)

60°

3

Queen Maud Land

60°

*Weddell
Sea*

Coats
Land

*Enderby
Land*

*Antarctic
Peninsula*

ANTARCTICA

80°

S

F

*Ronne
Ice Shelf*

*East
Antarctica*

80°

4

80°

*Bellingshausen
Sea*

Vinson Massif
▲ 5,140m
(16,863ft)

+ South Pole

Transantarctic Mountains

R

*Ellsworth
Land*

G

*West
Antarctica*

4

100°

*Amundsen
Sea*

Marie Byrd Land

100°

Wilkes Land

Q

*Ross
Ice Shelf*

H

120°

80°

Ross Sea   **3**

*Victoria
Land*

120°

+ South Magnetic
Pole

70°

P

Antarctic Circle

*S O U T H E R N
O C E A N*

J

60°S

2

140°

1

140°

N   160°W   **M**   180°   **L**   160°E   **K**

WORLD RECORDS

Here are some of the Earth's longest rivers, highest mountains and other amazing world records. But the world is always changing; mountains wear down, rivers change shape, and new buildings are constructed. Ways of measuring things can also change. That's why you may find slightly different figures in different books.

Highest mountains	
Everest, Nepal/China	8,850m (29,035ft)
K2, Pakistan/China	8,611m (28,251ft)
Kanchenjunga, India/Nepal	8,586m (28,169ft)
Lhotse I, Nepal/China	8,516m (27,940ft)
Makalu I, Nepal/China	8,462m (27,762ft)
Lhotse II, Nepal/China	8,400m (27,560ft)
Dhaulagiri, Nepal	8,167m (26,795ft)
Manaslu I, Nepal	8,156m (26,759ft)
Cho Oyu, Nepal/China	8,201m (26,906ft)
Nanga Parbat, Pakistan	8,126m (26,660ft)

Longest rivers	
Nile, Africa	6,650km (4,132 miles)
Amazon, South America	6,437km (4,000 miles)
Chang Jiang (Yangtze), China	6,380km (3,915 miles)
Mississippi/Missouri, U.S.A.	6,019km (3,741 miles)
Yenisey/Angara, Russia	5,539km (3,445 miles)
Huang He (Yellow), China	5,464km (3,398 miles)
Ob/Irtysh/Black Irtysh, Asia	5,411km (3,362 miles)
Amur/Shilka/Onon, Asia	4,416km (2,744 miles)
Lena, Russia	4,472km (2,734 miles)
Congo, Africa	4,700km (2,922 miles)

Biggest natural lakes	
Caspian Sea	371,000 sq km (143,000 sq mi)
Lake Superior	82,400 sq km (31,820 sq mi)
Lake Victoria	68,800 sq km (26,560 sq mi)
Lake Huron	59,600 sq km (23,010 sq mi)
Lake Michigan	58,000 sq km (22,400 sq mi)
Lake Tanganyika	32,900 sq km (12 702 sq mi)
Lake Baikal	31,494 sq km (12,160 sq mi)
Great Bear Lake	31,153 sq km (12,028 sq mi)
Lake Nyasa	29,600 sq km (11 428 sq mi)
Aral Sea	28,600 sq km (11,042 sq mi)

Deepest ocean
The Mariana Trench, part of the Pacific Ocean, is the deepest part of the sea at 10,911 meters (35,798ft) deep.

Deepest lake
Lake Baikal in Russia is the deepest lake in the world. At its deepest point it is 1,637m (5,370ft) deep.

Biggest islands	
Greenland	2,130,800 sq km (822,706 sq mi)
New Guinea	785,753 sq km (303,381 sq mi)
Borneo	748,168 sq km (288,869 sq mi)
Madagascar	587,713 sq km (226,917 sq mi)
Baffin Island	507,451 sq km (195,928 sq mi)
Sumatra	443,066 sq km (171,069 sq mi)
Honshu	225,800 sq km (87,182 sq mi)
Victoria Island	217,291 sq km (83,897 sq mi)
Great Britain	209,331 sq km (80,823 sq mi)
Ellesmere Island	196,236 sq km (75,767 sq mi)

Tallest inhabited buildings	
Taipei 101, Taipei	509m (1,670ft)
Shanghai WFC, Shanghai	492m (1,614ft)
Petronas Tower, Kuala Lumpur	452m (1,483ft)
Sears Tower, Chicago	442m (1,451ft)
Jin Mao Building, Shanghai	421m (1,381ft)
Two International FC, Hong Kong	415m (1,362ft)
CITIC Plaza, China	391m (1,283ft)
Shun Hing Square, China	384m (1,260ft)
Empire State Building, USA	381m (1,250ft)
Central Plaza, Hong Kong	374m (1,227ft)

Biggest cities/urban areas	
Tokyo-Yokohama, Japan	34.7 million
Jakarta, Indonesia	23.4 million
New York, U.S.A.	21.3 million
Mumbai, India	20.4 million
Manila, Philippines	20.1 million
Delhi, India	19.8 million
Seoul-Incheon, South Korea	19.7 million
Sao Paulo, Brazil	19.5 million
Mexico City, Mexico	18.6 million
Osaka-Kobe-Kyoto, Japan	17.3 million

Famous waterfalls	Height
Angel Falls, Venezuela	979m (3,212ft)
Sutherland Falls, New Zealand	580m (1,904ft)
Mardalfossen, Norway	517m (1,696ft)
Jog Falls, India	253m (830ft)
Victoria Falls, Zimbabwe/Zambia	108m (355ft)
Iguacu Falls, Brazil/Argentina	82m (269ft)
Niagara Falls, Canada/U.S.A.	52m (167ft)

Natural disasters

Natural disasters can be measured in different ways. For example, some earthquakes score highly on the Richter scale, while others cause more destruction. The events listed here are among the most famous and destructive disasters in history.

Earthquakes	Richter scale	Deaths and other effects
San Francisco, U.S.A., 1906	7.9	3,000; deadliest in U.S.; Great Fire
Messina, Italy, 1908	7.5	70-100,000; tsunami killed many
Tokyo-Kanto, Japan, 1923	8.3	142,807; caused Great Tokyo Fire
Quetta, Pakistan, 1935	7.5	30-60,000; Quetta city destroyed
Concepcion, Chile, 1960	8.7	2,000; strongest quake ever
Alaska, U.S.A., 1964	8.6	125; strongest quake ever in U.S.A.
Tangshan, China, 1976	7.9	655,237; deadliest quake of 1900s
Manjil-Rudbar, Iran, 1990	7.7	50,000; landslides; cities destroyed
Kobe, Japan, 1995	6.8	5,500; over $147bn damage
Gujarat, India, 2001	8.0	20,085; strongest quake in India ever

Volcanic eruptions	Disastrous effects
Mount Vesuvius, Italy, AD79	Pompeii flattened; up to 20,000 died
Tambora, Indonesia, 1815	92,000 people starved to death
Krakatoa, Indonesia, 1883	36,500 drowned in resulting tsunami
Mount Pelee, Martinique, 1902	Nearly 30,000 people buried in ash flows
Kelut, Indonesia, 1919	Over 5,000 people drowned in mud
Agung, Indonesia, 1963	1,200 people suffocated in hot ash
Mount St. Helens, U.S.A., 1980	Only 61 died but a large area was destroyed
Ruiz, Colombia, 1985	25,000 people died in giant mud flows
Mt. Pinatubo, Philippines, 1991	800 killed by collapsing roofs and disease
Island of Montserrat, 1995	Volcano left most of the island uninhabitable

Floods	Disastrous effects
Holland, 1228	100,000 drowned by a sea flood
Kaifeng, China, 1642	300,000 died after rebels destroyed a dyke
Johnstown, U.S.A., 1889	2,200 killed in a flood caused by rain
Frejus, France, 1959	More than 500 died after dam burst
Italy, 1963	Vaoint Dam overflowed; 2-3,000 killed
East Pakistan, 1970	Giant wave caused by cyclone killed 250,000
Bangladesh, 1988	1,300 died, 30m homeless in monsoon flood
Southern U.S.A., 1993	$12bn of damage after Mississippi flooded
China, 1998	Chang Jiang overflow left 14m homeless
Indian Ocean, 2004	Devastating tsunami killed 229, 896 people

Storms	Disastrous effects
Caribbean "Great Hurricane", 1780	Biggest ever hurricane killed over 20,000
Hong Kong typhoon, China, 1906	10,000 people died in this giant hurricane
Killer tornado, U.S.A., 1925	Up to 700 people died in Ellington, Missouri
Hurricane Fifi, Honduras, 1974	8,000 people died and 100,000 left homeless
Hurricane Georges, U.S.A., 1998	Caribbean and U.S.A. hit; $5bn of damage
Hurricane Mitch, C. America, 1998	Over 9,000 killed across Central America
Hurricane Katrina, U.S.A., 2005	Over 1,800 killed and $90 bn of damage

Amazing Earth facts

The Earth is 12,103km (7,520 miles) across. Its circumference (the distance around the Equator) is 38,022km (23,627 miles) and it is 149,503,000km (92,897,000 miles) away from the Sun.

To make one complete orbit around the Sun, the Earth has to travel 938,900,000km (583,400,000 miles). To do this in just a year, it has to travel very fast. Because of the atmosphere surrounding the Earth, you can't feel it moving. But you're zooming through space faster than any rocket.

• **Orbit speed** The Earth travels around the Sun at a speed of about 106,000kph (65,868mph).

• **Spinning speed** The Earth spins around an axis, but the speed you're spinning at depends on where you live. Places on the Equator move at 1,600kph (995mph). New York moves at around 1,100kph (684mph). Near the poles, the spinning is not very fast at all.

• **Solar System speed** The whole Solar System, including the Sun, the Earth and its moon, and the other planets and their moons, is moving at 72,400kph (45,000mph) through the galaxy.

• **Galaxy speed** Our galaxy, the Milky Way, whizzes through the universe at 2,172,150kph (1,350,000mph).

Internet links

For links to websites about landscapes, habitats and animals around the world, go to **www.usborne-quicklinks.com**

TIME ZONES

When it's midday in Rio de Janeiro, it's midnight in Tokyo. This is because we divide the Earth into different time zones. Within each zone, people usually set their clocks to the same time. If you fly between two zones, you change your watch to the time of the new zone.

Dividing up time

There are 25 different time zones. They are separated by one-hour intervals and there is a new time zone roughly every 15 degrees of longitude*. The zones are measured in hours ahead of or behind Greenwich Mean Time, or GMT, which is the time at the Prime Meridian Line*.

Governments can change their countries' time zones. So, for convenience, whole countries usually keep the same local time instead of sticking to the zones exactly. For example, China could be divided into several time zones, but instead the whole country keeps the same time. A few areas, such as India, Iran and parts of Australia, use non-standard half-hour deviations.

Summer time

Some countries adjust their clocks in summer. For example, in the U.K. everybody's clocks go forward one hour. This is known as Daylight Saving Time or Summer Time. It is a way of getting more out of the days by giving people an extra hour of daylight in the evening. It reduces energy use because people don't use as much electricity for lights.

Changing dates

On the opposite side of the world from the Prime Meridian Line is the International Date Line, which runs mostly through the Pacific Ocean and bends to avoid land. Places to the west of it are 24 hours ahead of places to the east. This means that if you travel east across it you lose a day and if you travel west across you gain a day.

This map shows the different times zones. The times at the top of the map tell you the time it is in the different zones when it is noon at the Prime Meridian Line. the numbers in circles tell you how many hours ahead of or behind Greenwich Mean Time an area is.

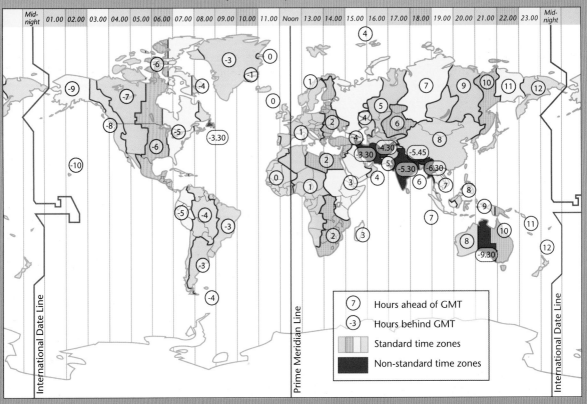

*Longitude, 6; Prime Meridian Line, 6

TYPES OF GOVERNMENTS

Most states have one main leader along with a parliament or assembly of politicians. The main types of governments are listed and explained below. A state can have a combination of more than one of these types of governments. For example, the United States of America is a federal republic.

Anarchy
Anarchy means a situation where there is no government. This can happen after a civil war, when a government has been destroyed and rival groups are battling to take its place.

Capitalist state
In a Capitalist or free-market state, people can own their own businesses and property, and buy services such as healthcare privately. However, most Capitalist governments also provide national health, education and welfare services.

Commonwealth
This word is sometimes used to mean a democratic republic, in which all the state's citizens are seen as having an equal interest in the functioning of the state.

Communist state
Under Communism, the state owns things like factories, farms and businesses, and provides healthcare, welfare and education for its people.

Democracy
In a democracy, the government is elected by the people, using a voting system.

Dictatorship
This is a state run by a single, unelected leader, who may use force to keep control. In a military dictatorship, the army is in power.

Federal government
In a federal system, such as that of the U.S.A., a central government shares power with a number of smaller regional governments.

Monarchy
A monarchy is a state with a king or queen. In some traditional monarchies, the monarch has complete power. A constitutional monarchy, however, also has a separate, usually democratic, government and the monarch's powers are limited.

Regional or local government
A government that controls a smaller area within a state. Some regional governments have very limited powers, and are largely directed by the central government. Others, such as the regional governments in the U.S.A., have much more power and can make their own laws.

Republic
A republic is a state with no monarch. The head of state is usually an elected president.

Revolutionary government
After a revolution, when a government is overthrown by force, the new regime is sometimes called a revolutionary government.

Totalitarian state
This is a state with only one political party, in which individuals are forced to obey the government and may also be prevented from leaving the country.

Transitional government
A government that is changing from one system to another is known as a transitional government. For example, a dictatorship may become a democracy after the dictator dies, but the transition between the systems can take several years.

GAZETTEER OF STATES

Afghanistan

Albania

Algeria

Andorra

Angola

Antigua and Barbuda

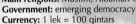

• **Argentina**

This gazetteer lists the world's 194 independent states, along with key facts about each one. In the lists of languages, the language that is most widely spoken is given first, even if it is not the official language. In the lists of religions, the one followed by the most people is also placed first. Every state has a national flag, which is usually used to represent the country abroad. A few states also have a state flag which they prefer to use instead. The state flags appear here with a dot beside them.

AFGHANISTAN (Asia)
Area: 647,500 sq km (250,001 sq miles)
Population: 33,609,937
Capital city: Kabul
Main languages: Dari, Pashto
Main religion: Muslim
Government: transitional
Currency: 1 afghani = 100 puls

ALBANIA (Europe)
Area: 28,748 sq km (11,100 sq miles)
Population: 3,639,453
Capital city: Tirana
Main language: Albanian
Main religions: Muslim, Albanian Orthodox
Government: emerging democracy
Currency: 1 lek = 100 qintars

ALGERIA (Africa)
Area: 2,381,740 sq km (919,595 sq miles)
Population: 34,178,188
Capital city: Algiers
Main languages: Arabic, French, Berber dialects
Main religion: Sunni Muslim
Government: republic
Currency: 1 Algerian dinar = 100 centimes

ANDORRA (Europe)
Area: 468 sq km (181 sq miles)
Population: 83,888
Capital city: Andorra la Vella
Main languages: Catalan, Spanish
Main religion: Roman Catholic
Government: parliamentary democracy
Currency: 1 euro = 100 cents

ANGOLA (Africa)
Area: 1,246,700 sq km (481,354 sq miles)
Population: 12,799,293
Capital city: Luanda
Main languages: Kilongo, Kimbundu, other Bantu languages, Portuguese
Main religions: indigenous, Roman Catholic, Protestant
Government: presidential republic
Currency: 1 kwanza = 100 lwei

ANTIGUA AND BARBUDA (North America)
Area: 443 sq km (171 sq miles)
Population: 85,632
Capital city: Saint John's
Main languages: Caribbean Creole, English
Main religion: Protestant
Government: constitutional monarchy
Currency: 1 East Caribbean dollar = 100 cents

ARGENTINA (South America)
Area: 2,766,890 sq km (1,068,302 sq miles)
Population: 40,913,584
Capital city: Buenos Aires
Main language: Spanish
Main religion: Roman Catholic
Government: republic
Currency: 1 peso = 100 centavos

ARMENIA (Asia)
Area: 29,743 sq km (11,484 sq miles)
Population: 2,967,004
Capital city: Yerevan
Main language: Armenian
Main religion: Armenian Orthodox
Government: republic
Currency: 1 dram = 100 luma

AUSTRALIA (Australasia/Oceania)
Area: 7,741,220 sq km (2,967,909 sq miles)
Population: 21,262,641
Capital city: Canberra
Main language: English
Main religion: Christian
Government: federal democratic monarchy
Currency: 1 Australian dollar = 100 cents

AUSTRIA (Europe)
Area: 83,870 sq km (32,382 sq miles)
Population: 8,210,281
Capital city: Vienna
Main language: German
Main religion: Roman Catholic
Government: federal republic
Currency: 1 euro = 100 cents

Armenia

Australia

Austria

Azerbaijan

Bahamas, The

Bahrain

Bangladesh

Internet links

For links to websites with flags, maps, quizzes, and facts about
every country in the world, go to www.usborne-quicklinks.com

Barbados

Belarus

Belgium

Belize

Benin

Bhutan

Bolivia

AZERBAIJAN (Asia)
Area: 86,600 sq km (33,436 sq miles)
Population: 8,238,672
Capital city: Baku
Main language: Azeri
Main religion: Muslim
Government: republic
Currency: 1 manat = 100 gopiks

BAHAMAS, THE (North America)
Area: 13,940 sq km (5,382 sq miles)
Population: 309,156
Capital city: Nassau
Main languages: Bahamian Creole, English
Main religion: Christian
Government: parliamentary democracy
Currency: 1 Bahamian dollar = 100 cents

BAHRAIN (Asia)
Area: 665 sq km (257 sq miles)
Population: 727,785
Capital city: Manama
Main languages: Arabic, English
Main religion: Muslim
Government: constitutional monarchy
Currency: 1 Bahraini dinar = 1,000 fils

BANGLADESH (Asia)
Area: 144,000 sq km (55,599 sq miles)
Population: 156,050,883
Capital city: Dhaka
Main languages: Bengali, English
Main religions: Muslim, Hindu
Government: parliamentary democracy
Currency: 1 taka = 100 poisha

BARBADOS (North America)
Area: 431 sq km (166 sq miles)
Population: 284,589
Capital city: Bridgetown
Main languages: Bajan, English
Main religion: Christian
Government: parliamentary democracy
Currency: 1 Barbadian dollar = 100 cents

BELARUS (Europe)
Area: 207,600 sq km (80,155 sq miles)
Population: 9,648,533
Capital city: Minsk
Main language: Belarusian
Main religion: Eastern Orthodox
Government: republic
Currency: 1 Belarusian ruble = 100 kopecks

BELGIUM (Europe)
Area: 30,528 sq km (11,787 sq miles)
Population: 10,414,336
Capital city: Brussels
Main languages: Dutch, French, German
Main religions: Roman Catholic, Protestant
Government: constitutional monarchy
Currency: 1 euro = 100 cents

BELIZE (North America)
Area: 22,966 sq km (8,867 sq miles)
Population: 307,899
Capital city: Belmopan
Main languages: Spanish, Belize
Creole, English, Garifuna, Maya

Main religions: Roman Catholic, Protestant
Government: parliamentary democracy
Currency: 1 Belizean dollar = 100 cents

BENIN (Africa)
Area: 112,620 sq km (43,483 sq miles)
Population: 8,791,832
Capital city: Porto-Novo
Main languages: Fon, French, Yoruba, Adja
Main religions: indigenous, Christian, Muslim
Government: republic
Currency: 1 CFA* franc = 100 centimes

BHUTAN (Asia)
Area: 47,000 sq km (18,147 sq miles)
Population: 691,141
Capital city: Thimphu
Main languages: Dzongkha, Nepali
Main religions: Buddist, Hindu
Government: constitutional monarchy
Currency: 1 ngultrum = 100 chetrum

BOLIVIA (South America)
Area: 1,098,580 sq km (424,164 sq miles)
Population: 9,775,246
Capital cities: La Paz/Sucre
Main languages: Spanish, Quechua, Aymara
Main religion: Roman Catholic
Government: republic
Currency: 1 boliviano = 100 centavos

BOSNIA AND HERZEGOVINA (Europe)
Area: 51,209 sq km (19,772 sq miles)
Population: 4,613,414
Capital city: Sarajevo
Main languages: Bosnian, Serbian, Croatian
Main religions: Muslim, Orthodox, Roman
Catholic
Government: emerging federal republic
Currency: 1 marka = 100 pfenninga

BOTSWANA (Africa)
Area: 600,370 sq km (231,804 sq miles)
Population: 1,990,876
Capital city: Gaborone
Main languages: Setswana, Kalanga,
English
Main religions: indigenous, Christian
Government: parliamentary republic
Currency: 1 pula = 100 thebe

BRAZIL (South America)
Area: 8,511,965 sq km (3,286,488 sq miles)
Population: 198,739,269
Capital city: Brasilia
Main language: Portuguese
Main religion: Roman Catholic
Government: federal republic
Currency: 1 real = 100 centavos

BRUNEI (Asia)
Area: 5,770 sq km (2,228 sq miles)
Population: 388,190
Capital city: Bandar Seri Begawan
Main languages: Malay, English, Chinese
Main religions: Muslim, Buddhist
Government: constitutional sultanate (a type
of monarchy)
Currency: 1 Bruneian dollar = 100 cents

**Bosnia and
Herzegovina**

Botswana

Brazil

Brunei

Bulgaria

Burkina Faso

Burma (Myanmar)

CFA = Communaute Financiere Africaine

GAZETTEER OF STATES CONTINUED:

Burundi

Cambodia

Cameroon

Canada

Cape Verde

Central African Republic

Chad

BULGARIA (Europe)
Area: 110,910 sq km (42,823 sq miles)
Population: 7,204,687
Capital city: Sofia
Main language: Bulgarian
Main religions: Bulgarian Orthodox, Muslim
Government: parliamentary democracy
Currency: 1 lev = 100 stotinki

BURKINA FASO (Africa)
Area: 274,200 sq km (105,869 sq miles)
Population: 15,746,232
Capital city: Ouagadougou
Main languages: Moore, Jula, French
Main religions: Muslim, indigenous
Government: parliamentary republic
Currency: 1 CFA* franc = 100 centimes

BURMA (MYANMAR) (Asia)
Area: 678,500 sq km (261,970 sq miles)
Population: 48,137,741
Capital city: Rangoon, Naypyidaw
Main language: Burmese
Main religion: Buddhist
Government: military dictatorship
Currency: 1 kyat = 100 pyas

BURUNDI (Africa)
Area: 27,830 sq km (10,745 sq miles)
Population: 8,988,091
Capital city: Bujumbura
Main languages: Kirundi, French, Swahili
Main religions: Christian, indigenous
Government: republic
Currency: 1 Burundi franc = 100 centimes

CAMBODIA (Asia)
Area: 181,040 sq km (69,900 sq miles)
Population: 14,494,293
Capital city: Phnom Penh
Main language: Khmer, French
Main religion: Buddhist
Government: constitutional monarchy
Currency: 1 new riel = 100 sen

CAMEROON (Africa)
Area: 475,440 sq km (183,568 sq miles)
Population: 18,879,301
Capital city: Yaounde
Main languages: Cameroon Pidgin English, Ewondo, Fula, French, English
Main religions: indigenous, Christian, Muslim
Government: republic
Currency: 1 CFA* franc = 100 centimes

CANADA (North America)
Area: 9,984,670 sq km (3,855,103 sq miles)
Population: 33,487,208
Capital city: Ottawa
Main languages: English, French
Main religions: Roman Catholic, Protestant
Government: federal democracy
Currency: 1 Canadian dollar = 100 cents

CAPE VERDE (Africa)
Area: 4,033 sq km (1,557 sq miles)
Population: 429,474
Capital city: Praia
Main languages: Crioulo*, Portuguese

Main religions: Roman Catholic, Protestant
Government: republic
Currency: 1 Cape Verdean escudo = 100 centavos

CENTRAL AFRICAN REPUBLIC (Africa)
Area: 622,984 sq km (240,535 sq miles)
Population: 4,511,488
Capital city: Bangui
Main languages: Sangho, French
Main religions: indigenous, Christian, Muslim
Government: republic
Currency: 1 CFA* franc = 100 centimes

CHAD (Africa)
Area: 1,284,000 sq km (495,755 sq miles)
Population: 10,329,208
Capital city: N'Djamena
Main languages: Arabic, Sara, French
Main religions: Muslim, Christian, indigenous
Government: republic
Currency: 1 CFA* franc = 100 centimes

CHILE (South America)
Area: 756,950 sq km (292,260 sq miles)
Population: 16,601,707
Capital city: Santiago
Main language: Spanish
Main religions: Roman Catholic, Protestant
Government: republic
Currency: 1 Chilean peso = 100 centavos

CHINA (Asia)
Area: 9,596,960 sq km (3,705,407 sq miles)
Population: 1,338,612,968
Capital city: Beijing
Main languages: Mandarin Chinese, Yue, Wu
Main religions: Taoist, Buddhist
Government: communist republic
Currency: 1 yuan = 10 jiao

COLOMBIA (South America)
Area: 1,138,910 sq km (439,736 sq miles)
Population: 45,644,023
Capital city: Bogota
Main language: Spanish
Main religion: Roman Catholic
Government: republic
Currency: 1 Colombian peso = 100 centavos

COMOROS (Africa)
Area: 2,170 sq km (838 sq miles)
Population: 752,438
Capital city: Moroni
Main languages: Comorian*, French, Arabic
Main religion: Sunni Muslim
Government: republic
Currency: 1 Comoran franc = 100 centimes

CONGO (Africa)
Area: 342,000 sq km (132,047 sq miles)
Population: 4,012,809
Capital city: Brazzaville
Main languages: Munukutuba, Lingala, French
Main religions: Christian, animist
Government: republic
Currency: 1 CFA* franc = 100 centimes

Chile

China

Colombia

Comoros

Congo

Congo (Democratic Republic)

Costa Rica

*CFA = Communaute Financiere Africaine; Comorian = a blend of Swahili and Arabic; Crioulo = a blend of Portuguese and West African

Croatia

Cuba

Cyprus

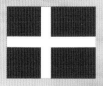

Czech Republic

Denmark

Djibouti

Dominica

CONGO (DEMOCRATIC REPUBLIC) (Africa)
Area: 2,345,410 sq km (905,568 sq miles)
Population: 68,692,542
Capital city: Kinshasa
Main languages: Lingala, Swahili, Kikongo, Tshiluba, French, Kingwana
Main religions: Roman Catholic, Protestant, Kimbanguist, Muslim
Government: republic
Currency: 1 Congolese franc = 100 centimes

COSTA RICA (North America)
Area: 51,100 sq km (19,730 sq miles)
Population: 4,253,877
Capital city: San Jose
Main language: Spanish
Main religions: Roman Catholic, Evangelical
Government: democratic republic
Currency: 1 Costa Rican colon = 100 centimos

CROATIA (Europe)
Area: 56,542 sq km (21,831 sq miles)
Population: 4,489,409
Capital city: Zagreb
Main language: Croatian
Main religions: Roman Catholic, Orthodox
Government: republic
Currency: 1 kuna = 100 lipas

CUBA (North America)
Area: 110,860 sq km (42,803 sq miles)
Population: 11,451,652
Capital city: Havana
Main language: Spanish
Main religion: Roman Catholic
Government: communist republic
Currency: 1 Cuban peso = 100 centavos

CYPRUS (Europe)
Area: 9,250 sq km (3,571 sq miles)
Population: 796,740
Capital city: Nicosia
Main languages: Greek, Turkish, English
Main religions: Greek Orthodox, Muslim
Government: republic with a self-proclaimed independent Turkish area
Currency: Greek Cypriot area: 1 euro = 100 cents; Turkish Cypriot area: 1 Turkish lira = 100 kurus

CZECH REPUBLIC (Europe)
Area: 78,866 sq km (30,450 sq miles)
Population: 10,211,904
Capital city: Prague
Main language: Czech
Main religion: Roman Catholic
Government: republic
Currency: 1 koruna = 100 haleru

DENMARK (Europe)
Area: 43,094 sq km (16,639 sq miles)
Population: 5,500,510
Capital city: Copenhagen
Main language: Danish
Main religion: Evangelical Lutheran
Government: constitutional monarchy
Currency: 1 Danish krone = 100 oere

DJIBOUTI (Africa)
Area: 23,000 sq km (8,880 sq miles)
Population: 516,055
Capital city: Djibouti
Main languages: Afar, Somali, Arabic, French
Main religion: Muslim
Government: republic
Currency: 1 Djiboutian franc = 100 centimes

DOMINICA (North America)
Area: 754 sq km (291 sq miles)
Population: 72,660
Capital city: Roseau
Main languages: English, French patois
Main religions: Roman Catholic, Protestant
Government: democratic republic
Currency: 1 East Caribbean dollar = 100 cents

DOMINICAN REPUBLIC (North America)
Area: 48,380 sq km (18,815 sq miles)
Population: 9,650,054
Capital city: Santo Domingo
Main language: Spanish
Main religion: Roman Catholic
Government: democratic republic
Currency: 1 Dominican peso = 100 centavos

EAST TIMOR (TIMOR-LESTE) (Asia)
Area: 15,007 sq km (5,794 sq miles)
Population: 1,131,612
Capital city: Dili
Main languages: Tetun (Tetum), Bahasa Indonesia, Portuguese
Main religions: Roman Catholic, animist
Government: republic
Currency: 1 U.S. dollar = 100 cents

ECUADOR (South America)
Area: 283,560 sq km (109,483 sq miles)
Population: 14,573,101
Capital city: Quito
Main languages: Spanish, Quechua
Main religion: Roman Catholic
Government: republic
Currency: 1 U.S. dollar = 100 cents

EGYPT (Africa)
Area: 1,001,450 sq km (386,662 sq miles)
Population: 83,082,869
Capital city: Cairo
Main language: Arabic
Main religion: Sunni Muslim
Government: republic
Currency: 1 Egyptian pound = 100 piasters

EL SALVADOR (North America)
Area: 21,040 sq km (8,124 sq miles)
Population: 7,185,218
Capital city: San Salvador
Main language: Spanish
Main religion: Roman Catholic
Government: republic
Currency: 1 U.S. dollar = 100 cents

EQUATORIAL GUINEA (Africa)
Area: 28,050 sq km (10,831 sq miles)
Population: 633,441
Capital city: Malabo
Main languages: Fang, Bubi, other Bantu

• Dominican Republic

East Timor

• Ecuador

Egypt

• El Salvador

Equatorial Guinea

Eritrea

*CFA = Communaute Financiere Africaine

GAZETTEER OF STATES CONTINUED:

Estonia

Ethiopia

Federated States of Micronesia

Fiji

Finland

France

Gabon

languages, Spanish, French, Pidgin English
Main religion: Christian
Government: republic
Currency: 1 CFA* franc = 100 centimes

ERITREA (Africa)
Area: 121,320 sq km (46,842 sq miles)
Population: 5,647,168
Capital city: Asmara
Main languages: Tigrinya, Afar, Arabic
Main religions: Muslim, Coptic Christian, Roman Catholic, Protestant
Government: republic
Currency: 1 nafka = 100 cents

ESTONIA (Europe)
Area: 45,226 sq km (17,462 sq miles)
Population: 1,299,371
Capital city: Tallinn
Main languages: Estonian, Russian
Main religions: Evangelical Lutheran, Russian and Estonian Orthodox, other Christian
Government: parliamentary democracy
Currency: 1 Estonian kroon = 100 senti

ETHIOPIA (Africa)
Area: 1,127,127 sq km (435,186 sq miles)
Population: 85,237,338
Capital city: Addis Ababa
Main languages: Amharic, Tigrinya, Arabic
Main religions: Muslim, Ethiopian Orthodox, animist
Government: federal republic
Currency: 1 birr = 100 santim

FEDERATED STATES OF MICRONESIA (Australasia/Oceania)
Area: 702 sq km (271 sq miles)
Population: 107,434
Capital city: Palikir
Main languages: Chuuk, Ponapean, English
Main religions: Roman Catholic, Protestant
Government: federal republic
Currency: 1 U.S. dollar = 100 cents

FIJI (Australasia/Oceania)
Area: 18,270 sq km (7,054 sq miles)
Population: 944,720
Capital city: Suva
Main languages: Fijian, Hindustani, English
Main religions: Christian, Hindu
Government: republic
Currency: 1 Fijian dollar = 100 cents

FINLAND (Europe)
Area: 338,145 sq km (130,559 sq miles)
Population: 5,250,275
Capital city: Helsinki
Main language: Finnish, Swedish
Main religion: Evangelical Lutheran
Government: republic
Currency: 1 euro = 100 cents

FRANCE (Europe)
Area: 547,030 sq km (211,209 sq miles)
Population: 62,150,775
Capital city: Paris
Main language: French

Main religion: Roman Catholic
Government: republic
Currency: 1 euro = 100 cents

GABON (Africa)
Area: 267,667 sq km (103,347 sq miles)
Population: 1,514,993
Capital city: Libreville
Main languages: Fang, Myene, French
Main religions: Christian, animist
Government: republic
Currency: 1 CFA* franc = 100 centimes

GAMBIA, THE (Africa)
Area: 11,300 sq km (4,363 sq miles)
Population: 1,782,893
Capital city: Banjul
Main languages: Mandinka, Fula, Wolof, English
Main religion: Muslim
Government: democratic republic
Currency: 1 dalasi = 100 butut

GEORGIA (Asia)
Area: 69,700 sq km (26,911 sq miles)
Population: 4,615,807
Capital city: Tbilisi
Main languages: Georgian, Russian
Main religions: Georgian Orthodox, Muslim, Russian Orthodox
Government: republic
Currency: 1 lari = 100 tetri

GERMANY (Europe)
Area: 357,021 sq km (137,847 sq miles)
Population: 82,329,758
Capital city: Berlin
Main language: German
Main religions: Protestant, Roman Catholic
Government: federal republic
Currency: 1 euro = 100 cents

GHANA (Africa)
Area: 239,460 sq km (92,456 sq miles)
Population: 23,832,495
Capital city: Accra
Main languages: Twi, Fante, Ga, Hausa, Dagbani, Ewe, Nzemi, English
Main religions: indigenous, Muslim, Christian
Government: republic
Currency: 1 new cedi = 100 pesewas

GREECE (Europe)
Area: 131,940 sq km (50,942 sq miles)
Population: 10,737,428
Capital city: Athens
Main language: Greek
Main religion: Greek Orthodox
Government: parliamentary republic
Currency: 1 euro = 100 cents

GRENADA (North America)
Area: 344 sq km (133 sq miles)
Population: 90,739
Capital city: Saint George's
Main languages: English, French patois
Main religions: Roman Catholic, Protestant
Government: parliamentary democracy
Currency: 1 East Caribbean dollar = 100 cents

Gambia, The

Georgia

Germany

Ghana

Greece

Grenada

Guatemala

*CFA = Communaute Financiere Africaine

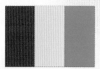

Guinea

Guinea-Bissau

Guyana

Haiti

Honduras

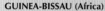

Hungary

Iceland

GUATEMALA (North America)
Area: 108,890 sq km (42,042 sq miles)
Population: 13,276,517
Capital city: Guatemala City
Main languages: Spanish, Amerindian languages including Quiche, Kekchi, Cakchiquel, Mam
Main religions: Roman Catholic, Protestant, indigenous Mayan beliefs
Government: democratic republic
Currency: 1 quetzal = 100 centavos

GUINEA (Africa)
Area: 245,857 sq km (94,925 sq miles)
Population: 10,057,975
Capital city: Conakry
Main languages: Fuuta Jalon, Mallinke, Susu, French
Main religion: Muslim
Government: republic
Currency: 1 Guinean franc = 100 centimes

GUINEA-BISSAU (Africa)
Area: 36,120 sq km (13,946 sq miles)
Population: 1,533,964
Capital city: Bissau
Main languages: Crioulo*, Balante, Pulaar, Mandjak, Mandinka, Portuguese
Main religions: indigenous, Muslim
Government: republic
Currency: 1 CFA* franc = 100 centimes

GUYANA (South America)
Area: 214,970 sq km (83,000 sq miles)
Population: 772,298
Capital city: Georgetown
Main languages: Guyanese Creole, English, Amerindian languages, Caribbean Hindi
Main religions: Christian, Hindu
Government: republic
Currency: 1 Guyanese dollar = 100 cents

HAITI (North America)
Area: 27,750 sq km (10,714 sq miles)
Population: 9,035,536
Capital city: Port-au-Prince
Main languages: Haitian Creole, French
Main religions: Roman Catholic, Protestant, Voodoo
Government: republic
Currency: 1 gourde = 100 centimes

HONDURAS (North America)
Area: 112,090 sq km (43,278 sq miles)
Population: 7,792,854
Capital city: Tegucigalpa
Main language: Spanish
Main religion: Roman Catholic
Government: republic
Currency: 1 lempira = 100 centavos

HUNGARY (Europe)
Area: 93,030 sq km (35,919 sq miles)
Population: 9,905,596
Capital city: Budapest
Main language: Hungarian
Main religions: Roman Catholic, Calvinist
Government: republic
Currency: 1 forint = 100 filler

ICELAND (Europe)
Area: 103,000 sq km (39,769 sq miles)
Population: 306,694
Capital city: Reykjavik
Main language: Icelandic
Main religion: Evangelical Lutheran
Government: constitutional republic
Currency: 1 Icelandic krona = 100 aurar

INDIA (Asia)
Area: 3,287,590 sq km (1,269,345 sq miles)
Population: 1,166,079,217
Capital city: New Delhi
Main languages: Hindi, English, Bengali, Urdu, over 1,600 other languages and dialects
Main religions: Hindu, Muslim
Government: federal republic
Currency: 1 Indian rupee = 100 paise

INDONESIA (Asia)
Area: 1,919,440 sq km (741,100 sq miles)
Population: 240,271,522
Capital city: Jakarta
Main languages: Bahasa Indonesia, English, Dutch, Javanese
Main religion: Muslim
Government: republic
Currency: 1 Indonesian rupiah = 100 sen

IRAN (Asia)
Area: 1,648,000 sq km (636,296 sq miles)
Population: 66,429,284
Capital city: Tehran
Main languages: Farsi and other Persian dialects, Azeri
Main religions: Shi'a Muslim, Sunni Muslim
Government: Islamic republic
Currency: 10 Iranian rials = 1 toman

IRAQ (Asia)
Area: 437,072 sq km (168,754 sq miles)
Population: 28,945,657
Capital city: Baghdad
Main languages: Arabic, Kurdish
Main religion: Muslim
Government: transitional republic
Currency: 1 Iraqi dinar = 1,000 fils

IRELAND (Europe)
Area: 70,280 sq km (27,135 sq miles)
Population: 4,203,200
Capital city: Dublin
Main languages: English, Irish (Gaelic)
Main religion: Roman Catholic
Government: republic
Currency: 1 euro = 100 cents

ISRAEL (Asia)
Area: 20,770 sq km (8,019 sq miles)
Population: 7,233,701
Capital city: Jerusalem
Main languages: Hebrew, Arabic
Main religions: Jewish, Muslim
Government: republic
Currency: 1 Israeli shekel = 100 agorot

ITALY (Europe)
Area: 301,230 sq km (116,306 sq miles)

India

Indonesia

Iran

Iraq

Ireland

Israel

Italy

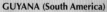

*CFA = Communaute Financiere Africaine;
Crioulo = a blend of Portuguese and West African

GAZETTEER OF STATES CONTINUED:

Ivory Coast

Population: 58,126,212
Capital city: Rome
Main language: Italian, French, German
Main religion: Roman Catholic
Government: republic
Currency: 1 euro = 100 cents

IVORY COAST (Africa)
Area: 322,460 sq km (124,503 sq miles)
Population: 20,617,068
Capital city: Yamoussoukro
Main languages: Baoule, Dioula, French
Main religions: Christian, Muslim, animist
Government: republic
Currency: 1 CFA* = 100 centimes

Jamaica

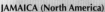

JAMAICA (North America)
Area: 10,991 sq km (4,244 sq miles)
Population: 2,825,928
Capital city: Kingston
Main languages: Southwestern Caribbean
Creole, English
Main religion: Protestant
Government: parliamentary democracy
Currency: 1 Jamaican dollar = 100 cents

Japan

JAPAN (Asia)
Area: 377,835 sq km (145,883 sq miles)
Population: 127,078,679
Capital city: Tokyo
Main language: Japanese
Main religions: Shinto, Buddhist
Government: parliamentary monarchy
Currency: 1 yen = 100 sen

Jordan

JORDAN (Asia)
Area: 92,300 sq km (35,637 sq miles)
Population: 6,342,948
Capital city: Amman
Main languages: Arabic, English
Main religion: Sunni Muslim
Government: constitutional monarchy
Currency: 1 Jordanian dinar = 1,000 fils

Kazakhstan

KAZAKHSTAN (Asia)
Area: 2,717,300 sq km (1,049,155 sq miles)
Population: 15,399,437
Capital city: Astana
Main languages: Kazakh, Russian
Main religions: Muslim, Russian Orthodox
Government: republic
Currency: 1 Kazakhstani tenge = 100 tiyn

Kenya

KENYA (Africa)
Area: 582,650 sq km (224,962 sq miles)
Population: 39,002,772
Capital city: Nairobi
Main languages: Swahili, English, Kiswahili,
Bantu languages
Main religions: Christian, indigenous
Government: republic
Currency: 1 Kenyan shilling = 100 cents

Kiribati

KIRIBATI (Australasia/Oceania)
Area: 811 sq km (313 sq miles)
Population: 112,850
Capital city: Bairiki
Main languages: Gilbertese, i-Kiribati, English
Main religions: Roman Catholic, Protestant

Government: republic
Currency: 1 Australian dollar = 100 cents

KOSOVO (Europe)
Area: 10,887 sq km (4 203 sq miles)
Population: 1,804,838
Capital city: Pristina
Main languages: Albanian, Serbian,
Bosnian, Turkish
Main religion: Muslim, Serbian Orthodox,
Roman Catholic
Government: republic
Currency: 1 euro = 100 cents

KUWAIT (Asia)
Area: 17,820 sq km (6,880 sq miles)
Population: 2,691,158
Capital city: Kuwait City
Main languages: Arabic, English
Main religion: Muslim
Government: constitutional monarchy
Currency: 1 Kuwaiti dinar = 1,000 fils

KYRGYZSTAN (Asia)
Area: 198,500 sq km (76,641 sq miles)
Population: 5,431,747
Capital city: Bishkek
Main languages: Kyrgyz, Russian, Uzbek
Main religions: Muslim, Russian Orthodox
Government: republic
Currency: 1 Kyrgyzstani som = 100 tyiyn

LAOS (Asia)
Area: 236,800 sq km (91,429 sq miles)
Population: 6,834,942
Capital city: Vientiane
Main languages: Lao, French, English
Main religions: Buddhist, animist
Government: communist republic
Currency: 1 new kip = 100 at

LATVIA (Europe)
Area: 64,589 sq km (24,938 sq miles)
Population: 2,231,503
Capital city: Riga
Main languages: Latvian, Russian
Main religions: Lutheran, Roman Catholic,
Russian Orthodox
Government: republic
Currency: 1 Latvian lat = 100 santims

LEBANON (Asia)
Area: 10,400 sq km (4,015 sq miles)
Population: 4,017,095
Capital city: Beirut
Main languages: Arabic, French, English
Main religions: Muslim, Christian
Government: republic
Currency: 1 Lebanese pound = 100 piasters

LESOTHO (Africa)
Area: 30,355 sq km (11,720 sq miles)
Population: 2,130,819
Capital cities: Maseru
Main languages: Sesotho, English, Zulu,
Xhosa
Main religions: Christian, indigenous
Government: constitutional monarchy
Currency: 1 loti = 100 lisente

Kosovo

Kuwait

Kyrgyzstan

Laos

Latvia

Lebanon

Lesotho

*CFA = Communaute Financiere Africaine

Liberia

LIBERIA (Africa)
Area: 111,370 sq km (43,000 sq miles)
Population: 3,441,790
Capital city: Monrovia
Main languages: Kpelle, English, Bassa
Main religions: indigenous, Christian, Muslim
Government: republic
Currency: 1 Liberian dollar = 100 cents

Libya

LIBYA (Africa)
Area: 1,759,540 sq km (679,362 sq miles)
Population: 6,310,434
Capital city: Tripoli
Main languages: Arabic, Italian, English
Main religion: Sunni Muslim
Government: military rule
Currency: 1 Libyan dinar = 1,000 dirhams

Liechtenstein

LIECHTENSTEIN (Europe)
Area: 160 sq km (62 sq miles)
Population: 34,761
Capital city: Vaduz
Main languages: German
Main religion: Roman Catholic
Government: constitutional monarchy
Currency: 1 Swiss franc = 100 centimes

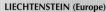

Lithuania

LITHUANIA (Europe)
Area: 65,300 sq km (25,212 sq miles)
Population: 3,555,179
Capital city: Vilnius
Main languages: Lithuanian, Polish, Russian
Main religions: Roman Catholic, Lutheran, Russian Orthodox
Government: parliamentary democracy
Currency: 1 Lithuanian litas = 100 centas

Luxembourg

LUXEMBOURG (Europe)
Area: 2,586 sq km (998 sq miles)
Population: 491,775
Capital city: Luxembourg
Main languages: Luxemburgish, German, French
Main religion: Roman Catholic
Government: constitutional monarchy
Currency: 1 euro = 100 cents

Macedonia

MACEDONIA (Europe)
Area: 25,333 sq km (9,781 sq miles)
Population: 2,066,718
Capital city: Skopje
Main languages: Macedonian, Albanian
Main religions: Macedonian Orthodox, Muslim
Government: republic
Currency: 1 Macedonian denar = 100 deni

Madagascar

MADAGASCAR (Africa)
Area: 587,040 sq km (226,657 sq miles)
Population: 20,653,556
Capital city: Antananarivo
Main languages: Malagasy, French, Cotiers
Main religions: indigenous beliefs, Christian
Government: republic
Currency: 1 ariary = 5 irainbilanja

MALAWI (Africa)
Area: 118,480 sq km (45,745 sq miles)
Population: 14,268,711

Capital city: Lilongwe
Main languages: Chichewa, English, Chinyanja
Main religions: Protestant, Roman Catholic, Muslim
Government: republic
Currency: 1 Malawian kwacha = 100 tambala

Malawi

MALAYSIA (Asia)
Area: 329,750 sq km (127,317 sq miles)
Population: 25,715,819
Capital city: Kuala Lumpur
Main languages: Bahasa Melayu, English, Chinese dialects, Tamil
Main religions: Muslim, Buddhist, Daoist
Government: constitutional monarchy
Currency: 1 ringgit = 100 sen

Malaysia

MALDIVES (Asia)
Area: 300 sq km (116 sq miles)
Population: 396,334
Capital city: Male
Main languages: Maldivian, English
Main religion: Sunni Muslim
Government: republic
Currency: 1 rufiyaa = 100 laari

Maldives

MALI (Africa)
Area: 1,240,000 sq km (478,767 sq miles)
Population: 12,666,987
Capital city: Bamako
Main languages: Bambara, Fulani, Songhai, French
Main religion: Muslim
Government: republic
Currency: 1 CFA* franc = 100 centimes

Mali

MALTA (Europe)
Area: 316 sq km (122 sq miles)
Population: 405,165
Capital city: Valletta
Main languages: Maltese, English
Main religion: Roman Catholic
Government: democratic republic
Currency: 1 euro = 100 cents

Malta

MARSHALL ISLANDS (Australasia/Oceania)
Area: 181 sq km (70 sq miles)
Population: 64,522
Capital city: Majuro
Main languages: Marshallese, English
Main religion: Protestant
Government: republic
Currency: 1 U.S. dollar = 100 cents

Marshall Islands

MAURITANIA (Africa)
Area: 1,030,700 sq km (397,955 sq miles)
Population: 3,129,486
Capital city: Nouakchott
Main languages: Arabic, Wolof, French
Main religion: Muslim
Government: miltary rule
Currency: 1 ouguiya = 5 khoums

Mauritania

MAURITIUS (Africa)
Area: 2,040 sq km (788 sq miles)
Population: 1,284,264
Capital city: Port Louis
Main languages: Mauritius Creole French, French, Hindi, Bhojpuri, Urdu, Tamil,

*CFA = Communaute Financiere Africaine

GAZETTEER OF STATES CONTINUED:

Mauritius

English
Main religions: Hindu, Christian, English
Government: parliamentary democracy
Currency: 1 Mauritian rupee = 100 cents

MEXICO (North America)
Nationality: Mexican
Area: 1,972,550 sq km (761,606 sq miles)
Population: 111,211,789
Capital city: Mexico City
Main languages: Spanish, Mayan, Nahuatl
Main religion: Roman Catholic, Protestant
Government: federal republic
Currency: 1 New Mexican peso = 100 centavos

Mexico

MOLDOVA (Europe)
Area: 33,843 sq km (13,067 sq miles)
Population: 4,320,7
Capital city: Chisinau
Main languages: Moldovan, Russian, Gagauz
Main religion: Eastern Orthodox
Government: republic
Currency: 1 Moldovan leu = 100 bani

Moldova

MONACO (Europe)
Area: 1.95 sq km (0.75 sq miles)
Population: 32,965
Capital city: Monaco
Main languages: French, Monegasque, Italian
Main religion: Roman Catholic
Government: constitutional monarchy
Currency: 1 euro = 100 cents

Monaco

MONGOLIA (Asia)
Area: 1,564,116 sq km (603,909 sq miles)
Population: 3,041,142
Capital city: Ulan Bator
Main language: Khalkha Mongol
Main religion: Tibetan Buddist Lamaist
Government: republic
Currency: 1 tugrik = 100 mongos

Mongolia

MONTENEGRO (Europe)
Area: 14,026 sq km (5,415 sq miles)
Population: 672,180
Capital city: Podgorica
Main language: Serbian, Montenegrin
Main religion: Orthodox Christian, Muslim
Government: republic
Currency: 1 euro = 100 cents

Montenegro

MOROCCO (Africa)
Area: 446,550 sq km (172,414 sq miles)
Population: 34,859,364
Capital city: Rabat
Main languages: Arabic, Berber, French
Main religion: Muslim
Government: constitutional monarchy
Currency: 1 Moroccan dirham = 100 centimes

Morocco

MOZAMBIQUE (Africa)
Area: 801,590 sq km (309,496 sq miles)
Population: 21,669,278
Capital city: Maputo
Main languages: Makua, Tsonga, Portuguese, Emskhuwa, Xichangana
Main religions: indigenous, Christian, Muslim
Government: republic
Currency: 1 metical = 100 centavos

NAMIBIA (Africa)
Area: 825,418 sq km (318,696 sq miles)
Population: 2,108,665
Capital city: Windhoek
Main languages: Afrikaans, German, English
Main religions: Christian, indigenous
Government: republic
Currency: 1 Namibian dollar = 100 cents

NAURU (Australasia/Oceania)
Area: 21 sq km (8 sq miles)
Population: 14,019
Capital: Yaren
Main languages: Nauruan, English
Main religion: Christian
Government: republic
Currency: 1 Australian dollar = 100 cents

NEPAL (Asia)
Area: 147,181 sq km (56,827 sq miles)
Population: 28,563,377
Capital city: Kathmandu
Main languages: Nepali, Maithili
Main religions: Hindu, Buddhist
Government: federal republic
Currency: 1 Nepalese rupee = 100 paisa

NETHERLANDS (Europe)
Area: 41,526 sq km (16,033 sq miles)
Population: 16,715,999
Capital cities: Amsterdam, The Hague
Main language: Dutch
Main religion: Protestant, Roman Catholic
Government: constitutional monarchy
Currency: 1 euro = 100 cents

NEW ZEALAND (Australasia/Oceania)
Area: 268,680 sq km (103,738 sq miles)
Population: 4,213,418
Capital city: Wellington
Main languages: English, Maori
Main religion: Christian
Government: parliamentary democracy
Currency: 1 New Zealand dollar = 100 cents

NICARAGUA (North America)
Area: 129,494 sq km (49,998 sq miles)
Population: 5,891,199
Capital city: Managua
Main language: Spanish
Main religion: Roman Catholic, Protestant
Government: republic
Currency: 1 gold cordoba = 100 centavos

NIGER (Africa)
Area: 1,267,000 sq km (489,191 sq miles)
Population: 15,306,252
Capital city: Niamey
Main languages: Hausa, Djerma, French
Main religion: Muslim
Government: republic
Currency: 1 CFA* franc = 100 centimes

NIGERIA (Africa)
Area: 923,768 sq km (356,669 sq miles)
Population: 149,229,090
Capital city: Abuja
Main languages: Hausa, Yoruba, Igbo, English, Fulani

Mozambique

Namibia

Nauru

Nepal

Netherlands

New Zealand

Nicaragua

*CFA = Communaute Financiere Africaine

Niger

Main religions: Muslim, Christian, indigenous
Government: federal republic
Currency: 1 naira = 100 kobo

NORTH KOREA (Asia)
Area: 120,540 sq km (46,541 sq miles)
Population: 22,665,345
Capital city: Pyongyang
Main language: Korean
Main religions: Buddhist, Confucianist
Government: authoritarian socialist
Currency: 1 North Korean won = 100 chon

NORWAY (Europe)
Area: 323,802 sq km (125,021 sq miles)
Population: 4,660,539
Capital city: Oslo
Main language: Norwegian
Main religion: Evangelical Lutheran
Government: constitutional monarchy
Currency: 1 Norwegian krone = 100 oere

OMAN (Asia)
Area: 212,460 sq km (82,031 sq miles)
Population: 3,418,085
Capital city: Muscat
Main languages: Arabic, English, Baluchi
Main religion: Muslim
Government: monarchy
Currency: 1 Omani rial = 1,000 baiza

PAKISTAN (Asia)
Area: 803,940 sq km (310,403 sq miles)
Population: 176,242,949
Capital city: Islamabad
Main languages: Punjabi, Sindhi, Urdu, English
Main religion: Muslim
Government: federal republic
Currency: 1 Pakistani rupee = 100 paisa

PALAU (Australasia/Oceania)
Area: 458 sq km (177 sq miles)
Population: 20,796
Capital city: Melekeok
Main languages: Palauan, English, Philipino
Main religions: Christian, Modekngei
Government: democratic republic
Currency: 1 U.S. dollar = 100 cents

PANAMA (North America)
Area: 78,200 sq km (30,193 sq miles)
Population: 3,360,474
Capital city: Panama City
Main languages: Spanish, English
Main religions: Roman Catholic, Protestant
Government: democracy
Currency: 1 balboa = 100 centesimos

PAPUA NEW GUINEA
(Australasia/Oceania)
Area: 462,840 sq km (178,704 sq miles)
Population: 6,057,263
Capital city: Port Moresby
Main languages: Tok Pisin, Hiri Motu, English
Main religions: Christian, indigenous
Government: parliamentary democracy
Currency: 1 kina = 100 toea

PARAGUAY (South America)
Area: 406,750 sq km (157,047 sq miles)
Population: 6,995,655
Capital city: Asuncion
Main languages: Guarani, Spanish
Main religion: Roman Catholic
Government: republic
Currency: 1 guarani = 100 centimos

PERU (South America)
Area: 1,285,220 sq km (496,226 sq miles)
Population: 29,546,963
Capital city: Lima
Main languages: Spanish, Quechua, Aymara
Main religion: Roman Catholic
Government: republic
Currency: 1 nuevo sol = 100 centimos

PHILIPPINES (Asia)
Area: 300,000 sq km (115,831 sq miles)
Population: 97,976,603
Capital city: Manila
Main languages: Tagalog, English, Ilocano, Cebuano
Main religion: Roman Catholic
Government: republic
Currency: 1 Philippine peso = 100 centavos

POLAND (Europe)
Area: 312,679 sq km (120,726 sq miles)
Population: 38,482,919
Capital city: Warsaw
Main language: Polish
Main religion: Roman Catholic
Government: democratic republic
Currency: 1 zloty = 100 groszy

PORTUGAL (Europe)
Area: 92,391 sq km (35,672 sq miles)
Population: 10,707,924
Capital city: Lisbon
Main language: Portuguese
Main religion: Roman Catholic
Government: democratic republic
Currency: 1 euro = 100 cents

QATAR (Asia)
Area: 11,437 sq km (4,416 sq miles)
Population: 833,285
Capital city: Doha
Main languages: Arabic, English
Main religion: Muslim
Government: monarchy
Currency: 1 Qatari riyal = 100 dirhams

ROMANIA (Europe)
Area: 237,500 sq km (91,699 sq miles)
Population: 22,215,421
Capital city: Bucharest
Main languages: Romanian, Hungarian, German
Main religion: Romanian Orthodox
Government: republic
Currency: 1 leu = 100 bani

RUSSIA (Europe and Asia)
Area: 17,075,200 sq km (6,592,772 sq miles)
Population: 140,041,247
Capital city: Moscow

Nigeria

North Korea

Norway

Oman

Pakistan

Palau

Panama

Papua New Guinea

Paraguay

• **Peru**

Philippines

Poland

Portugal

GAZETTEER OF STATES CONTINUED:

Qatar

Main language: Russian
Main religions: Russian Orthodox, Muslim
Government: federal government
Currency: 1 ruble = 100 kopeks

RWANDA (Africa)
Area: 26,338 sq km (10,169 sq miles)
Population: 10,473,282
Capital city: Kigali
Main languages: Kinyarwanda, French,
English, Swahili
Main religions: Roman Catholic, Protestant,
Adventist
Government: republic
Currency: 1 Rwandan franc = 100 centimes

Romania

**SAINT KITTS AND NEVIS
(North America)**
Area: 261 sq km (101 sq miles)
Population: 40,131
Capital city: Basseterre
Main language: English
Main religions: Protestant, Roman Catholic
Government: constitutional monarchy
Currency: 1 East Caribbean dollar = 100 cents

Russia

SAINT LUCIA (North America)
Area: 616 sq km (239 sq miles)
Population: 160,267
Capital city: Castries
Main languages: French patois, English
Main religion: Roman Catholic, Protestant
Government: parliamentary democracy
Currency: 1 East Caribbean dollar = 100 cents

Rwanda

**SAINT VINCENT AND THE GRENADINES
(North America)**
Area: 389 sq km (150 sq miles)
Population: 104,574
Capital city: Kingstown
Main languages: English, French patois
Main religions: Protestant, Roman Catholic
Government: parliamentary democracy
Currency: 1 East Caribbean dollar = 100 cents

**Saint Kitts
and Nevis**

SAMOA (Australasia/Oceania)
Area: 2,944 sq km (1,137 sq miles)
Population: 217,083
Capital city: Apia
Main languages: Samoan, English
Main religion: Christian
Government: constitutional monarchy
Currency: 1 tala = 100 sene

Saint Lucia

SAN MARINO (Europe)
Area: 61 sq km (24 sq miles)
Population: 30,324
Capital city: San Marino
Main language: Italian
Main religion: Roman Catholic
Government: republic
Currency: 1 euro = 100 cents

**Saint Vincent and
the Grenadines**

SÃO TOMÉ AND PRINCIPE (Africa)
Area: 1,001 sq km (386 sq miles)
Population: 212,679
Capital city: Sao Tome
Main languages: Crioulo* dialects, Portuguese
Main religion: Christian

Government: republic
Currency: 1 dobra = 100 centimos

SAUDI ARABIA (Asia)
Area: 2,149,690 sq km (830,000 sq miles)
Population: 28,686,633
Capital city: Riyadh
Main language: Arabic
Main religion: Muslim
Government: monarchy
Currency: 1 Saudi riyal = 100 halalah

SENEGAL (Africa)
Area: 196,190 sq km (75,749 sq miles)
Population: 13,711,597
Capital city: Dakar
Main languages: Wolof, French, Pulaar
Main religion: Muslim
Government: democratic republic
Currency: 1 CFA* franc = 100 centimes

SERBIA (Europe)
Area: 77,474 sq km (29,913 sq miles)
Population: 8,354,208
Capital city: Belgrade
Main language: Serbian, Hungarian
Main religion: Serbian Orthodox, Roman
Catholic, Muslim
Government: republic
Currency: 1 Serbian dinar = 100 para

SEYCHELLES (Africa)
Area: 455 sq km (176 sq miles)
Population: 87,476
Capital city: Victoria
Main language: Seselwa, English
Main religion: Roman Catholic
Government: republic
Currency: 1 Seychelles rupee = 100 cents

SIERRA LEONE (Africa)
Area: 71,740 sq km (27,699 sq miles)
Population: 6,440,053
Capital city: Freetown
Main languages: Mende, Temne, Krio,
English
Main religions: Muslim, indigenous,
Christian
Government: republic
Currency: 1 leone = 100 cents

SINGAPORE (Asia)
Area: 693 sq km (267 sq miles)
Population: 4,657,542
Capital city: Singapore
Main languages: Chinese, Malay, English,
Tamil
Main religions: Buddhist, Muslim
Government: parliamentary republic
Currency: 1 Singapore dollar = 100 cents

SLOVAKIA (Europe)
Area: 48,845 sq km (18,859 sq miles)
Population: 5,463,046
Capital city: Bratislava
Main languages: Slovak, Hungarian
Main religion: Roman Catholic, Protestant
Government: parliamentary democracy
Currency: 1 euro = 100 cents

Samoa

• San Marino

**Sao Tome
and Principe**

Saudi Arabia

Senegal

• Serbia

Seychelles

*CFA = Communaute Financiere Africaine; Crioulo = a
blend of Portuguese and West African*

Sierra Leone

Singapore

Slovakia

Slovenia

Solomon Islands

Somalia

South Africa

SLOVENIA (Europe)
Area: 20,273 sq km (7,827 sq miles)
Population: 2,005,692
Capital city: Ljubljana
Main language: Slovenian
Main religion: Roman Catholic
Government: democratic republic
Currency: 1 euro = 100 cents

**SOLOMON ISLANDS
(Australasia/Oceania)**
Area: 28,450 sq km (10,985 sq miles)
Population: 595,613
Capital city: Honiara
Main languages: Solomon pidgin, Kwara'ae,
To'abaita, English
Main religion: Christian
Government: parliamentary democracy
Currency: 1 Solomon Islands dollar =
100 cents

SOMALIA (Africa)
Area: 637,657 sq km (246,201 sq miles)
Population: 9,832,017
Capital city: Mogadishu
Main languages: Somali, Arabic, Oromo
Main religion: Sunni Muslim
Government: currently has no government
Currency: 1 Somali shilling = 100 cents

SOUTH AFRICA (Africa)
Area: 1,219,912 sq km (471,011 sq miles)
Population: 49,052,489
Capital cities: Pretoria, Cape Town
Main languages: Zulu, Xhosa, Afrikaans, Pedi,
English, Tswana, Sotho, Tsonga, Swati, Venda,
Ndebele, Isi Zulu, Isi Xhosa
Main religions: Christian, indigenous
Government: republic
Currency: 1 rand = 100 cents

SOUTH KOREA (Asia)
Area: 98,480 sq km (38,023 sq miles)
Population: 48,508,972
Capital city: Seoul
Main language: Korean
Main religions: Christian, Buddhist
Government: republic
Currency: 1 South Korean won = 100 chun

SPAIN (Europe)
Area: 504,750 sq km (194,897 sq miles)
Population: 40,525,002
Capital city: Madrid
Main languages: Castilian Spanish, Catalan
Main religion: Roman Catholic
Government: constitutional monarchy
Currency: 1 euro = 100 cents

SRI LANKA (Asia)
Area: 65,610 sq km (25,332 sq miles)
Population: 21,324,791
Capital cities: Colombo, Sri Jayewardenepura
Kotte
Main languages: Sinhala, Tamil, English
Main religions: Buddhist, Hindu, Muslim
Government: republic
Currency: 1 Sri Lankan rupee =
100 cents

SUDAN (Africa)
Area: 2,505,810 sq km (967,499 sq miles)
Population: 41,087,825
Capital city: Khartoum
Main languages: Arabic, English
Main religions: Sunni Muslim, indigenous
Government: Islamic republic
Currency: 1 Sudanese pound = 100 piastres

SURINAME (South America)
Area: 163,270 sq km (63,039 sq miles)
Population: 481,267
Capital city: Paramaribo
Main languages: Sranang Tongo, Dutch, English
Main religions: Hindu, Christian, Muslim
Government: republic
Currency: 1 Surinamese dollar = 100 cents

SWAZILAND (Africa)
Area: 17,363 sq km (6,704 sq miles)
Population: 1,123,913
Capital cities: Mbabane, Lobamba
Main languages: Swati, English
Main religions: Christian, indigenous, Muslim
Government: monarchy
Currency: 1 lilangeni = 100 cents

SWEDEN (Europe)
Area: 449,964 sq km (173,732 sq miles)
Population: 9,059,651
Capital city: Stockholm
Main language: Swedish
Main religion: Lutheran
Government: constitutional monarchy
Currency: 1 Swedish krona = 100 oere

SWITZERLAND (Europe)
Area: 41,290 sq km (15,942 sq miles)
Population: 7,604,467
Capital city: Bern
Main languages: German, French, Italian
Main religions: Roman Catholic, Protestant
Government: federal republic
Currency: 1 Swiss franc, franken or frano =
100 centimes, rappen or centesimi

SYRIA (Asia)
Area: 185,180 sq km (71,498 sq miles)
Population: 20,178,485
Capital city: Damascus
Main languages: Arabic, Kurdish
Main religions: Muslim, Christian
Government: republic under military regime
Currency: 1 Syrian pound = 100 piastres

TAJIKISTAN (Asia)
Area: 143,100 sq km (55,251 sq miles)
Population: 7,349,145
Capital city: Dushanbe
Main languages: Tajik, Russian
Main religion: Sunni Muslim
Government: republic
Currency: 1 somoni = 100 dirams

TANZANIA (Africa)
Area: 945,087 sq km (364,900 sq miles)
Population: 41,048,532
Capital cities: Dar es Salaam, Dodoma
Main languages: Swahili, English, Sukuma

South Korea

Spain

Sri Lanka

Sudan

Suriname

Swaziland

Sweden

GAZETTEER OF STATES CONTINUED:

Switzerland

Main religions: Christian, Muslim, indigenous
Government: republic
Currency: 1 Tanzanian shilling = 100 cents

THAILAND (Asia)
Area: 514,000 sq km (198,457 sq miles)
Population: 65,905,410
Capital city: Bangkok
Main languages: Thai, English, Chaochow
Main religion: Buddhist
Government: constitutional monarchy
Currency: 1 baht = 100 satang

TOGO (Africa)
Area: 56,785 sq km (21,925 sq miles)
Population: 6,019,877
Capital city: Lome
Main languages: Mina, Ewe, Kabye, French
Main religions: indigenous, Christian, Muslim
Government: republic
Currency: 1 CFA* franc = 100 centimes

Syria

TONGA (Australasia/Oceania)
Area: 748 sq km (289 sq miles)
Population: 120,898
Capital city: Nukualofa
Main languages: Tongan, English
Main religion: Christian
Government: constitutional monarchy
Currency: 1 pa'anga = 100 seniti

Tajikistan

TRINIDAD AND TOBAGO (North America)
Area: 5,128 sq km (1,980 sq miles)
Population: 1,229,953
Capital city: Port-of-Spain
Main languages: English, French, Spanish, Hindi
Main religions: Christian, Hindu
Government: parliamentary democracy
Currency: 1 Trinidad and Tobago dollar = 100 cents

TUNISIA (Africa)
Area: 163,610 sq km (63,170 sq miles)
Population: 10,486,339
Capital city: Tunis
Main languages: Arabic, French
Main religion: Muslim
Government: republic
Currency: 1 Tunisian dinar = 1,000 millimes

Tanzania

TURKEY (Europe and Asia)
Area: 780,580 sq km (301,384 sq miles)
Population: 76,805,524
Capital city: Ankara
Main language: Turkish
Main religion: Muslim
Government: democratic republic
Currency: 1 Turkish lira = 100 kurus

Thailand

TURKMENISTAN (Asia)
Area: 488,100 sq km (188,456 sq miles)
Population: 4,884,887
Capital city: Ashgabat (Ashkhabad)
Main languages: Turkmen, Russian
Main religion: Muslim
Government: republic
Currency: 1 Turkmen manat = 100 tenesi

Togo

TUVALU (Australasia/Oceania)
Area: 26 sq km (10 sq miles)
Population: 12,373
Capital city: Funafuti
Main languages: Tuvaluan, English
Main religion: Congregationalist
Government: constitutional monarchy
Currency: 1 Tuvaluan dollar or 1 Australian dollar = 100 cents

UGANDA (Africa)
Area: 236,040 sq km (91,135 sq miles)
Population: 32,369,558
Capital city: Kampala
Main languages: Luganda, English, Swahili
Main religion: Christian, Muslim, indigenous
Government: republic
Currency: 1 Ugandan shilling = 100 cents

UKRAINE (Europe)
Area: 603,700 sq km (233,090 sq miles)
Population: 45,700,395
Capital city: Kiev
Main languages: Ukrainian, Russian
Main religion: Ukrainain Orthodox
Government: republic
Currency: 1 hryvnia = 100 kopiykas

UNITED ARAB EMIRATES (Asia)
Area: 83,600 sq km (32,278 sq miles)
Population: 4,798,491
Capital city: Abu Dhabi
Main languages: Arabic, English
Main religion: Muslim
Government: federation
Currency: 1 Emirati dirham = 100 fils

UNITED KINGDOM (Europe)
Area: 244,820 sq km (94,526 sq miles)
Population: 61,113,205
Capital city: London
Main language: English
Main religions: Anglican, Roman Catholic
Government: constitutional monarchy
Currency: 1 British pound = 100 pence

UNITED STATES OF AMERICA (North America)
Area: 9,826,630 sq km (3,794,083 sq miles)
Population: 307,212,123
Capital city: Washington D.C.
Main language: English
Main religions: Protestant, Roman Catholic
Government: federal republic
Currency: 1 U.S. dollar = 100 cents

URUGUAY (South America)
Area: 176,220 sq km (68,039 sq miles)
Population: 3,494,382
Capital city: Montevideo
Main language: Spanish
Main religion: Roman Catholic
Government: republic
Currency: 1 Uruguayan peso = 100 centesimos

UZBEKISTAN (Asia)
Area: 447,400 sq km (172,742 sq miles)
Population: 27,606,007

Tonga

Trinidad and Tobago

Tunisia

Turkey

Turkmenistan

Tuvalu

Uganda

96

Ukraine

United Arab Emirates

United Kingdom

United States of America

Uruguay

Uzbekistan

Vanuatu

Capital city: Tashkent
Main languages: Uzbek, Russian
Main religions: Muslim, Eastern Orthodox
Government: republic
Currency: 1 Uzbekistani sum = 100 tyyn

VANUATU (Australasia/Oceania)
Area: 12,200 sq km (4,710 sq miles)
Population: 218,519
Capital city: Port-Vila
Main languages: Bislama, French, English
Main religion: Christian
Government: republic
Currency: 1 vatu = 100 centimes

VATICAN CITY (Europe)
Area: 0.44 sq km (0.17 sq miles)
Population: 826
Capital city: Vatican City
Main languages: Italian, Latin
Main religion: Roman Catholic
Government: led by the Pope
Currency: 1 euro = 100 cents

VENEZUELA (South America)
Area: 912,050 sq km (352,144 sq miles)
Population: 26,814,843
Capital city: Caracas
Main language: Spanish
Main religion: Roman Catholic
Government: federal republic
Currency: 1 bolivar = 100 centimos

VIETNAM (Asia)
Area: 329,560 sq km (127,244 sq miles)

Population: 86,967,524
Capital city: Hanoi
Main languages: Vietnamese, French, English, Khmer, Chinese
Main religion: Buddhist
Government: communist state
Currency: 1 new dong = 100 xu

YEMEN (Asia)
Area: 527,970 sq km (203,850 sq miles)
Population: 23,822,783
Capital city: Sana
Main language: Arabic
Main religion: Muslim
Government: republic
Currency: 1 Yemeni rial = 100 fils

ZAMBIA (Africa)
Area: 752,614 sq km (290,586 sq miles)
Population: 11,862,740
Capital city: Lusaka
Main languages: Bemba, Tonga, Nyanja, English, Kaonda, Lozi, Lunda, Luvale
Main religions: Christian, Muslim, Hindu
Government: republic
Currency: 1 Zambian kwacha = 100 ngwee

ZIMBABWE (Africa)
Area: 390,580 sq km (150,804 sq miles)
Population: 11,392,629
Capital city: Harare
Main languages: Shona, Ndebele, English
Main religions: Christian, indigenous
Government: republic
Currency: 1 Zimbabwean dollar = 100 cents

Vatican City

Venezuela

Vietnam

Yemen

Zambia

Zimbabwe

The United Nations

The United Nations (U.N.) is an organization which aims to bring countries together to work for peace and development. Of the world's 194 states, 192 are members of the U.N. Those that don't belong are Kosovo and the Vatican City.

Internet links

For links to websites with flags, facts, maps, quizzes, and more information about the U.N., go to
www.usborne-quicklinks.com

Ban Ki-moon, the Secretary-General of the U.N., shakes hands with Hillary Clinton, the Secretary of State of the U.S.A.

MAP INDEX

This is an index of the places and features named on the maps. Each entry consists of the following parts: the name (given in bold type), the country or region within which it is located (given in italics), the page on which the name can be found (given in bold type), and the grid reference (also given in bold type). For some names, there is also a description explaining what kind of place it is – for example a country, internal administrative area (state or province), national capital or internal capital. To find a place on a map, first find the map indicated by the page reference. Then use the grid reference to find the square containing the name or town symbol. See page 7 for help with using the grid.

a

Abaco, *The Bahamas,* **27 L5**
Abadan, *Iran,* **53 E5**
Abakan, *Russia,* **54 E3**
Abaya, Lake, *Ethiopia,* **73 G2**
Abeche, *Chad,* **68 F6**
Abeokuta, *Nigeria,* **71 F7**
Aberdeen, *United Kingdom,* **62 D2**
Aberystwyth, *United Kingdom,* **62 C3**
Abha, *Saudi Arabia,* **53 D8**
Abidjan, *Ivory Coast,* **71 E7**
Abilene, *U.S.A.,* **26 G4**
Abomey, *Benin,* **71 F7**
Abu Dhabi, *United Arab Emirates, national capital,* **53 F7**
Abuja, *Nigeria, national capital,* **71 G7**
Abu Kamal, *Syria,* **52 D5**
Abu Simbel, *Egypt,* **69 H4**
Acapulco, *Mexico,* **28 E4**
Accra, *Ghana, national capital,* **71 E7**
Acklins Island, *The Bahamas,* **27 L6**
Aconcagua, *Argentina,* **34 E6**
Adana, *Turkey,* **52 C4**
Adapazari, *Turkey,* **65 J3**
Ad Dakhla, *Western Sahara,* **70 B4**
Ad Dammam, *Saudi Arabia,* **53 F6**
Addis Ababa, *Ethiopia, national capital,* **73 G2**
Adelaide, *Australia, internal capital,* **40 G6**
Aden, *Yemen,* **53 E9**
Aden, Gulf of, *Africa/Asia,* **53 E9**
Admiralty Islands, *Papua New Guinea,* **45 L4**
Adrar, *Algeria,* **70 E3**
Adriatic Sea, *Europe,* **64 E3**
Adzope, *Ivory Coast,* **71 E7**
Aegean Sea, *Europe,* **65 H4**
Afghanistan, *Asia, country,* **50 A4**
Africa, **21**
Agadez, *Niger,* **68 C5**
Agadir, *Morocco,* **70 D2**
Agra, *India,* **50 D5**
Agrigento, *Italy,* **64 E4**
Agua Prieta, *Mexico,* **28 C1**
Aguascalientes, *Mexico,* **28 D3**
Agulhas, Cape, *South Africa,* **74 C6**
Agulhas Negras, Mount, *Brazil,* **34 K4**
Ahaggar Mountains, *Algeria,* **70 G4**
Ahmadabad, *India,* **51 C6**
Ahvaz, *Iran,* **53 E5**
Aix-en-Provence, *France,* **63 F6**
Aizawl, *India,* **51 G6**
Ajaccio, *France,* **63 G6**
Ajdabiya, *Libya,* **68 F2**
Ajmer, *India,* **50 C5**
Akhisar, *Turkey,* **65 H4**
Akita, *Japan,* **49 P3**
Akjoujt, *Mauritania,* **70 C5**
Akola, *India,* **51 D6**
Aksaray, *Turkey,* **65 K4**
Aksu, *China,* **50 E2**
Alabama, *U.S.A., internal admin. area,* **27 J4**
Al Amarah, *Iraq,* **53 E5**
Aland Islands, *Finland,* **60 F3**
Alanya, *Turkey,* **65 J4**
Al Aqabah, *Jordan,* **53 C6**
Alaska, *U.S.A., internal admin. area,* **24 D2**
Alaska, Gulf of, *North America,* **24 E3**

Alaska Peninsula, *U.S.A.,* **24 D3**
Alaska Range, *U.S.A.,* **24 D2**
Alavus, *Finland,* **60 G3**
Al Ayn, *United Arab Emirates,* **53 G7**
Albacete, *Spain,* **63 D7**
Albania, *Europe, country,* **65 F3**
Albany, *Australia,* **40 C7**
Albany, *Georgia, U.S.A.,* **27 K4**
Albany, *New York, U.S.A., internal capital,* **27 M2**
Al Bayda, *Libya,* **68 F2**
Alberta, *Canada, internal admin. area,* **24 H3**
Albert, Lake, *Africa,* **73 F3**
Albino Point, *Angola,* **74 B3**
Alboran Island, *Spain,* **63 D7**
Alborg, *Denmark,* **61 D4**
Albuquerque, *U.S.A.,* **26 E3**
Aldabra Group, *Seychelles,* **75 J1**
Aleppo, *Syria,* **52 C4**
Alesund, *Norway,* **60 C3**
Aleutian Islands, *U.S.A.,* **25 A3**
Alexander Archipelago, *Canada,* **24 F3**
Alexander Bay, *South Africa,* **74 C5**
Alexandria, *Egypt,* **69 H2**
Algeciras, *Spain,* **63 C7**
Algeria, *Africa, country,* **70 F3**
Algiers, *Algeria, national capital,* **70 F1**
Al Hillah, *Iraq,* **52 D5**
Al Hoceima, *Morocco,* **70 E1**
Al Hudaydah, *Yemen,* **53 D9**
Ali Bayramli, *Azerbaijan,* **52 E4**
Alicante, *Spain,* **63 D7**
Alice Springs, *Australia,* **40 F4**
Aligarh, *India,* **50 D5**
Al Jawf, *Libya,* **68 F4**
Al Khums, *Libya,* **68 D2**
Al Kut, *Iraq,* **53 E5**
Allahabad, *India,* **50 E5**
Almaty, *Kazakhstan,* **50 D2**
Almeria, *Spain,* **63 D7**
Almetyevsk, *Russia,* **59 G3**
Almirante, *Panama,* **29 H6**
Al Mubarrez, *Saudi Arabia,* **53 E6**
Al Mukalla, *Yemen,* **53 E9**
Alor Setar, *Malaysia,* **44 B2**
Alps, *Europe,* **64 D2**
Al Qamishli, *Syria,* **52 D4**
Alta, *Norway,* **60 G1**
Altai Mountains, *Asia,* **48 D1**
Altamira, *Brazil,* **33 H4**
Altay, *China,* **50 F1**
Altay, *Mongolia,* **48 E1**
Altun Mountains, *China,* **50 G3**
Aluksne, *Latvia,* **61 H4**
Alytus, *Lithuania,* **61 H5**
Amadjuak Lake, *Canada,* **25 M2**
Amami, *Japan,* **49 L5**
Amarillo, *U.S.A.,* **26 F3**
Amazon, *South America,* **32 H4**
Amazon Delta, *Brazil,* **33 J3**
Ambanja, *Madagascar,* **75 J2**
Ambato, *Ecuador,* **32 C4**
Amber, Cape, *Madagascar,* **75 J2**
Ambilobe, *Madagascar,* **75 J2**
Ambon, *Indonesia,* **45 G4**
Ambositra, *Madagascar,* **75 J4**
American Samoa, *Oceania, dependency,* **38 F6**

America, United States of, *North America, country,* **26 F3**
Amiens, *France,* **62 E4**
Amman, *Jordan, national capital,* **53 C5**
Amravati, *India,* **51 D6**
Amritsar, *India,* **50 C4**
Amsterdam, *Netherlands, national capital,* **62 F3**
Am Timan, *Chad,* **68 F6**
Amu Darya, *Asia,* **52 H4**
Amundsen Gulf, *Canada,* **24 G1**
Amundsen Sea, *Antarctica,* **79 Q3**
Amur, *Asia,* **55 G3**
Anadyr, *Russia,* **55 J2**
Anadyr, Gulf of, *Asia,* **55 K2**
Analalava, *Madagascar,* **75 J2**
Anambas Islands, *Indonesia,* **44 C3**
Anchorage, *U.S.A.,* **24 E2**
Ancona, *Italy,* **64 E3**
Andaman Islands, *India,* **51 G8**
Andaman Sea, *Asia,* **46 C5**
Andara, *Namibia,* **74 D3**
Andes, *South America,* **34 E5**
Andorra, *Europe, country,* **63 E6**
Andorra la Vella, *Andorra, national capital,* **63 E6**
Androka, *Madagascar,* **75 H5**
Andros, *The Bahamas,* **27 L6**
Aneto, Pico de, *Spain,* **63 E6**
Angel Falls, *Venezuela,* **32 F2**
Angers, *France,* **62 D5**
Angkor, *Cambodia,* **46 D5**
Angoche, *Mozambique,* **75 G3**
Angola, *Africa, country,* **74 C2**
Angra do Heroismo, *Azores,* **70 K10**
Angren, *Uzbekistan,* **50 C2**
Anguilla, *North America,* **28 M4**
Anjouan Island, *Comoros,* **75 H2**
Ankara, *Turkey, national capital,* **65 K3**
Annaba, *Algeria,* **70 G1**
An Najaf, *Iraq,* **53 D5**
Annapolis, *U.S.A., internal capital,* **27 L3**
An Nasiriyah, *Iraq,* **53 E5**
Anqing, *China,* **49 J4**
Anshan, *China,* **49 K2**
Antalya, *Turkey,* **65 J4**
Antalya, Gulf of, *Turkey,* **65 J4**
Antananarivo, *Madagascar, national capital,* **75 J3**
Antarctica, **79 B4**
Antarctic Peninsula, *Antarctica,* **79 T2**
Anticosti Island, *Canada,* **25 N4**
Antigua and Barbuda, *North America, country,* **28 M4**
Antofagasta, *Chile,* **34 D4**
Antsalova, *Madagascar,* **75 H3**
Antsirabe, *Madagascar,* **75 J3**
Antsiranana, *Madagascar,* **75 J2**
Antwerp, *Belgium,* **62 F4**
Aomori, *Japan,* **49 P2**
Aoraki, *New Zealand,* **41 P8**
Apalachee Bay, *U.S.A.,* **27 K5**
Aparri, *Philippines,* **47 H4**
Apatity, *Russia,* **60 K2**
Apennines, *Italy,* **64 E3**
Apia, *Samoa, national capital,* **38 F6**

Appalachian Mountains, *U.S.A.,* **27 K3**
Aqsay, *Kazakhstan,* **59 G3**
Aqtau, *Kazakhstan,* **52 F3**
Aqtobe, *Kazakhstan,* **59 H3**
Arabian Desert, *Africa,* **69 H3**
Arabian Peninsula, *Asia,* **53 E7**
Arabian Sea, *Asia,* **53 G8**
Aracaju, *Brazil,* **33 L6**
Arad, *Romania,* **65 G2**
Arafura Sea, *Asia/Australasia,* **45 H5**
Araguaia, *Brazil,* **33 H6**
Araguaina, *Brazil,* **33 J5**
Arak, *Iran,* **52 E5**
Aral, *Kazakhstan,* **52 H2**
Aral Sea, *Asia,* **52 G2**
Arapiraca, *Brazil,* **33 L5**
Araraquara, *Brazil,* **34 J4**
Araure, *Venezuela,* **32 E2**
Arbil, *Iraq,* **52 D4**
Arctic Ocean, **77 A4**
Ardabil, *Iran,* **52 E4**
Arendal, *Norway,* **60 D4**
Arequipa, *Peru,* **32 D7**
Argentina, *South America, country,* **35 E7**
Argentino, Lake, *Argentina,* **35 D10**
Arhus, *Denmark,* **61 D4**
Arica, *Chile,* **34 D3**
Arica, Gulf of, *South America,* **32 D7**
Arizona, *U.S.A., internal admin. area,* **26 D4**
Arkansas, *U.S.A.,* **27 G3**
Arkansas, *U.S.A., internal admin. area,* **27 H4**
Arkhangelsk, *Russia,* **54 C2**
Armenia, *Asia, country,* **52 D3**
Armidale, *Australia,* **41 K6**
Arnhem, *Netherlands,* **62 F4**
Arnhem Land, *Australia,* **40 F2**
Arqalyq, *Kazakhstan,* **52 J1**
Ar Ramadi, *Iraq,* **52 D5**
Ar Raqqah, *Syria,* **52 C4**
Aruba, *North America,* **29 K5**
Aru Islands, *Indonesia,* **45 J5**
Arusha, *Tanzania,* **73 G4**
Arzamas, *Russia,* **58 E2**
Asahikawa, *Japan,* **49 P2**
Asansol, *India,* **51 F6**
Ashgabat, *Turkmenistan, national capital,* **52 G4**
Ashkhabad, *Turkmenistan, national capital,* **52 G4**
Asia, **21**
Asir, *Saudi Arabia,* **53 D7**
Asmara, *Eritrea, national capital,* **69 J5**
Assab, *Eritrea,* **69 K6**
As Sulaymaniyah, *Iraq,* **52 E4**
Assumption, *Seychelles,* **75 J1**
Astana, *Kazakhstan, national capital,* **54 D3**
Astove, *Seychelles,* **75 J2**
Astrakhan, *Russia,* **59 F4**
Asuncion, *Paraguay, national capital,* **34 G5**
Aswan, *Egypt,* **69 H4**
Aswan High Dam, *Egypt,* **69 H4**
Asyut, *Egypt,* **69 H3**
Atacama Desert, *Chile,* **34 E3**

Atalaia do Norte, *Brazil*, 32 D4
Atar, *Mauritania*, 70 C4
Atbarah, *Sudan*, 69 H5
Atbasar, *Kazakhstan*, 52 J1
Athabasca, *Canada*, 24 H3
Athabasca, Lake, *Canada*, 24 J3
Athens, *Greece, national capital*, 65 G4
Atka Island, *U.S.A.*, 25 B3
Atlanta, *U.S.A., internal capital*, 27 K4
Atlantic City, *U.S.A.*, 27 M3
Atlantic Ocean, 20
Atlas Mountains, *Africa*, 70 D2
At Taif, *Saudi Arabia*, 53 D7
Attapu, *Laos*, 46 E5
Attu Island, *U.S.A.*, 25 A3
Atyrau, *Kazakhstan*, 59 G4
Auckland, *New Zealand*, 41 P7
Augsburg, *Germany*, 62 G4
Augusta, *U.S.A., internal capital*, 27 N2
Aurangabad, *India*, 51 D7
Austin, *U.S.A., internal capital*, 26 G4
Australasia and Oceania, 21
Australia, *Australasia, country*, 40 E4
Australian Capital Territory, *Australia, internal admin. area*, 41 J6
Austria, *Europe, country*, 64 E2
Awasa, *Ethiopia*, 73 G2
Ayacucho, *Peru*, 32 D6
Aydin, *Turkey*, 65 H4
Ayers Rock, *Australia*, 40 F5
Ayoun el Atrous, *Mauritania*, 71 D5
Azerbaijan, *Asia, country*, 52 E3
Azores, *Atlantic Ocean*, 70 K10
Azov, Sea of, *Europe*, 65 K2
Az Zarqa, *Jordan*, 53 C5

b

Baardheere, *Somalia*, 73 H3
Babahoyo, *Ecuador*, 32 C4
Bab al Mandab, *Africa/Asia*, 69 K6
Babruysk, *Belarus*, 61 J5
Babuyan Islands, *Philippines*, 47 H4
Babylon, *Iraq*, 52 D5
Bacabal, *Brazil*, 33 K4
Bacau, *Romania*, 65 H2
Bac Lieu, *Vietnam*, 46 E6
Bacolod, *Philippines*, 47 H5
Badajoz, *Spain*, 63 C7
Baffin Bay, *Canada*, 25 N1
Baffin Island, *Canada*, 25 M2
Bafoussam, *Cameroon*, 72 B2
Bage, *Brazil*, 34 H6
Baghdad, *Iraq, national capital*, 52 D5
Bahamas, The, *North America, country*, 27 L5
Bahawalpur, *Pakistan*, 50 C5
Bahia, *Brazil*, 33 L6
Bahia Blanca, *Argentina*, 35 F7
Bahir Dar, *Ethiopia*, 73 G1
Bahrain, *Asia, country*, 53 F6
Baia Mare, *Romania*, 65 G2
Baie-Comeau, *Canada*, 25 N4
Baikal, Lake, *Russia*, 55 F3
Bairiki, *Kiribati, national capital*, 38 E4
Bakersfield, *U.S.A.*, 26 C3
Baku, *Azerbaijan, national capital*, 52 E3
Balakovo, *Russia*, 59 F3
Balaton, Lake, *Hungary*, 61 F7
Balbina Reservoir, *Brazil*, 33 G4
Baldy Peak, *U.S.A.*, 26 E4
Balearic Islands, *Spain*, 63 E7
Bali, *Indonesia*, 44 E5
Balikesir, *Turkey*, 65 H4
Balikpapan, *Indonesia*, 44 E4
Balkanabat, *Turkmenistan*, 52 F4
Balkan Mountains, *Europe*, 65 G3
Balkhash, Lake, *Kazakhstan*, 50 D1
Balkuduk, *Kazakhstan*, 59 F4
Balqash, *Kazakhstan*, 50 D1
Balti, *Moldova*, 65 H2
Baltic Sea, *Europe*, 61 F4
Baltimore, *U.S.A.*, 27 L3
Bamako, *Mali, national capital*, 71 D6
Bamenda, *Cameroon*, 72 B2
Bancs Providence, *Seychelles*, 75 K1
Banda Aceh, *Indonesia*, 44 A2

Bandar-e Abbas, *Iran*, 53 G6
Bandar Seri Begawan, *Brunei, national capital*, 44 D2
Banda Sea, *Indonesia*, 45 G5
Bandundu, *Democratic Republic of Congo*, 72 C4
Bandung, *Indonesia*, 44 C5
Banfora, *Burkina Faso*, 71 E6
Bangalore, *India*, 51 D8
Bangassou, *Central African Republic*, 72 D3
Bangka, *Indonesia*, 44 C4
Bangkok, *Thailand, national capital*, 46 D5
Bangladesh, *Asia, country*, 51 F6
Bangor, *U.S.A.*, 27 N2
Bangui, *Central African Republic, national capital*, 72 C3
Bangweulu, Lake, *Zambia*, 74 E2
Banja Luka, *Bosnia and Herzegovina*, 64 F2
Banjarmasin, *Indonesia*, 44 D4
Banjul, *The Gambia, national capital*, 71 B6
Banks Island, *Canada*, 24 G1
Banks Islands, *Vanuatu*, 41 N2
Banska Bystrica, *Slovakia*, 61 F6
Baoding, *China*, 49 J3
Baoji, *China*, 48 G4
Baotou, *China*, 48 G2
Baqubah, *Iraq*, 52 D5
Baranavichy, *Belarus*, 61 H5
Barbacena, *Brazil*, 34 K4
Barbados, *North America, country*, 28 N5
Barcelona, *Spain*, 63 E6
Barcelona, *Venezuela*, 32 F1
Bareilly, *India*, 50 D5
Barents Sea, *Europe*, 54 B2
Bari, *Italy*, 64 F3
Barinas, *Venezuela*, 32 D2
Barkly Tableland, *Australia*, 40 G3
Barnaul, *Russia*, 54 E3
Barquisimeto, *Venezuela*, 32 E1
Barra Falsa Point, *Mozambique*, 75 G4
Barranquilla, *Colombia*, 32 D1
Barra Point, *Mozambique*, 75 G4
Barreiras, *Brazil*, 34 J2
Barrow, Point, *U.S.A.*, 24 D1
Barysaw, *Belarus*, 61 J5
Basel, *Switzerland*, 64 C2
Basra, *Iraq*, 53 E5
Bassas da India, *Africa*, 75 G4
Basse-Terre, *Guadeloupe*, 28 M4
Basseterre, *St. Kitts and Nevis, national capital*, 28 M4
Bass Strait, *Australia*, 40 J7
Bastia, *France*, 63 G6
Bata, *Equatorial Guinea*, 72 A3
Batan Islands, *Philippines*, 47 H3
Batdambang, *Cambodia*, 46 D5
Bathurst, *Canada*, 25 N4
Bathurst, *U.S.A.*, 27 N1
Bathurst Island, *Canada*, 25 K1
Batna, *Algeria*, 70 G1
Baton Rouge, *U.S.A., internal capital*, 27 H4
Batumi, *Georgia*, 52 D3
Baturaja, *Indonesia*, 44 B4
Bawku, *Ghana*, 71 E6
Bayamo, *Cuba*, 29 J3
Baydhabo, *Somalia*, 73 H3
Bealanana, *Madagascar*, 75 J2
Beaufort Sea, *North America*, 24 F1
Beaufort West, *South Africa*, 74 D6
Beaumont, *U.S.A.*, 27 H4
Bechar, *Algeria*, 70 E2
Beer Sheva, *Israel*, 53 B5
Beijing, *China, national capital*, 49 J3
Beira, *Mozambique*, 75 G3
Beirut, *Lebanon, national capital*, 52 C5
Bejaia, *Algeria*, 70 F1
Bekescsaba, *Hungary*, 61 G7
Bekily, *Madagascar*, 75 J4
Belarus, *Europe, country*, 61 J5
Belaya, *Russia*, 59 G2
Belcher Islands, *Canada*, 25 L3
Beledweyne, *Somalia*, 73 J3

Belem, *Brazil*, 33 J4
Belfast, *United Kingdom, internal capital*, 62 C3
Belgaum, *India*, 51 C7
Belgium, *Europe, country*, 62 E4
Belgrade, *Serbia, national capital*, 65 G2
Belitung, *Indonesia*, 44 C4
Belize, *North America, country*, 28 G4
Bellingham, *U.S.A.*, 26 B1
Bellingshausen Sea, *Antarctica*, 79 R2
Belmopan, *Belize, national capital*, 28 G4
Belo Horizonte, *Brazil*, 34 K3
Belomorsk, *Russia*, 60 K2
Beloretsk, *Russia*, 59 H3
Belo-Tsiribihina, *Madagascar*, 75 H3
Bendigo, *Australia*, 40 H7
Bengal, Bay of, *Asia*, 51 F7
Benghazi, *Libya*, 68 F2
Bengkulu, *Indonesia*, 44 B4
Benguela, *Angola*, 74 B2
Beni Mellal, *Morocco*, 70 D2
Benin, *Africa, country*, 71 F6
Benin, Bight of, *Africa*, 71 F7
Benin City, *Nigeria*, 71 G7
Beni Suef, *Egypt*, 69 H3
Ben Nevis, *United Kingdom*, 62 C2
Benoni, *South Africa*, 74 E5
Berbera, *Somalia*, 73 J1
Berberati, *Central African Republic*, 72 C3
Berdyansk, *Ukraine*, 58 D4
Berezniki, *Russia*, 59 H2
Bergamo, *Italy*, 64 D2
Bergen, *Norway*, 60 C3
Bering Sea, *North America*, 24 C2
Bering Strait, *U.S.A.*, 24 B2
Berlin, *Germany, national capital*, 62 H3
Bern, *Switzerland, national capital*, 64 C2
Beroroha, *Madagascar*, 75 J4
Bertoua, *Cameroon*, 72 B3
Besalampy, *Madagascar*, 75 H3
Besancon, *France*, 63 F5
Bethel, *U.S.A.*, 24 C2
Bethlehem, *South Africa*, 74 E5
Betroka, *Madagascar*, 75 J4
Beyneu, *Kazakhstan*, 52 G2
Beysehir Lake, *Turkey*, 65 J4
Beziers, *France*, 63 E6
Bhagalpur, *India*, 50 F5
Bhavnagar, *India*, 51 C6
Bhopal, *India*, 51 D6
Bhutan, *Asia, country*, 50 G5
Biak, *Indonesia*, 45 J4
Bialystok, *Poland*, 61 G5
Bida, *Nigeria*, 71 G7
Biel, *Switzerland*, 64 C2
Bielefeld, *Germany*, 62 G3
Bien Hoa, *Vietnam*, 46 E5
Bie Plateau, *Angola*, 74 B2
Bignona, *Senegal*, 71 B6
Bikaner, *India*, 50 C5
Bila Tserkva, *Ukraine*, 61 J6
Bilbao, *Spain*, 63 E6
Bilhorod Dnistrovskyy, *Ukraine*, 58 C4
Billings, *U.S.A.*, 26 E1
Bindura, *Zimbabwe*, 74 F3
Binga, *Zimbabwe*, 74 E3
Bintulu, *Malaysia*, 44 D3
Bioco, *Equatorial Guinea*, 72 A3
Birao, *Central African Republic*, 72 D1
Biratnagar, *Nepal*, 50 F5
Birjand, *Iran*, 52 G5
Birmingham, *United Kingdom*, 62 D3
Birmingham, *U.S.A.*, 27 J4
Birnin-Kebbi, *Nigeria*, 71 F6
Biscay, Bay of, *Europe*, 63 C5
Bishkek, *Kyrgyzstan, national capital*, 50 D2
Bisho, *South Africa*, 74 E6
Biskra, *Algeria*, 70 G2
Bismarck, *U.S.A., internal capital*, 26 F1
Bismarck Sea, *Papua New Guinea*, 45 L4
Bissagos Archipelago, *Guinea-Bissau*, 71 B6
Bissau, *Guinea-Bissau, national capital*, 71 B6

Bitola, *Macedonia*, 65 G3
Bitterfontein, *South Africa*, 74 C6
Bizerte, *Tunisia*, 68 C1
Blackpool, *United Kingdom*, 62 D3
Black Sea, *Asia/Europe*, 54 B3
Black Volta, *Africa*, 71 E6
Blagoevgrad, *Bulgaria*, 65 G3
Blagoveshchensk, *Russia*, 55 G3
Blanca Bay, *Argentina*, 35 F7
Blanc, Cape, *Africa*, 70 B4
Blanc, Mont, *Europe*, 63 F5
Blantyre, *Malawi*, 75 F3
Blida, *Algeria*, 70 F1
Bloemfontein, *South Africa, national capital*, 74 E5
Blue Nile, *Africa*, 69 H6
Bo, *Sierra Leone*, 71 C7
Boa Vista, *Brazil*, 32 F3
Boa Vista, *Cape Verde*, 71 M11
Bobo Dioulasso, *Burkina Faso*, 71 E6
Bodele Depression, *Africa*, 68 E5
Boden, *Sweden*, 60 G2
Bodo, *Norway*, 60 F3
Bogor, *Indonesia*, 44 C5
Bogota, *Colombia, national capital*, 32 D3
Bohol, *Philippines*, 47 H6
Boise, *U.S.A., internal capital*, 26 C2
Bojnurd, *Iran*, 52 G4
Boke, *Guinea*, 71 C6
Bolivar Peak, *Venezuela*, 32 D2
Bolivia, *South America, country*, 34 E3
Bologna, *Italy*, 64 D2
Bolzano, *Italy*, 64 D2
Bombay, *India*, 51 C7
Bondoukou, *Ivory Coast*, 71 E7
Bongor, *Chad*, 72 C1
Bonin Islands, *Japan*, 38 B2
Bonn, *Germany*, 62 F4
Boosaaso, *Somalia*, 73 J1
Boothia, Gulf of, *Canada*, 25 K1
Boothia Peninsula, *Canada*, 25 K1
Bordeaux, *France*, 63 D5
Bordj Bou Arreridj, *Algeria*, 70 F1
Borlange, *Sweden*, 60 E3
Borneo, *Asia*, 44 D4
Bornholm, *Denmark*, 61 E5
Borovichi, *Russia*, 60 K4
Bosnia and Herzegovina, *Europe, country*, 64 F2
Bosporus, *Turkey*, 65 J3
Bossangoa, *Central African Republic*, 72 C2
Bossembele, *Central African Republic*, 72 C2
Bosten Lake, *China*, 50 F2
Boston, *U.S.A., internal capital*, 27 M2
Bothnia, Gulf of, *Europe*, 60 F3
Botosani, *Romania*, 65 H2
Botswana, *Africa, country*, 74 D4
Bouake, *Ivory Coast*, 71 E7
Bouar, *Central African Republic*, 72 C2
Boujdour, *Western Sahara*, 70 C3
Bouna, *Ivory Coast*, 71 E7
Bozoum, *Central African Republic*, 72 C2
Braga, *Portugal*, 63 B6
Braganca, *Brazil*, 33 J4
Brahmapur, *India*, 51 E7
Brahmaputra, *Asia*, 50 G5
Braila, *Romania*, 65 H2
Brandon, *Canada*, 25 K4
Brandon, *U.S.A.*, 26 G1
Brasilia, *Brazil, national capital*, 34 J3
Brasov, *Romania*, 65 H2
Bratislava, *Slovakia, national capital*, 61 F6
Brazil, *South America, country*, 33 H5
Brazilian Highlands, *Brazil*, 34 K2
Brazzaville, *Congo, national capital*, 72 C4
Bremen, *Germany*, 62 G3
Bremerhaven, *Germany*, 62 G3
Brescia, *Italy*, 64 D2
Brest, *Belarus*, 61 G5
Brest, *France*, 62 C4
Bria, *Central African Republic*, 72 D2
Bridgetown, *Barbados, national capital*, 28 N5

Brisbane, *Australia, internal capital,* 41 K5
Bristol, *United Kingdom,* 62 D4
Bristol Bay, *U.S.A.,* 24 C3
British Columbia, *Canada, internal admin. area,* 24 G3
Brno, *Czech Republic,* 64 F1
Broken Hill, *Australia,* 40 H6
Brokopondo, *Suriname,* 33 G2
Brooks Range, *U.S.A.,* 24 D2
Brownsville, *U.S.A.,* 26 G5
Bruges, *Belgium,* 62 E4
Brunei, *Asia, country,* 44 D3
Brussels, *Belgium, national capital,* 62 F4
Bryansk, *Russia,* 58 C4
Bucaramanga, *Colombia,* 32 D2
Bucharest, *Romania, national capital,* 65 H2
Budapest, *Hungary, national capital,* 61 F7
Buenaventura, *Colombia,* 32 C3
Buenos Aires, *Argentina, national capital,* 34 G6
Buenos Aires, Lake, *South America,* 35 D9
Buffalo, *U.S.A.,* 27 L2
Buga, *Colombia,* 32 C3
Buinsk, *Russia,* 59 F3
Bujumbura, *Burundi, national capital,* 72 E4
Bukavu, *Democratic Republic of Congo,* 72 E4
Bulawayo, *Zimbabwe,* 74 E4
Bulgan, *Mongolia,* 48 F1
Bulgaria, *Europe, country,* 65 H3
Bunbury, *Australia,* 40 C6
Bundaberg, *Australia,* 41 K4
Buon Me Thuot, *Vietnam,* 46 E5
Buraydah, *Saudi Arabia,* 53 D6
Burgas, *Bulgaria,* 65 H3
Burgos, *Spain,* 63 D6
Burkina Faso, *Africa, country,* 71 E6
Burma, *Asia, country,* 46 C3
Bursa, *Turkey,* 65 J3
Buru, *Indonesia,* 45 G4
Burundi, *Africa, country,* 72 E4
Bushehr, *Iran,* 53 F6
Buta, *Democratic Republic of Congo,* 72 D3
Butare, *Rwanda,* 72 E4
Butembo, *Democratic Republic of Congo,* 72 E3
Buton, *Indonesia,* 45 F4
Butuan, *Philippines,* 47 J6
Buxoro, *Uzbekistan,* 50 A3
Buzau, *Romania,* 65 H2
Buzuluk, *Russia,* 59 G3
Bydgoszcz, *Poland,* 61 F5

C
Cabanatuan, *Philippines,* 47 H4
Cabinda, *Angola, enclave,* 72 B5
Cabonga Reservoir, *Canada,* 27 L1
Cabora Bassa Reservoir, *Mozambique,* 74 F3
Caceres, *Brazil,* 34 G3
Caceres, *Colombia,* 32 C2
Caceres, *Spain,* 63 C7
Cachoeiro de Itapemirim, *Brazil,* 34 K4
Cadiz, *Spain,* 63 C7
Cadiz, Gulf of, *Europe,* 63 C7
Caen, *France,* 62 D4
Cagayan de Oro, *Philippines,* 47 H6
Cagliari, *Italy,* 64 D4
Caicara, *Venezuela,* 32 E2
Cairns, *Australia,* 40 J3
Cairo, *Egypt, national capital,* 69 H3
Caiundo, *Angola,* 74 C3
Cajamarca, *Peru,* 32 C5
Calabar, *Nigeria,* 72 A2
Calais, *France,* 62 E4
Calama, *Chile,* 34 E4
Calamian Group, *Philippines,* 47 G5
Calapan, *Philippines,* 47 H5
Calbayog, *Philippines,* 47 H5
Calcutta, *India,* 51 F6
Calgary, *Canada,* 24 H3

Cali, *Colombia,* 32 C3
Calicut, *India,* 51 D8
California, *U.S.A., internal admin. area,* 26 C3
California, Gulf of, *Mexico,* 28 B2
Camaguey, *Cuba,* 29 J3
Cambodia, *Asia, country,* 46 E5
Cambridge, *United Kingdom,* 62 E3
Cameroon, *Africa, country,* 72 B2
Cameroon Mountain, *Cameroon,* 72 A3
Cameta, *Brazil,* 33 J4
Campeche, *Mexico,* 28 F4
Campeche, Bay of, *Mexico,* 28 F3
Campina Grande, *Brazil,* 33 L5
Campinas, *Brazil,* 34 J4
Campo Grande, *Brazil,* 34 H4
Campos, *Brazil,* 34 K4
Canada, *North America, country,* 24 J3
Canadian, *U.S.A.,* 26 F3
Canakkale, *Turkey,* 65 H3
Canary Islands, *Atlantic Ocean,* 70 B3
Canaveral, Cape, *U.S.A.,* 27 K5
Canberra, *Australia, national capital,* 41 J7
Cancun, *Mexico,* 29 G3
Cangombe, *Angola,* 74 D2
Cannes, *France,* 63 F6
Can Tho, *Vietnam,* 46 E6
Canton, *China,* 49 H6
Cape Coast, *Ghana,* 71 E7
Cape Town, *South Africa, national capital,* 74 C6
Cape Verde, *Atlantic Ocean, country,* 71 L11
Cape York Peninsula, *Australia,* 40 H2
Cap-Haitien, *Haiti,* 29 K4
Caprivi Strip, *Namibia,* 74 D3
Caracas, *Venezuela, national capital,* 32 E1
Cardiff, *United Kingdom, internal capital,* 62 D4
Caribbean Sea, *North/South America,* 29 J4
Carlisle, *United Kingdom,* 62 D3
Carnarvon, *Australia,* 40 B4
Carnarvon, *South Africa,* 74 D6
Carnot, Cape, *Australia,* 40 G7
Caroline Islands, *Federated States of Micronesia,* 38 B4
Carpathian Mountains, *Europe,* 61 H7
Carpentaria, Gulf of, *Australia,* 40 G2
Carson City, *U.S.A., internal capital,* 26 C3
Cartagena, *Colombia,* 32 C1
Cartagena, *Spain,* 63 D7
Carthage, *Tunisia,* 68 D1
Cartwright, *Canada,* 25 P3
Caruaru, *Brazil,* 33 L5
Casablanca, *Morocco,* 70 D2
Cascade Range, *U.S.A.,* 26 B2
Cascais, *Portugal,* 63 B7
Cascavel, *Brazil,* 34 H4
Casper, *U.S.A.,* 26 E2
Caspian Depression, *Asia,* 52 F2
Caspian Sea, *Asia,* 59 G4
Castellon de la Plana, *Spain,* 63 D7
Castelo Branco, *Portugal,* 63 C7
Castries, *St. Lucia, national capital,* 28 M5
Catamarca, *Argentina,* 34 E5
Catania, *Italy,* 64 E4
Catanzaro, *Italy,* 64 F4
Cat Island, *The Bahamas,* 27 L6
Caucasus Mountains, *Asia/Europe,* 52 D3
Caxias do Sul, *Brazil,* 34 H5
Cayenne, *French Guiana, national capital,* 33 H3
Cayman Islands, *North America,* 29 H4
Cebu, *Philippines,* 47 H5
Cedar Lake *Canada,* 24 J3
Cedar Rapids, *U.S.A.,* 27 H2
Cedros Island, *Mexico,* 28 A2
Ceduna, *Australia,* 40 F6
Celaya, *Mexico,* 28 D3
Celebes, *Indonesia,* 45 F4

Celebes Sea, *Asia,* 47 H7
Celtic Sea, *Europe,* 62 C4
Central African Republic, *Africa, country,* 72 C2
Central Cordillera, *Peru,* 32 C5
Central Russian Uplands, *Russia,* 58 D3
Central Siberian Plateau, *Russia,* 55 F2
Central Sierras, *Spain,* 63 D6
Ceram, *Indonesia,* 45 G4
Ceram Sea, *Indonesia,* 45 G4
Cerro de Pasco, *Peru,* 32 C6
Cesis, *Latvia,* 61 H4
Ceske Budejovice, *Czech Republic,* 64 E1
Ceuta, *Africa,* 63 C8
Chacabuco, *Argentina,* 34 F6
Chad, *Africa, country,* 68 E5
Chad, Lake, *Africa,* 68 D6
Chala, *Peru,* 32 D7
Chalan Kanoa, *Northern Marianas,* 38 B3
Chalkida, *Greece,* 65 G4
Challapata, *Bolivia,* 34 E3
Chalon-sur-Saone, *France,* 63 F5
Chanaral, *Chile,* 34 D5
Chandigarh, *India,* 50 D4
Chandrapur, *India,* 51 D7
Changchun, *China,* 49 L2
Changde, *China,* 48 H5
Changhua, *China,* 49 K6
Chang Jiang, *China,* 49 J4
Changsha, *China,* 49 H5
Changzhi, *China,* 49 H4
Chania, *Greece,* 65 G5
Channel Islands, *Europe,* 62 D4
Channel Islands, *U.S.A.,* 26 C4
Chapaev, *Kazakhstan,* 59 G3
Charagua, *Bolivia,* 34 F3
Charleroi, *Belgium,* 62 F4
Charleston, *South Carolina, U.S.A.,* 27 L4
Charleston, *West Virginia, U.S.A., internal capital,* 27 K3
Charlotte, *U.S.A.,* 27 K3
Charlottesville, *U.S.A.,* 27 L3
Charlottetown, *Canada, internal capital,* 25 N4
Chatham Islands, *New Zealand,* 41 R8
Chattanooga, *U.S.A.,* 27 J3
Chavuma, *Zambia,* 74 D2
Cheboksary, *Russia,* 59 F2
Chech Erg, *Africa,* 70 E3
Cheju, *South Korea,* 49 L4
Chelyabinsk, *Russia,* 59 J3
Chemnitz, *Germany,* 62 H4
Chengdu, *China,* 48 F4
Chennai, *India,* 51 E8
Chenzhou, *China,* 49 H5
Cherbourg, *France,* 62 D4
Cherepovets, *Russia,* 58 D2
Cherkasy, *Ukraine,* 58 C4
Chernihiv, *Ukraine,* 58 C3
Chernivtsi, *Ukraine,* 61 H6
Chesterfield Islands, *New Caledonia,* 41 M3
Cheyenne, *U.S.A., internal capital,* 26 F2
Chiang Mai, *Thailand,* 46 C4
Chicago, *U.S.A.,* 27 J2
Chiclayo, *Peru,* 32 C5
Chico, *U.S.A.,* 26 B3
Chicoutimi, *Canada,* 25 M4
Chidley, Cape, *Canada,* 25 N2
Chifeng, *China,* 49 J2
Chigubo, *Mozambique,* 75 F4
Chihli, Gulf of, *China,* 49 J3
Chihuahua, *Mexico,* 28 C2
Chile, *South America, country,* 34 D6
Chillan, *Chile,* 35 D7
Chiloe Island, *Chile,* 35 C8
Chilung, *China,* 49 K5
Chilwa, Lake, *Africa,* 75 G3
Chimanimani, *Zimbabwe,* 75 F3
Chimbote, *Peru,* 32 C5
China, *Asia, country,* 48 E3
Chincha Alta, *Peru,* 32 C6
Chingola, *Zambia,* 74 E2
Chinhoyi, *Zimbabwe,* 74 F3
Chios, *Greece,* 65 H4
Chipata, *Zambia,* 75 F2

Chiredzi, *Zimbabwe,* 74 F4
Chisinau, *Moldova, national capital,* 61 J2
Chittagong, *Bangladesh,* 51 G6
Chongjin, *North Korea,* 49 L2
Chongju, *South Korea,* 49 L3
Chongqing, *China,* 48 G5
Chonos Archipelago, *Chile,* 35 C8
Chott el Jerid, *Tunisia,* 68 C2
Christchurch, *New Zealand,* 41 P8
Christmas Island, *Asia,* 44 C6
Chukchi Sea, *Arctic Ocean,* 77 B2
Chulucanas, *Peru,* 32 B5
Chumphon, *Thailand,* 46 C5
Churchill, *Canada,* 25 K3
Churchill Falls, *Canada,* 25 N3
Cienfuegos, *Cuba,* 29 H3
Cilacap, *Indonesia,* 44 C5
Cincinnati, *U.S.A.,* 27 K3
Ciudad Bolivar, *Venezuela,* 32 F2
Ciudad del Carmen, *Mexico,* 28 F4
Ciudad del Este, *Paraguay,* 34 H5
Ciudad Guayana, *Venezuela,* 32 F2
Ciudad Juarez, *Mexico,* 28 C1
Ciudad Obregon, *Mexico,* 28 C2
Ciudad Real, *Spain,* 63 D7
Ciudad Victoria, *Mexico,* 28 E3
Clark Hill Lake, *U.S.A.,* 27 K4
Clermont-Ferrand, *France,* 63 E5
Cleveland, *U.S.A.,* 27 K2
Cluj-Napoca, *Romania,* 65 G2
Coast Mountains, *Canada,* 24 F3
Coast Ranges, *U.S.A.,* 26 B2
Coats Land, *Antarctica,* 79 A3
Coatzacoalcos, *Mexico,* 28 F4
Cobija, *Bolivia,* 34 E2
Cochabamba, *Bolivia,* 34 E3
Cochin, *India,* 51 D9
Cocos Island, *Costa Rica,* 29 G6
Cod, Cape, *U.S.A.,* 27 N2
Coeur d'Alene, *U.S.A.,* 26 C1
Coiba Island, *Panama,* 29 H6
Coihaique, *Chile,* 35 D9
Coimbatore, *India,* 51 D8
Coimbra, *Portugal,* 63 B6
Colima, *Mexico,* 28 D4
Cologne, *Germany,* 62 F4
Colombia, *South America, country,* 32 D3
Colombo, *Sri Lanka, national capital,* 51 D9
Colon, *Panama,* 29 J6
Colorado, *Argentina,* 35 F7
Colorado, *U.S.A.,* 26 D4
Colorado, *U.S.A., internal admin. area,* 26 E3
Colorado Plateau, *U.S.A.,* 26 D3
Colorado Springs, *U.S.A.,* 26 F3
Columbia, *U.S.A.,* 26 C1
Columbia, *U.S.A., internal capital,* 27 K4
Columbine, Cape, *South Africa,* 74 C6
Columbus, *U.S.A., internal capital,* 27 K3
Colwyn Bay, *United Kingdom,* 62 D3
Communism Peak, *Tajikistan,* 50 C3
Como, Lake, *Italy,* 64 D2
Comodoro Rivadavia, *Argentina,* 35 E9
Comoros, *Africa, country,* 75 H2
Conakry, *Guinea, national capital,* 71 C7
Concepcion, *Bolivia,* 34 F3
Concepcion, *Chile,* 35 D7
Concepcion, *Paraguay,* 34 G4
Concord, *U.S.A., internal capital,* 27 M2
Concordia, *Argentina,* 34 G6
Congo, *Africa,* 72 C4
Congo, *Africa, country,* 72 C4
Congo, Democratic Republic of, *Africa, country,* 72 D4
Connecticut, *U.S.A., internal admin. area,* 27 M2
Con Son, *Vietnam,* 46 E6
Constanta, *Romania,* 65 J2
Constantine, *Algeria,* 70 G1
Cook Islands, *Oceania,* 38 G7
Cook, Mount, *New Zealand,* 41 P8
Cook Strait, *New Zealand,* 41 P8
Copenhagen, *Denmark, national capital,* 61 E5
Copiapo, *Chile,* 34 D5

Coquimbo, *Chile,* **34 D5**
Coral Sea, *Oceania,* **41 K2**
Coral Sea Islands Territory, *Oceania, dependency,* **41 K3**
Cordoba, *Argentina,* **34 F6**
Cordoba, *Spain,* **63 C7**
Corfu, *Greece,* **65 F4**
Cork, *Ireland,* **62 B4**
Corner Brook, *Canada,* **25 P4**
Coro, *Venezuela,* **32 E1**
Coropuna, Mount, *Peru,* **32 D6**
Corpus Christi, *U.S.A.,* **26 G5**
Corrientes, *Argentina,* **34 G5**
Corsica, *France,* **63 G6**
Corum, *Turkey,* **65 K3**
Corumba, *Brazil,* **34 G3**
Cosenza, *Italy,* **64 F4**
Cosmoledo Group, *Seychelles,* **75 J1**
Costa Rica, *North America, country,* **29 G6**
Cotonou, *Benin,* **71 F7**
Cottbus, *Germany,* **62 H4**
Cradock, *South Africa,* **74 E6**
Craiova, *Romania,* **65 G2**
Cravo Norte, *Colombia,* **32 D2**
Crete, *Greece,* **65 H5**
Criciuma, *Brazil,* **34 J5**
Crimea, *Ukraine,* **65 K2**
Cristobal Colon, *Colombia,* **32 D1**
Croatia, *Europe, country,* **64 F2**
Cruzeiro do Sul, *Brazil,* **32 D5**
Cuamba, *Mozambique,* **75 G2**
Cuangar, *Angola,* **74 C3**
Cuango, *Africa,* **74 C1**
Cuanza, *Angola,* **74 C2**
Cuba, *North America, country,* **29 J3**
Cucuta, *Colombia,* **32 D2**
Cuenca, *Ecuador,* **32 C4**
Cuiaba, *Brazil,* **34 G3**
Culiacan, *Mexico,* **28 C3**
Cumana, *Venezuela,* **32 F1**
Cumberland Peninsula, *Canada,* **25 N2**
Cunene, *Africa,* **74 C3**
Curitiba, *Brazil,* **34 J5**
Cusco, *Peru,* **32 D6**
Cuttack, *India,* **51 F6**
Cuxhaven, *Germany,* **62 G3**
Cyclades, *Greece,* **65 H4**
Cyprus, *Asia, country,* **65 J5**
Cyrene, *Libya,* **68 F2**
Czech Republic, *Europe, country,* **64 E1**
Czestochowa, *Poland,* **61 F6**

d

Dabeiba, *Colombia,* **32 C2**
Dagupan, *Philippines,* **47 H4**
Dahlak Archipelago, *Eritrea,* **69 K5**
Dakar, *Senegal, national capital,* **71 B6**
Dal, *Sweden,* **60 F3**
Da Lat, *Vietnam,* **46 E5**
Dali, *China,* **48 F5**
Dalian, *China,* **49 K3**
Dallas, *U.S.A.,* **27 G4**
Daloa, *Ivory Coast,* **71 D7**
Damascus, *Syria, national capital,* **52 C5**
Damavand, *Iran,* **52 F4**
Damongo, *Ghana,* **71 E7**
Da Nang, *Vietnam,* **46 E4**
Dandong, *China,* **49 K2**
Danube, *Europe,* **61 F7**
Danube, Mouths of the, *Europe,* **65 J2**
Daqing, *China,* **49 L1**
Darbhanga, *India,* **50 F5**
Dar es Salaam, *Tanzania, national capital,* **73 G5**
Darien, Gulf of, *Colombia,* **32 C2**
Darjeeling, *India,* **50 F5**
Darling, *Australia,* **40 H6**
Darnah, *Libya,* **68 F2**
Darwin, *Australia, internal capital,* **40 F2**
Darwin, Mount, *Zimbabwe,* **74 F3**
Dasht-e Kavir, *Iran,* **52 F5**
Dasoguz, *Turkmenistan,* **52 G3**
Datong, *China,* **49 H2**
Daugavpils, *Latvia,* **61 H5**
Davangere, *India,* **51 D8**

Davao, *Philippines,* **47 J6**
David, *Panama,* **29 H6**
Davis Strait, *Canada,* **25 P2**
Dawson, *Canada,* **24 F2**
Dayr az Zawr, *Syria,* **52 D4**
Daytona Beach, *U.S.A.,* **27 K5**
De Aar, *South Africa,* **74 D6**
Dease Lake, *Canada,* **24 G3**
Death Valley, *U.S.A.,* **26 C3**
Debrecen, *Hungary,* **61 G7**
Debre Zeyit, *Ethiopia,* **73 G2**
Deccan Plateau, *India,* **51 D7**
Delaware, *U.S.A., internal admin. area,* **27 L3**
Delgado, Cape, *Mozambique,* **75 H2**
Delhi, *India,* **50 D5**
Del Rio, *U.S.A.,* **26 F5**
Democratic Republic of Congo, *Africa, country,* **72 D4**
Denizli, *Turkey,* **65 J4**
Denmark, *Europe, country,* **61 D5**
Denpasar, *Indonesia,* **44 E5**
D'Entrecasteaux Islands, *Papua New Guinea,* **45 M5**
Denver, *U.S.A., internal capital,* **26 E3**
Dera Ghazi Khan, *Pakistan,* **50 C4**
Derbent, *Russia,* **52 E3**
Dese, *Ethiopia,* **73 G1**
Des Moines, *U.S.A., internal capital,* **27 H2**
Desna, *Europe,* **58 C3**
Detroit, *U.S.A.,* **27 K2**
Devon Island, *Canada,* **25 L1**
Devonport, *Australia,* **40 J8**
Dhaka, *Bangladesh, national capital,* **51 G6**
Dhamar, *Yemen,* **53 D9**
Dhule, *India,* **51 C6**
Dibrugarh, *India,* **50 G5**
Dijon, *France,* **63 F5**
Dikhil, *Djibouti,* **69 K6**
Dili, *East Timor, national capital,* **45 G5**
Dilolo, *Democratic Republic of Congo,* **72 D6**
Dinaric Alps, *Europe,* **64 E2**
Dire Dawa, *Ethiopia,* **73 H2**
Divo, *Ivory Coast,* **71 D7**
Diyarbakir, *Turkey,* **52 D4**
Djado Plateau, *Africa,* **68 D4**
Djambala, *Congo,* **72 B4**
Djelfa, *Algeria,* **70 F2**
Djema, *Central African Republic,* **72 E2**
Djemila, *Algeria,* **70 G1**
Djibouti, *Africa, country,* **69 K6**
Djibouti, *Djibouti, national capital,* **69 K6**
Djougou, *Benin,* **71 F7**
Dnieper, *Europe,* **58 C4**
Dniester, *Europe,* **61 H6**
Dniprodzerzhynsk, *Ukraine,* **58 C4**
Dnipropetrovsk, *Ukraine,* **58 D4**
Doba, *Chad,* **72 C2**
Dobrich, *Bulgaria,* **65 H3**
Dodecanese, *Greece,* **65 H4**
Dodoma, *Tanzania, national capital,* **73 G5**
Doha, *Qatar, national capital,* **53 F6**
Dolak, *Indonesia,* **45 J5**
Dolores, *Argentina,* **35 G7**
Dominica, *North America, country,* **28 M4**
Dominican Republic, *North America, country,* **29 L3**
Don, *Russia,* **58 E4**
Dondo, *Angola,* **74 B1**
Donets, *Europe,* **58 D4**
Donetsk, *Ukraine,* **58 D4**
Dongting Lake, *China,* **49 H5**
Dori, *Burkina Faso,* **71 E6**
Dosso, *Niger,* **71 F6**
Douala, *Cameroon,* **72 A3**
Douglas, *South Africa,* **74 D5**
Dourados, *Brazil,* **34 H4**
Douro, *Europe,* **63 C6**
Dover, *United Kingdom,* **62 E4**
Dover, *U.S.A., internal capital,* **27 L3**

Dover, Strait of, *Europe,* **62 E4**
Drakensberg, *South Africa,* **74 E6**
Drake Passage, *South America,* **35 E11**
Drammen, *Norway,* **60 D4**
Dresden, *Germany,* **62 H4**
Drobeta-Turnu Severin, *Romania,* **65 G2**
Dryden, *Canada,* **25 K4**
Dubai, *United Arab Emirates,* **53 G6**
Dubawnt Lake, *Canada,* **24 J2**
Dubbo, *Australia,* **41 J6**
Dublin, *Ireland, national capital,* **62 C3**
Dubrovnik, *Croatia,* **65 F3**
Duisburg, *Germany,* **62 F4**
Duitama, *Colombia,* **32 D2**
Duluth, *U.S.A.,* **27 H1**
Dumaguete, *Philippines,* **47 H6**
Dundee, *United Kingdom,* **62 D2**
Dunedin, *New Zealand,* **41 P9**
Durango, *Mexico,* **28 D3**
Durazno, *Uruguay,* **34 G6**
Durban, *South Africa,* **74 F5**
Durres, *Albania,* **65 F3**
Dushanbe, *Tajikistan, national capital,* **50 B3**
Dusseldorf, *Germany,* **62 F4**
Dzhankoy, *Ukraine,* **65 K2**
Dzungarian Basin, *China,* **50 F1**

e

East Antarctica, *Antarctica,* **79 E3**
East Cape, *New Zealand,* **41 Q7**
East China Sea, *Asia,* **49 K5**
Easter Island, *Pacific Ocean,* **39 N7**
Eastern Cordillera, *Colombia,* **32 D3**
Eastern Cordillera, *Peru,* **32 D6**
Eastern Ghats, *India,* **51 D8**
Eastern Sierra Madre, *Mexico,* **28 D2**
East Falkland, *Falkland Islands,* **35 G10**
East London, *South Africa,* **74 E6**
East Siberian Sea, *Russia,* **55 J2**
East Timor (Timor Leste), *Asia, country,* **45 G5**
Ebolowa, *Cameroon,* **72 B3**
Ebro, *Spain,* **63 D6**
Ecuador, *South America, country,* **32 B4**
Edinburgh, *United Kingdom, internal capital,* **62 D2**
Edirne, *Turkey,* **65 H3**
Edmonton, *Canada, internal capital,* **24 H3**
Edmundston, *Canada,* **25 N4**
Edward, Lake, *Africa,* **72 E4**
Edwards Plateau, *U.S.A.,* **26 F4**
Efate, *Vanuatu,* **41 N3**
Egypt, *Africa, country,* **69 G3**
Eindhoven, *Netherlands,* **62 F4**
Elat, *Israel,* **53 B6**
Elazig, *Turkey,* **52 C4**
Elba, *Italy,* **64 D3**
Elbasan, *Albania,* **65 G3**
Elbe, *Europe,* **62 G3**
Elbrus, Mount, *Russia,* **52 D3**
Elche, *Spain,* **63 D6**
Eldorado, *Argentina,* **34 H5**
Eldoret, *Kenya,* **73 G3**
Elephant Island, *Atlantic Ocean,* **35 H12**
Eleuthera, *The Bahamas,* **27 L5**
El Fasher, *Sudan,* **69 G6**
Elgon, Mount, *Uganda,* **73 F3**
El Hierro, *Canary Islands,* **70 B3**
Elista, *Russia,* **52 D2**
El Jadida, *Morocco,* **70 D2**
El Jem, *Tunisia,* **68 D1**
El Mansura, *Egypt,* **69 H2**
El Minya, *Egypt,* **69 H3**
El Obeid, *Sudan,* **69 H6**
El Oued, *Algeria,* **70 G2**
El Paso, *U.S.A.,* **26 E4**
El Salvador, *North America, country,* **28 G5**
Ellesmere Island, *Canada,* **77 R3**
Ellsworth Land, *Antarctica,* **79 R3**
Embi, *Kazakhstan,* **52 G2**
Emi Koussi, *Chad,* **68 E4**
Empty Quarter, *Asia,* **53 E8**
Encarnacion, *Paraguay,* **34 G5**

Ende, *Indonesia,* **45 F5**
Enderby Land, *Antarctica,* **79 E3**
Engels, *Russia,* **59 F3**
England, *United Kingdom, internal admin. area,* **62 D3**
English Channel, *Europe,* **62 D4**
Ennedi Plateau, *Africa,* **68 F5**
Enschede, *Netherlands,* **62 F3**
Entebbe, *Uganda,* **73 F3**
Enugu, *Nigeria,* **71 G7**
Ephesus, *Turkey,* **65 H4**
Equatorial Guinea, *Africa, country,* **72 A3**
Erenhot, *China,* **48 H2**
Erfurt, *Germany,* **62 G4**
Erie, *U.S.A.,* **27 K2**
Erie, Lake, *U.S.A.,* **27 K2**
Eritrea, *Africa, country,* **69 J5**
Er Rachidia, *Morocco,* **70 E2**
Ershovka, *Kazakhstan,* **59 K3**
Erzurum, *Turkey,* **52 D4**
Esbjerg, *Denmark,* **61 D5**
Esfahan, *Iran,* **52 F5**
Eskilstuna, *Sweden,* **60 F4**
Eskisehir, *Turkey,* **65 J4**
Esmeraldas, *Ecuador,* **32 C3**
Esperance, *Australia,* **40 D6**
Espinosa, *Brazil,* **34 K2**
Espiritu Santo, *Vanuatu,* **41 N3**
Espoo, *Finland,* **60 H3**
Espungabera, *Mozambique,* **75 F4**
Esquel, *Argentina,* **35 D8**
Essaouira, *Morocco,* **70 D2**
Es Semara, *Western Sahara,* **70 C3**
Essen, *Germany,* **62 F4**
Estevan, *Canada,* **24 J4**
Estonia, *Europe, country,* **60 H4**
Ethiopia, *Africa, country,* **73 G2**
Ethiopian Highlands, *Ethiopia,* **73 G1**
Etna, Mount, *Italy,* **64 E4**
Etosha Pan, *Namibia,* **74 C3**
Euboea, *Greece,* **65 G4**
Eugene, *U.S.A.,* **26 B2**
Eugenia, Point, *Mexico,* **28 A2**
Euphrates, *Asia,* **53 E5**
Europa Island, *Africa,* **75 H4**
Europe, **21**
Evansville, *U.S.A.,* **27 J3**
Everest, Mount, *Asia,* **50 F5**
Everglades, The, *U.S.A.,* **27 K5**
Evora, *Portugal,* **63 C7**
Evry, *France,* **62 E4**
Exeter, *United Kingdom,* **62 D4**
Eyl, *Somalia,* **73 J2**
Eyre, Lake, *Australia,* **40 G5**

f

Fada-Ngourma, *Burkina Faso,* **71 F6**
Fairbanks, *U.S.A.,* **24 E2**
Faisalabad, *Pakistan,* **50 C4**
Fakfak, *Indonesia,* **45 H4**
Falkland Islands, *Atlantic Ocean,* **35 F10**
Farasan Islands, *Saudi Arabia,* **53 D8**
Farewell, Cape, *New Zealand,* **41 P8**
Fargo, *U.S.A.,* **27 G1**
Fargona, *Uzbekistan,* **50 C2**
Farmington, *U.S.A.,* **26 E3**
Faro, *Portugal,* **63 C7**
Farquhar Group, *Seychelles,* **75 K1**
Faxafloi, *Iceland,* **60 N2**
Faya-Largeau, *Chad,* **68 E5**
Federated States of Micronesia, *Oceania, country,* **38 C4**
Feira de Santana, *Brazil,* **34 L2**
Feodosiya, *Ukraine,* **65 K2**
Fernandina, *Ecuador,* **32 N10**
Ferrara, *Italy,* **64 D2**
Fes, *Morocco,* **70 E2**
Fianarantsoa, *Madagascar,* **75 J4**
Fiji, *Oceania, country,* **41 Q3**
Finland, *Europe, country,* **60 H2**
Finland, Gulf of, *Europe,* **60 H4**
Flagstaff, *U.S.A.,* **26 D3**
Flensburg, *Germany,* **62 G3**
Flinders Island, *Australia,* **41 J7**
Flin Flon, *Canada,* **24 J3**
Florence, *Italy,* **64 D3**

Florencia, *Colombia*, 32 C3
Flores, *Azores*, 70 J10
Flores, *Indonesia*, 45 F5
Flores Sea, *Indonesia*, 45 F5
Floresta, *Brazil*, 33 L5
Floriano, *Brazil*, 33 K5
Florianopolis, *Brazil*, 34 J5
Florida, *U.S.A., internal admin. area,* 27 K5
Florida Keys, *U.S.A.,* 27 K6
Florida, Straits of, *North America,* 27 K6
Focsani, *Romania,* 65 H2
Foggia, *Italy,* 64 E3
Fogo, *Cape Verde,* 71 M12
Fomboni, *Comoros,* 75 H2
Formosa, *Argentina,* 34 G5
Fort Albany, *Canada,* 25 L3
Fortaleza, *Brazil,* 33 L4
Fort Chipewyan, *Canada,* 24 H3
Fort-de-France, *Martinique,* 28 M5
Fort Lauderdale, *U.S.A.,* 27 K5
Fort McMurray, *Canada,* 24 H3
Fort Nelson, *Canada,* 24 G3
Fort Peck Lake, *U.S.A.,* 26 E1
Fort Providence, *Canada,* 24 H2
Fort St. John, *Canada,* 24 G3
Fort Severn, *Canada,* 25 L3
Fort Vermilion, *Canada,* 24 H3
Fort Wayne, *U.S.A.,* 27 J2
Fort Worth, *U.S.A.,* 26 G4
Foumban, *Cameroon,* 72 B2
Foxe Basin, *Canada,* 25 M2
Foxe Peninsula, *Canada,* 25 M2
Fox Islands, *U.S.A.,* 25 C3
Foz do Cunene, *Angola,* 74 B3
Foz do Iguacu, *Brazil,* 34 H5
France, *Europe, country,* 63 E5
Franceville, *Gabon,* 72 B4
Francistown, *Botswana,* 74 E4
Frankfort, *U.S.A., internal capital,* 27 K3
Frankfurt, *Germany,* 62 G4
Franz Josef Land, *Russia,* 54 C1
Fraser Island, *Australia,* 41 K5
Fredericton, *Canada, internal capital,* 25 N4
Fredrikstad, *Norway,* 60 D4
Freeport City, *The Bahamas,* 27 L5
Freetown, *Sierra Leone, national capital,* 71 C7
Freiburg, *Germany,* 62 F4
French Guiana, *South America, dependency,* 33 H3
French Polynesia, *Oceania, dependency,* 39 J6
Fresno, *U.S.A.,* 26 C3
Frisian Islands, *Europe,* 62 F3
Froya, *Norway,* 60 D3
Fuerteventura, *Canary Islands,* 70 B3
Fuji, Mount, *Japan,* 49 N3
Fukui, *Japan,* 49 N3
Fukuoka, *Japan,* 49 M4
Fukushima, *Japan,* 49 P3
Funafuti, *Tuvalu, national capital,* 38 E5
Funchal, *Madeira,* 70 B2
Furnas Reservoir, *Brazil,* 34 J4
Fushun, *China,* 49 K2
Fuxin, *China,* 49 K2
Fyn, *Denmark,* 61 D5

g
Gabes, *Tunisia,* 68 D2
Gabes, Gulf of, *Africa,* 68 D2
Gabon, *Africa, country,* 72 B4
Gaborone, *Botswana, national capital,* 74 E4
Gafsa, *Tunisia,* 68 C2
Gagnoa, *Ivory Coast,* 71 D7
Gairdner, Lake, *Australia,* 40 F6
Galapagos Islands, *Ecuador,* 32 N9
Galati, *Romania,* 65 J2
Galdhopiggen, *Norway,* 60 D3
Galle, *Sri Lanka,* 51 E9
Gallinas, Cape, *Colombia,* 32 D1
Galveston, *U.S.A.,* 27 H5
Galway, *Ireland,* 62 B3
Gambela, *Ethiopia,* 73 F2

Gambia, The, *Africa, country,* 71 B6
Ganca, *Azerbaijan,* 52 E3
Gander, *Canada,* 25 P4
Ganges, *Asia,* 50 E5
Ganges, Mouths of the, *Asia,* 51 F6
Ganzhou, *China,* 49 H5
Gao, *Mali,* 71 F5
Garda, Lake, *Italy,* 64 D2
Garissa, *Kenya,* 73 G4
Garonne, *France,* 63 E5
Garoua, *Cameroon,* 72 B2
Gaspe, *Canada,* 25 N4
Gatchina, *Russia,* 60 J4
Gavle, *Sweden,* 60 F3
Gaza, *Israel,* 53 B5
Gaziantep, *Turkey,* 52 C4
Gdansk, *Poland,* 61 F5
Gdansk, Gulf of, *Poland,* 61 F5
Gdynia, *Poland,* 61 F5
Gedaref, *Sudan,* 69 J6
Geelong, *Australia,* 40 H7
Gejiu, *China,* 48 F6
Gemena, *Democratic Republic of Congo,* 72 C3
General Roca, *Argentina,* 35 E7
General Santos, *Philippines,* 47 J6
General Villegas, *Argentina,* 34 F7
Geneva, *Switzerland,* 64 C2
Geneva, Lake, *Europe,* 64 C2
Genoa, *Italy,* 64 D2
Genoa, Gulf of, *Italy,* 64 D2
Gent, *Belgium,* 62 E4
Georgetown, *Guyana, national capital,* 33 G2
George Town, *Malaysia,* 44 B2
Georgia, *Asia, country,* 52 D3
Georgia, *U.S.A., internal admin. area,* 27 K4
Gera, *Germany,* 62 H4
Geraldton, *Australia,* 40 B5
Gerlachovsky stit, *Slovakia,* 61 G6
Germany, *Europe, country,* 62 G4
Gerona, *Spain,* 63 E6
Ghadamis, *Libya,* 68 C2
Ghana, *Africa, country,* 71 E7
Ghardaia, *Algeria,* 70 F2
Gharyan, *Libya,* 68 D2
Ghat, *Libya,* 68 D3
Gibraltar, *Europe,* 63 C7
Gibson Desert, *Australia,* 40 E4
Gijon, *Spain,* 63 C6
Gilbert Islands, *Kiribati,* 38 E5
Gilgit, *Pakistan,* 50 C3
Girardeau, Cape, *U.S.A.,* 27 J3
Giza, Pyramids of, *Egypt,* 69 H3
Gladstone, *Australia,* 41 K4
Glama, *Norway,* 60 D3
Glasgow, *United Kingdom,* 62 C3
Glazov, *Russia,* 59 G2
Glorioso Islands, *Africa,* 75 J2
Gloucester, *United Kingdom,* 62 D4
Gobabis, *Namibia,* 74 C4
Gobi Desert, *Asia,* 48 F2
Gochas, *Namibia,* 74 C4
Godavari, *India,* 51 D7
Gode, *Ethiopia,* 73 H2
Goiania, *Brazil,* 34 J3
Gold Coast, *Australia,* 41 K5
Golmud, *China,* 50 G3
Goma, *Democratic Republic of Congo,* 72 E4
Gonaives, *Haiti,* 29 K4
Gonder, *Ethiopia,* 73 G1
Gongga Shan, *China,* 48 F5
Good Hope, Cape of, *South Africa,* 74 C6
Goose Lake, *U.S.A.,* 26 B2
Gorakhpur, *India,* 51 E5
Gorgan, *Iran,* 52 F4
Gori, *Georgia,* 52 D3
Gorki Reservoir, *Russia,* 58 E2
Gorontalo, *Indonesia,* 45 F3
Gorzow Wielkopolski, *Poland,* 61 E5
Gothenburg, *Sweden,* 61 E4
Gotland, *Sweden,* 61 F4
Gottingen, *Germany,* 62 G4

Gouin Reservoir, *Canada,* 27 L1
Goundam, *Mali,* 71 E5
Governador Valadares, *Brazil,* 34 K3
Graaff-Reinet, *South Africa,* 74 D6
Grafton, *Australia,* 41 K5
Grahamstown, *South Africa,* 74 E6
Granada, *Spain,* 63 D7
Gran Canaria, *Canary Islands,* 70 B3
Gran Chaco, *South America,* 34 F4
Grand Bahama, The *Bahamas,* 27 L5
Grand Canal, *China,* 49 J4
Grand Canyon, *U.S.A.,* 26 D3
Grand Comoro, *Comoros,* 75 H2
Grande Bay, *Argentina,* 35 E10
Grande Prairie, *Canada,* 24 H3
Grand Forks, *U.S.A.,* 27 G1
Grand Island, *U.S.A.,* 26 G2
Grand Junction, *U.S.A.,* 26 E3
Grand Rapids, *Canada,* 25 K3
Grand Rapids, *U.S.A.,* 27 J2
Grand Teton, *U.S.A.,* 26 D2
Graskop, *South Africa,* 74 F5
Graz, *Austria,* 64 E2
Great Australian Bight, *Australia,* 40 F6
Great Barrier Reef, *Australia,* 40 J3
Great Basin, *U.S.A.,* 26 C2
Great Bear Lake, *Canada,* 24 G2
Great Dividing Range, *Australia,* 41 J6
Great Eastern Erg, *Algeria,* 70 G3
Greater Antilles, *North America,* 29 J4
Greater Khingan Range, *China,* 49 J1
Greater Sunda Islands, *Asia,* 44 C4
Great Falls, *U.S.A.,* 26 D1
Great Inagua, *The Bahamas,* 29 K3
Great Karoo, *South Africa,* 74 D6
Great Plains, *U.S.A.,* 26 F2
Great Rift Valley, *Africa,* 73 F5
Great Salt Desert, *Iran,* 52 F5
Great Salt Lake, *U.S.A.,* 26 D2
Great Salt Lake Desert, *U.S.A.,* 26 D2
Great Sandy Desert, *Australia,* 40 D4
Great Slave Lake, *Canada,* 24 H2
Great Victoria Desert, *Australia,* 40 D5
Great Wall of China, *China,* 48 F3
Great Western Erg, *Algeria,* 70 E2
Greece, *Europe, country,* 65 G4
Green Bay, *U.S.A.,* 27 J2
Greenland, *North America, dependency,* 77 P3
Greenland Sea, *Atlantic Ocean,* 77 M3
Greensboro, *U.S.A.,* 27 L3
Greenville, *U.S.A.,* 27 H4
Grenada, *North America, country,* 28 M5
Grenoble, *France,* 63 F5
Griffith, *Australia,* 40 J6
Groningen, *Netherlands,* 62 F3
Groot, *South Africa,* 74 D6
Groote Eylandt, *Australia,* 40 G2
Grossglockner, *Austria,* 64 E2
Groznyy, *Russia,* 52 E3
Grudziadz, *Poland,* 61 F5
Grunau, *Namibia,* 74 C5
Grytviken, *South Georgia,* 35 L10
Guadalajara, *Mexico,* 28 D3
Guadalquivir, *Spain,* 63 C7
Guadalupe Island, *Mexico,* 28 A2
Guadeloupe, *North America,* 28 M4
Guadiana, *Europe,* 63 C7
Gualeguaychu, *Argentina,* 34 G6
Guam, *Oceania,* 38 B3
Guangzhou, *China,* 49 H6
Guantanamo, *Cuba,* 29 J3
Guapuava, *Brazil,* 34 H5
Guardafui, Cape, *Somalia,* 73 K1
Guatemala, *North America, country,* 28 F4
Guatemala City, *Guatemala, national capital,* 28 F5
Guaviare, *Colombia,* 32 E3
Guayaquil, *Ecuador,* 32 B4
Guayaquil, Gulf of, *Ecuador,* 32 B4
Gueckedou, *Guinea,* 71 C7
Guelma, *Algeria,* 64 C4
Guiana Highlands, *Venezuela,* 32 E2
Guilin, *China,* 48 H5
Guinea, *Africa, country,* 71 C6

Guinea-Bissau, *Africa, country,* 71 B6
Guinea, Gulf of, *Africa,* 71 F8
Guiria, *Venezuela,* 32 F1
Guiyang, *China,* 48 G5
Gujranwala, *Pakistan,* 50 C4
Gujrat, *Pakistan,* 50 C4
Gulbarga, *India,* 51 D7
Gulf, The, *Asia,* 53 F6
Gulu, *Uganda,* 73 F3
Gunung Kerinci, *Indonesia,* 44 B4
Gunung Tahan, *Malaysia,* 44 B3
Gurupi, *Brazil,* 34 J2
Gusau, *Nigeria,* 71 G6
Guwahati, *India,* 50 G5
Guyana, *South America, country,* 33 G2
Gwalior, *India,* 50 D5
Gweru, *Zimbabwe,* 74 E3
Gympie, *Australia,* 41 K5
Gyor, *Hungary,* 61 F7

h
Haapsalu, *Estonia,* 60 G4
Haarlem, *Netherlands,* 62 F3
Hadhramaut, *Yemen,* 53 E9
Ha Giang, *Vietnam,* 46 E3
Hague, The, *Netherlands, national capital,* 62 F3
Haifa, *Israel,* 52 B5
Haikou, *China,* 48 H6
Hail, *Saudi Arabia,* 53 D6
Hailar, *China,* 49 J1
Hainan, *China,* 48 H7
Hai Phong, *Vietnam,* 46 E3
Haiti, *North America, country,* 29 K4
Hakodate, *Japan,* 49 P2
Halifax, *Canada, internal capital,* 25 N4
Halmahera, *Indonesia,* 45 G3
Halmstad, *Sweden,* 61 E4
Hamadan, *Iran,* 52 E5
Hamah, *Syria,* 52 C4
Hamamatsu, *Japan,* 49 N4
Hamburg, *Germany,* 62 G3
Hameenlinna, *Finland,* 60 H3
Hamhung, *North Korea,* 49 L3
Hami, *China,* 50 G2
Hamilton, *Canada,* 25 M4
Hamilton, *New Zealand,* 41 Q7
Hammerfest, *Norway,* 60 G1
Handan, *China,* 49 H3
Hangzhou, *China,* 49 K4
Hannover, *Germany,* 62 G3
Hanoi, *Vietnam, national capital,* 46 E3
Happy Valley-Goose Bay, *Canada,* 25 N3
Haradh, *Saudi Arabia,* 53 E7
Harare, *Zimbabwe, national capital,* 74 F3
Harbin, *China,* 49 L1
Harer, *Ethiopia,* 73 H2
Hargeysa, *Somalia,* 73 H2
Harney Basin, *U.S.A.,* 26 C2
Harper, *Liberia,* 71 D8
Harrisburg, *U.S.A., internal capital,* 27 L2
Harrismith, *South Africa,* 74 E5
Hartford, *U.S.A., internal capital,* 27 M2
Hatteras, Cape, *U.S.A.,* 27 L3
Hattiesburg, *U.S.A.,* 27 J4
Hat Yai, *Thailand,* 46 D6
Hauki Lake, *Finland,* 60 J3
Havana, *Cuba, national capital,* 29 H3
Hawaii, *Pacific Ocean, internal admin. area,* 27 P7
Hawaiian Islands, *Pacific Ocean,* 27 P7
Hebrides, *United Kingdom,* 62 C2
Hefei, *China,* 49 J4
Hegang, *China,* 49 M1
Hejaz, *Saudi Arabia,* 53 C6
Helena, *U.S.A., internal capital,* 26 D1
Helmand, *Asia,* 50 B4
Helsingborg, *Sweden,* 61 E4
Helsinki, *Finland, national capital,* 60 H3
Hengyang, *China,* 48 H5
Henzada, *Burma,* 46 C4
Herat, *Afghanistan,* 50 A4
Hermosillo, *Mexico,* 28 B2
Hiiumaa, *Estonia,* 60 G4
Hilo, *U.S.A.,* 27 P8

Himalayas, *Asia*, 50 E4
Hindu Kush, *Asia*, 50 B3
Hinton, *Canada*, 24 H3
Hiroshima, *Japan*, 49 M4
Hispaniola, *North America*, 29 K4
Hitra, *Norway*, 60 D3
Ho Chi Minh City, *Vietnam*, 46 E5
Hohhot, *China*, 48 H2
Hokkaido, *Japan*, 49 P2
Holguin, *Cuba*, 29 J3
Homs, *Syria*, 52 C5
Homyel, *Belarus*, 61 J5
Honduras, *North America, country*, 29 G4
Honduras, Gulf of, *North America*, 29 G4
Honefoss, *Norway*, 60 D3
Hong Kong, *China*, 49 H6
Honiara, *Solomon Islands, national capital*, 38 D5
Honolulu, *U.S.A., internal capital*, 27 P7
Honshu, *Japan*, 49 N3
Horlivka, *Ukraine*, 58 D4
Hormuz, Strait of, *Asia*, 53 G6
Horn, Cape, *Chile*, 35 H4
Horn Lake, *Sweden*, 60 F2
Hotan, *China*, 50 D3
Hotazel, *South Africa*, 74 D5
Houston, *U.S.A.*, 27 G5
Hradec Kralove, *Czech Republic*, 64 E1
Hrodna, *Belarus*, 61 G5
Huacrachuco, *Peru*, 32 C5
Huaihua, *China*, 48 H5
Huambo, *Angola*, 74 C2
Huancayo, *Peru*, 32 C6
Huang He, *China*, 49 H3
Huanuco, *Peru*, 32 C5
Huascaran, Mount, *Peru*, 32 C5
Hubli, *India*, 51 D7
Hudiksvall, *Sweden*, 60 F3
Hudson Bay, *Canada*, 25 L3
Hudson Strait, *Canada*, 25 M2
Hue, *Vietnam*, 46 E4
Huelva, *Spain*, 63 C7
Hull, *United Kingdom*, 62 D3
Hulun Lake, *China*, 49 J1
Hungary, *Europe, country*, 61 F7
Huntsville, *Canada*, 25 M4
Huntsville, *U.S.A.*, 27 J4
Hurghada, *Egypt*, 69 H3
Huron, Lake, *U.S.A.*, 27 K2
Hvannadalshnukur, *Iceland*, 60 P2
Hwange, *Zimbabwe*, 74 E3
Hyderabad, *India*, 51 D7
Hyderabad, *Pakistan*, 50 B5
Hyesan, *North Korea*, 49 L2

i

Iasi, *Romania*, 65 H2
Ibadan, *Nigeria*, 71 F7
Ibague, *Colombia*, 32 C3
Ibarra, *Ecuador*, 32 C3
Ibb, *Yemen*, 53 D9
Iberian Mountains, *Spain*, 63 D6
Ibiza, *Spain*, 63 E7
Ica, *Peru*, 32 C6
Iceland, *Europe, country*, 60 P2
Idaho, *U.S.A., internal admin. area*, 26 C2
Idaho Falls, *U.S.A.*, 26 D2
Ierapetra, *Greece*, 65 H5
Iguacu Falls, *South America*, 34 H5
Ihosy, *Madagascar*, 75 J4
Ikopa, *Madagascar*, 75 J3
Ilagan, *Philippines*, 47 H4
Ilebo, *Democratic Republic of Congo*, 72 D4
Ilheus, *Brazil*, 34 L2
Iliamna Lake, *U.S.A.*, 24 D2
Iligan, *Philippines*, 47 H6
Illapel, *Chile*, 34 D6
Illimani, Mount, *Bolivia*, 34 E3
Illinois, *U.S.A., internal admin. area*, 27 J2
Illizi, *Algeria*, 70 G3
Ilmen, Lake, *Russia*, 60 M3
Iloilo, *Philippines*, 47 H5
Ilonga, *Tanzania*, 73 G5
Ilorin, *Nigeria*, 71 F7

Imperatriz, *Brazil*, 33 J5
Imphal, *India*, 51 G6
Inari, Lake, *Finland*, 60 H1
Inchon, *South Korea*, 49 L3
Indals, *Sweden*, 60 E3
Inderbor, *Kazakhstan*, 59 G4
India, *Asia, country*, 51 D6
Indiana, *U.S.A., internal admin. area*, 27 J2
Indianapolis, *U.S.A., internal capital*, 27 J3
Indian Ocean, 21
Indonesia, *Asia, country*, 44 C5
Indore, *India*, 51 D6
Indus, *Asia*, 50 B5
Ingolstadt, *Germany*, 62 G4
Inhambane, *Mozambique*, 75 G4
Inner Mongolia, *China*, 49 H2
Innsbruck, *Austria*, 64 D2
Inukjuak, *Canada*, 25 M3
Inuvik, *Canada*, 24 F2
Invercargill, *New Zealand*, 41 N9
Inyangani, *Zimbabwe*, 75 F3
Ioannina, *Greece*, 65 G4
Ionian Sea, *Europe*, 65 F4
Iowa, *U.S.A., internal admin. area*, 27 H2
Ipiales, *Colombia*, 32 C3
Ipoh, *Malaysia*, 44 B3
Ipswich, *United Kingdom*, 62 E3
Iqaluit, *Canada, internal capital*, 25 N2
Iquique, *Chile*, 34 D4
Iquitos, *Peru*, 32 D4
Irakleio, *Greece*, 65 H5
Iran, *Asia, country*, 52 F5
Iranshahr, *Iran*, 53 H6
Iraq, *Asia, country*, 52 D5
Irbid, *Jordan*, 52 C5
Ireland, *Europe, country*, 62 B3
Iringa, *Tanzania*, 73 G5
Irish Sea, *Europe*, 62 C3
Irkutsk, *Russia*, 55 F3
Irrawaddy, *Burma*, 46 C4
Irrawaddy, Mouths of the, *Burma*, 46 B4
Irtysh, *Asia*, 54 D3
Isabela, *Ecuador*, 32 N10
Isafjordhur, *Iceland*, 60 N2
Isiro, *Democratic Republic of Congo*, 72 E3
Islamabad, *Pakistan, national capital*, 50 C4
Isle of Man, *Europe*, 62 C3
Isle of Wight, *United Kingdom*, 62 D4
Ismailia, *Egypt*, 69 H2
Isoka, *Zambia*, 75 F2
Isparta, *Turkey*, 65 J4
Israel, *Asia, country*, 53 B5
Issyk, Lake, *Kyrgyzstan*, 50 D2
Istanbul, *Turkey*, 65 J3
Itaituba, *Brazil*, 33 G4
Itajai, *Brazil*, 34 J5
Italy, *Europe, country*, 64 D2
Itapetininga, *Brazil*, 34 J4
Ivano-Frankivsk, *Ukraine*, 61 H6
Ivanovo, *Russia*, 58 E2
Ivdel, *Russia*, 59 J1
Ivory Coast, *Africa, country*, 71 D7
Ivujivik, *Canada*, 25 M2
Izhevsk, *Russia*, 59 G2
Izmir, *Turkey*, 65 H4

j

Jabalpur, *India*, 51 D6
Jackson, *Mississippi, U.S.A., internal capital*, 27 H4
Jackson, *Tennessee, U.S.A.*, 27 J3
Jacksonville, *U.S.A.*, 27 K4
Jaen, *Spain*, 63 D7
Jaffna, *Sri Lanka*, 51 E9
Jaipur, *India*, 50 D5
Jakarta, *Indonesia, national capital*, 44 C5
Jalalabad, *Afghanistan*, 50 C4
Jalal-Abad, *Kyrgyzstan*, 50 C2
Jamaica, *North America, country*, 29 J4
Jambi, *Indonesia*, 44 B4
James Bay, *Canada*, 25 L3
Jamestown, *U.S.A.*, 27 L2

Jammu, *India*, 50 C4
Jammu and Kashmir, *Asia*, 50 D4
Jamnagar, *India*, 51 C6
Jamshedpur, *India*, 51 F6
Japan, *Asia, country*, 49 N3
Japan, Sea of, *Asia*, 49 M2
Japura, *Brazil*, 32 E4
Jatai, *Brazil*, 34 H3
Java, *Indonesia*, 44 C5
Java Sea, *Indonesia*, 44 C5
Jayapura, *Indonesia*, 45 K4
Jedda, *Saudi Arabia*, 53 C7
Jefferson City, *U.S.A., internal capital*, 27 H3
Jekabpils, *Latvia*, 61 H4
Jelgava, *Latvia*, 61 G4
Jember, *Indonesia*, 44 D5
Jerba, *Tunisia*, 68 D1
Jerez de la Frontera, *Spain*, 63 C7
Jerusalem, *Israel, national capital*, 53 C5
Jhansi, *India*, 50 D5
Jiamusi, *China*, 49 M1
Jilin, *China*, 49 L2
Jima, *Ethiopia*, 73 G2
Jinhua, *China*, 49 J5
Jining, *China*, 49 J3
Jinja, *Uganda*, 73 F3
Jinzhou, *China*, 49 K2
Jixi, *China*, 49 M1
Jizzax, *Uzbekistan*, 50 B2
Joao Pessoa, *Brazil*, 33 M5
Jodhpur, *India*, 50 C5
Johannesburg, *South Africa*, 74 E5
Johnston Atoll, *Oceania*, 38 G3
Johor Bahru, *Malaysia*, 44 B3
Jolo, *Philippines*, 47 H6
Jonesboro, *U.S.A.*, 27 H3
Jonkoping, *Sweden*, 61 E4
Jordan, *Asia, country*, 53 C5
Jorhat, *India*, 50 G5
Jos, *Nigeria*, 72 A2
Juan de Nova, *Africa*, 75 H3
Juazeiro, *Brazil*, 33 K5
Juazeiro do Norte, *Brazil*, 33 L5
Juba, *Africa*, 73 H3
Juba, *Sudan*, 73 F3
Juchitan, *Mexico*, 28 E4
Juiz de Fora, *Brazil*, 34 K4
Juliaca, *Peru*, 32 D7
Juneau, *U.S.A., internal capital*, 24 F3
Jurmala, *Latvia*, 61 G4
Jurua, *Brazil*, 32 E5
Jutland, *Europe*, 61 D4
Jyvaskyla, *Finland*, 60 H3

k

K2, *Asia*, 50 D3
Kaamanen, *Finland*, 60 H1
Kabinda, *Democratic Republic of Congo*, 72 D5
Kabul, *Afghanistan, national capital*, 50 B4
Kabunda, *Democratic Republic of Congo*, 72 E6
Kabwe, *Zambia*, 74 E2
Kadoma, *Zimbabwe*, 74 E3
Kaduna, *Nigeria*, 71 G6
Kaedi, *Mauritania*, 71 C5
Kafakumba, *Democratic Republic of Congo*, 72 D5
Kafue, *Zambia*, 74 E3
Kagoshima, *Japan*, 49 M4
Kahramanmaras, *Turkey*, 52 C4
Kahului, *U.S.A.*, 27 P7
Kainji Reservoir, *Nigeria*, 71 F6
Kairouan, *Tunisia*, 68 D1
Kajaani, *Finland*, 60 H2
Kakhovske Reservoir, *Ukraine*, 58 C4
Kalahari Desert, *Africa*, 74 D4
Kalamata, *Greece*, 65 G4
Kalemie, *Democratic Republic of Congo*, 72 E5
Kalgoorlie, *Australia*, 40 D6
Kaliningrad, *Russia*, 61 G5
Kalisz, *Poland*, 61 F6
Kalkrand, *Namibia*, 74 C4

Kalmar, *Sweden*, 61 F4
Kaluga, *Russia*, 58 D3
Kamanjab, *Namibia*, 74 B3
Kama Reservoir, *Russia*, 59 H2
Kamativi, *Zimbabwe*, 74 E3
Kamchatka Peninsula, *Russia*, 55 H3
Kamenka, *Russia*, 58 F2
Kamina, *Democratic Republic of Congo*, 72 E5
Kamloops, *Canada*, 24 G3
Kampala, *Uganda, national capital*, 73 F3
Kampong Cham, *Cambodia*, 46 E5
Kampong Chhnang, *Cambodia*, 46 D5
Kampong Saom, *Cambodia*, 46 D5
Kamyanets-Podilskyy, *Ukraine*, 61 H6
Kamyshin, *Russia*, 58 F3
Kananga, *Democratic Republic of Congo*, 72 D5
Kanazawa, *Japan*, 49 N3
Kandahar, *Afghanistan*, 50 B4
Kandalaksha, *Russia*, 60 K2
Kandi, *Benin*, 71 F6
Kandy, *Sri Lanka*, 51 E9
Kang, *Botswana*, 74 D4
Kangaroo Island, *Australia*, 40 G7
Kanggye, *North Korea*, 49 L2
Kankan, *Guinea*, 71 D6
Kano, *Nigeria*, 68 C6
Kanpur, *India*, 50 E5
Kansas, *U.S.A., internal admin. area*, 26 G3
Kansas City, *U.S.A.*, 27 H3
Kanye, *Botswana*, 74 E4
Kaohsiung, *China*, 49 K6
Kaolack, *Senegal*, 71 B6
Kara-Balta, *Kyrgyzstan*, 50 C2
Karabuk, *Turkey*, 65 K3
Karachi, *Pakistan*, 51 B6
Karaj, *Iran*, 52 F4
Karakol, *Kyrgyzstan*, 50 D2
Karakorum Range, *Asia*, 50 D3
Kara Kum Desert, *Turkmenistan*, 52 G3
Karaman, *Turkey*, 55 K4
Karamay, *China*, 50 E1
Kara Sea, *Russia*, 54 D2
Kariba, *Zimbabwe*, 74 E3
Kariba, Lake, *Africa*, 74 E3
Karibib, *Namibia*, 74 C4
Karimata Strait, *Indonesia*, 44 C4
Karlovac, *Croatia*, 64 E2
Karlovy Vary, *Czech Republic*, 64 E1
Karlshamn, *Sweden*, 61 E4
Karlsruhe, *Germany*, 62 G4
Karlstad, *Sweden*, 60 E4
Karmoy, *Norway*, 60 C4
Karonga, *Malawi*, 75 F1
Karora, *Eritrea*, 69 J5
Karpathos, *Greece*, 65 H5
Karratha, *Australia*, 40 C4
Kasai, *Africa*, 72 C4
Kasama, *Zambia*, 74 F2
Kashi, *China*, 50 D3
Kasama, *Sudan*, 69 J5
Kassel, *Germany*, 62 G4
Kasungu, *Malawi*, 75 F2
Kataba, *Zambia*, 74 E3
Kathmandu, *Nepal, national capital*, 50 F5
Katiola, *Ivory Coast*, 71 D7
Katowice, *Poland*, 61 F6
Katsina, *Nigeria*, 71 G6
Kattegat, *Europe*, 61 D4
Kauai, *U.S.A.*, 27 P7
Kaukau Veld, *Africa*, 74 C4
Kaunas, *Lithuania*, 61 G5
Kavala, *Greece*, 65 H3
Kawambwa, *Zambia*, 74 E1
Kayes, *Mali*, 71 C6
Kayseri, *Turkey*, 52 C4
Kazakhstan, *Asia, country*, 54 C3
Kazan, *Russia*, 59 F2
Kaztalovka, *Kazakhstan*, 59 F4
Kebnekaise, *Sweden*, 60 F2
Kecskemet, *Hungary*, 61 F7
Kedougou, *Senegal*, 71 C6
Keetmanshoop, *Namibia*, 74 C5

Kefallonia, *Greece*, 65 F4
Keflavik, *Iceland*, 60 N2
Kelowna, *Canada*, 24 H4
Kempten, *Germany*, 62 G5
Kendari, *Indonesia*, 45 F4
Kenema, *Sierra Leone*, 71 C7
Kenhardt, *South Africa*, 74 D5
Kenitra, *Morocco*, 70 D2
Kenora, *Canada*, 25 K4
Kentucky, *U.S.A., internal admin. area*, 27 J3
Kentucky Lake, *U.S.A.*, 27 J3
Kenya, *Africa, country*, 73 G3
Kenya, Mount, *Kenya*, 73 G4
Kerch, *Ukraine*, 65 L2
Kerema, *Papua New Guinea*, 45 L5
Keren, *Eritrea*, 69 J5
Kerkenah Islands, *Tunisia*, 68 D2
Kermadec Islands, *New Zealand*, 41 Q6
Kerman, *Iran*, 53 G5
Kermanshah, *Iran*, 52 E5
Key West, *U.S.A.*, 27 K6
Khabarovsk, *Russia*, 55 G3
Khanka, Lake, *Asia*, 49 M2
Kharkiv, *Ukraine*, 58 D3
Khartoum, *Sudan, national capital*, 69 H5
Kherson, *Ukraine*, 58 C4
Khmelnytskyy, *Ukraine*, 61 H6
Khon Kaen, *Thailand*, 46 D4
Khorugh, *Tajikistan*, 50 C3
Khouribga, *Morocco*, 70 D2
Khujand, *Tajikistan*, 50 B2
Khulna, *Bangladesh*, 51 F6
Kidal, *Mali*, 70 F5
Kiel, *Germany*, 62 G3
Kielce, *Poland*, 61 G6
Kiev, *Ukraine, national capital*, 61 J6
Kievske Reservoir, *Ukraine*, 58 C3
Kiffa, *Mauritania*, 71 C5
Kigali, *Rwanda, national capital*, 73 F4
Kigoma, *Tanzania*, 72 E4
Kikwit, *Democratic Republic of Congo*, 72 C5
Kilimanjaro, *Africa*, 73 G4
Kilwa, *Democratic Republic of Congo*, 72 E5
Kimberley, *South Africa*, 74 D5
Kimberley Plateau, *Australia*, 40 E3
Kimchaek, *North Korea*, 49 L2
Kindia, *Guinea*, 71 C6
Kindu, *Democratic Republic of Congo*, 72 E4
Kineshma, *Russia*, 58 E2
King George Island, *Atlantic Ocean*, 35 G12
Kingisepp, *Russia*, 60 J4
King Island, *Australia*, 40 H7
Kings Peak, *U.S.A.*, 26 D2
Kingston, *Canada*, 25 M4
Kingston, *Jamaica, national capital*, 29 J4
Kingstown, *St. Vincent and the Grenadines, national capital*, 28 M5
King William Island, *Canada*, 25 K2
Kinkala, *Congo*, 72 B4
Kinshasa, *Democratic Republic of Congo, national capital*, 72 C4
Kipushi, *Democratic Republic of Congo*, 72 E6
Kiribati, *Oceania, country*, 38 F5
Kirikkale, *Turkey*, 65 K4
Kirinyaga, *Kenya*, 73 G4
Kirishi, *Russia*, 60 K4
Kirkenes, *Norway*, 60 J1
Kirkland Lake, *Canada*, 25 L4
Kirkuk, *Iraq*, 52 D4
Kirkwall, *United Kingdom*, 62 D2
Kirov, *Russia*, 59 F2
Kirovohrad, *Ukraine*, 58 C4
Kiruna, *Sweden*, 60 G2
Kisangani, *Democratic Republic of Congo*, 72 E3
Kisii, *Kenya*, 73 F4
Kismaayo, *Somalia*, 73 H4
Kisumu, *Kenya*, 73 F4
Kita, *Mali*, 71 D6

Kitakyushu, *Japan*, 49 M4
Kitale, *Kenya*, 73 G3
Kitwe, *Zambia*, 74 E2
Kiuruvesi, *Finland*, 60 H3
Kivu, Lake, *Africa*, 72 E4
Klagenfurt, *Austria*, 64 E2
Klaipeda, *Lithuania*, 61 G5
Klar, *Europe*, 60 E3
Klintsy, *Russia*, 61 K5
Knittelfeld, *Austria*, 64 E2
Knoxville, *U.S.A.*, 27 K3
Kobar Sink, *Ethiopia*, 69 K6
Koblenz, *Germany*, 62 F4
Kochi, *India*, 51 D9
Kodiak Island, *U.S.A.*, 24 D3
Koforidua, *Ghana*, 71 E7
Kohtla-Jarve, *Estonia*, 60 H4
Kokkola, *Finland*, 60 G3
Kokshetau, *Kazakhstan*, 52 J1
Kola Peninsula, *Russia*, 60 L2
Kolda, *Senegal*, 71 C6
Kolding, *Denmark*, 61 D5
Kolhapur, *India*, 51 C7
Kolkata, *India*, 51 F6
Kolomna, *Russia*, 58 D2
Kolwezi, *Democratic Republic of Congo*, 72 E6
Kolyma Range, *Russia*, 55 H2
Komsomolets, *Kazakhstan*, 59 J3
Komsomolsk, *Russia*, 55 G3
Konduz, *Afghanistan*, 50 B3
Kongur Shan, *China*, 50 D3
Konosha, *Russia*, 58 E1
Konya, *Turkey*, 65 K4
Korce, *Albania*, 65 G3
Korea Bay, *Asia*, 49 K3
Korea Strait, *Asia*, 49 L4
Korhogo, *Ivory Coast*, 71 D7
Korla, *China*, 50 F2
Korosten, *Ukraine*, 61 J6
Kosciuszko, Mount, *Australia*, 41 J7
Kosice, *Slovakia*, 61 G6
Kosovo, *Europe, country*, 65 G3
Kosti, *Sudan*, 69 H6
Kostomuksha, *Russia*, 60 J2
Kostroma, *Russia*, 58 E2
Koszalin, *Poland*, 61 F5
Kota, *India*, 50 D5
Kota Bharu, *Malaysia*, 44 B2
Kota Kinabalu, *Malaysia*, 44 E2
Kotka, *Finland*, 60 H3
Kotlas, *Russia*, 59 F1
Koudougou, *Burkina Faso*, 71 E6
Koutiala, *Mali*, 71 D6
Kouvola, *Finland*, 60 H3
Kovel, *Ukraine*, 61 H6
Kozhikode, *India*, 51 D8
Kragujevac, *Serbia*, 65 G2
Krakatoa, *Indonesia*, 44 C5
Krakow, *Poland*, 61 G6
Kraljevo, *Serbia*, 65 G3
Kramatorsk, *Ukraine*, 58 D4
Kranj, *Slovenia*, 64 E2
Krasnodar, *Russia*, 52 C2
Krasnoyarsk, *Russia*, 54 E3
Kremenchuk, *Ukraine*, 58 C4
Kremenchukske Reservoir, *Ukraine*, 58 C4
Krishna, *India*, 51 D7
Kristiansand, *Norway*, 60 C4
Kristiansund, *Norway*, 60 C3
Krong Kaoh Kong, *Cambodia*, 46 D5
Kroonstad, *South Africa*, 74 E5
Krugersdorp, *South Africa*, 74 E5
Kryvyy Rih, *Ukraine*, 58 C4
Kuala Lumpur, *Malaysia, national capital*, 44 B3
Kuala Terengganu, *Malaysia*, 44 B2
Kuantan, *Malaysia*, 44 B3
Kuching, *Malaysia*, 44 D3
Kuhmo, *Finland*, 60 J2
Kuito, *Angola*, 74 C2
Kulob, *Tajikistan*, 50 B3
Kumamoto, *Japan*, 49 M4
Kumanovo, *Macedonia*, 65 G3
Kumasi, *Ghana*, 71 E7

Kumba, *Cameroon*, 72 A3
Kumo, *Nigeria*, 68 D6
Kunlun Mountains, *China*, 50 E3
Kunming, *China*, 48 F5
Kuopio, *Finland*, 60 H2
Kupang, *Indonesia*, 45 F6
Kuressaare, *Estonia*, 61 G4
Kurgan, *Russia*, 59 K2
Kurikka, *Finland*, 60 G3
Kuril Islands, *Russia*, 55 H3
Kursk, *Russia*, 58 D3
Kushiro, *Japan*, 49 P2
Kutahya, *Turkey*, 65 J4
Kutaisi, *Georgia*, 52 D3
Kutch, Rann of, *India*, 51 B6
Kuujjuaq, *Canada*, 25 N3
Kuusamo, *Finland*, 60 J2
Kuwait, *Asia, country*, 53 E6
Kuwait City, *Kuwait, national capital*, 53 E6
Kuybyshev Reservoir, *Russia*, 59 F3
Kuyto, Lake, *Russia*, 60 K2
Kuytun, *China*, 50 F2
Kwangju, *South Korea*, 49 L3
Kyoga, Lake, *Uganda*, 73 F3
Kyoto, *Japan*, 49 N3
Kyrenia, *Cyprus*, 65 K5
Kyrgyzstan, *Asia, country*, 50 C2
Kythira, *Greece*, 65 G4
Kyushu, *Japan*, 49 M4
Kyzyl, *Russia*, 54 E3

l

Laayoune, *Western Sahara, national capital*, 70 C2
Labe, *Guinea*, 71 C6
Labrador City, *Canada*, 25 N3
Labrador Sea, *North America*, 25 P2
La Chorrera, *Colombia*, 32 D4
La Coruna, *Spain*, 63 B6
Ladoga, Lake, *Russia*, 60 J3
Ladysmith, *South Africa*, 74 E5
Lae, *Papua New Guinea*, 45 L5
Lagdo Reservoir, *Cameroon*, 72 B2
La Gomera, *Canary Islands*, 70 B3
Lagos, *Nigeria*, 71 F7
Lagos, *Portugal*, 63 B7
La Grande Reservoir, *Canada*, 25 M3
Lagunillas, *Venezuela*, 32 D1
Lahat, *Indonesia*, 44 B4
Lahore, *Pakistan*, 50 C4
Lahti, *Finland*, 60 H3
Lai, *Chad*, 72 C2
La Libertad, *Ecuador*, 32 B4
Lambarene, *Gabon*, 72 B4
Lamia, *Greece*, 65 G4
Lancaster Sound, *Canada*, 25 L1
Land's End, *United Kingdom*, 62 C4
Langanes, *Iceland*, 60 Q2
Langsa, *Indonesia*, 44 A3
Lansing, *U.S.A., internal capital*, 27 K2
Lanzarote, *Canary Islands*, 70 C3
Lanzhou, *China*, 48 F3
Laoag, *Philippines*, 47 H4
Lao Cai, *Vietnam*, 46 D3
La Oroya, *Peru*, 32 C6
Laos, *Asia, country*, 46 D4
La Palma, *Canary Islands*, 70 B3
La Palma, *Panama*, 29 J6
La Paz, *Bolivia, national capital*, 34 E3
La Paz, *Mexico*, 28 B3
La Perouse Strait, *Asia*, 49 P1
Lapland, *Europe*, 60 H1
La Plata, *Argentina*, 34 G6
Lappeenranta, *Finland*, 60 J3
Laptev Sea, *Russia*, 55 G2
Larache, *Morocco*, 70 D1
Laredo, *U.S.A.*, 26 G5
La Rioja, *Argentina*, 34 E5
Larisa, *Greece*, 65 G4
Larkana, *Pakistan*, 50 B5
Larnaca, *Cyprus*, 65 K5
La Rochelle, *France*, 63 D5
La Romana, *Dominican Republic*, 29 L4
Larvik, *Norway*, 60 D4
Lashio, *Burma*, 46 C3

Lastoursville, *Gabon*, 72 B4
Las Vegas, *U.S.A.*, 26 C3
Latakia, *Syria*, 52 C4
Latvia, *Europe, country*, 61 H4
Launceston, *Australia*, 40 J8
Lausanne, *Switzerland*, 64 C2
Lautoka, *Fiji*, 41 Q3
Lebanon, *Asia, country*, 52 C5
Lecce, *Italy*, 65 F3
Ledo, Cape, *Angola*, 74 B1
Leeds, *United Kingdom*, 62 D3
Leeuwarden, *Netherlands*, 62 F3
Leeuwin, Cape, *Australia*, 40 B6
Leeward Islands, *North America*, 28 M4
Legaspi, *Philippines*, 47 H5
Legnica, *Poland*, 61 F6
Le Havre, *France*, 62 E4
Leipzig, *Germany*, 62 F4
Leiria, *Portugal*, 63 B7
Le Mans, *France*, 62 E4
Lena, *Russia*, 55 G2
Leon, *Mexico*, 28 D3
Leon, *Nicaragua*, 29 G5
Leon, *Spain*, 63 C6
Leonardville, *Namibia*, 74 C4
Lerida, *Spain*, 63 E6
Lerwick, *United Kingdom*, 62 D1
Les Cayes, *Haiti*, 29 K4
Leshan, *China*, 48 F5
Leskovac, *Serbia*, 65 G3
Lesotho, *Africa, country*, 74 E5
Lesser Antilles, *North America*, 28 M5
Lesser Sunda Islands, *Indonesia*, 44 E5
Lesvos, *Greece*, 65 H4
Lethbridge, *Canada*, 24 H4
Leticia, *Brazil*, 32 K4
Lewiston, *U.S.A.*, 26 C1
Lexington, *U.S.A.*, 27 K3
Lhasa, *China*, 50 F4
Lhokseumawe, *Indonesia*, 44 A2
Lianyungang, *China*, 49 J4
Liaoyuan, *China*, 49 L2
Liberec, *Czech Republic*, 64 E1
Liberia, *Africa, country*, 71 D7
Liberia, *Costa Rica*, 29 G5
Libreville, *Gabon, national capital*, 72 A3
Libya, *Africa, country*, 68 E3
Libyan Desert, *Africa*, 68 F3
Lichinga, *Mozambique*, 75 G2
Lida, *Belarus*, 61 H5
Lidkoping, *Sweden*, 60 E4
Liechtenstein, *Europe, country*, 64 D2
Liege, *Belgium*, 62 F4
Lieksa, *Finland*, 60 J3
Liepaja, *Latvia*, 61 G4
Ligurian Sea, *Europe*, 64 C3
Likasi, *Democratic Republic of Congo*, 72 E6
Lille, *France*, 62 E4
Lillehammer, *Norway*, 60 D3
Lilongwe, *Malawi, national capital*, 75 F2
Lima, *Peru, national capital*, 32 C6
Limassol, *Cyprus*, 65 K5
Limerick, *Ireland*, 62 B3
Limnos, *Greece*, 58 C3
Limoges, *France*, 63 E5
Limon, *Costa Rica*, 29 H5
Limpopo, *Africa*, 74 F4
Linares, *Chile*, 35 D7
Linchuan, *China*, 49 J5
Lincoln, *U.S.A., internal capital*, 27 G2
Lindi, *Tanzania*, 73 G6
Line Islands, *Kiribati*, 39 H4
Linhares, *Brazil*, 34 K3
Linkoping, *Sweden*, 60 E4
Linz, *Austria*, 64 E1
Lions, Gulf of, *Europe*, 63 F6
Lipari Islands, *Italy*, 64 E4
Lipetsk, *Russia*, 58 D3
Lisbon, *Portugal, national capital*, 63 B7
Lithuania, *Europe, country*, 61 G5
Little Andaman, *India*, 51 G8
Little Rock, *U.S.A., internal capital*, 27 H4
Liuzhou, *China*, 48 G6
Liverpool, *United Kingdom*, 62 D3

Livingstone, *Zambia*, 74 E3
Livorno, *Italy*, 64 D3
Liwale, *Tanzania*, 73 G5
Ljubljana, *Slovenia, national capital*, 64 E2
Llanos, *South America*, 32 D2
Lloydminster, *Canada*, 24 J3
Lobamba, *Swaziland, national capital*, 74 F5
Lodz, *Poland*, 61 F6
Lofoten, *Norway*, 60 E1
Logan, Mount, *Canada*, 24 F2
Logrono, *Spain*, 63 D6
Loire, *France*, 62 E5
Loja, *Ecuador*, 32 C4
Lokan Reservoir, *Finland*, 60 H2
Lolland, *Denmark*, 61 D5
Lombok, *Indonesia*, 44 E5
Lome, *Togo, national capital*, 71 F7
London, *Canada*, 25 L4
London, *United Kingdom, national capital*, 62 D4
Londonderry, *United Kingdom*, 62 C3
Londrina, *Brazil*, 34 H4
Long Island, *The Bahamas*, 27 L6
Long Xuyen, *Vietnam*, 46 E5
Lopez, Cape, *Gabon*, 72 A4
Lop Lake, *China*, 50 G2
Lord Howe Island, *Australia*, 41 L6
Los Angeles, *Chile*, 35 D7
Los Angeles, *U.S.A.*, 26 C4
Los Mochis, *Mexico*, 28 C2
Louangphrabang, *Laos*, 46 D4
Loubomo, *Congo*, 72 B4
Louga, *Senegal*, 71 B5
Louisiana, *U.S.A., internal admin. area*, 27 H4
Lower California, *Mexico*, 28 B2
Loyalty Islands, *New Caledonia*, 41 N4
Luacano, *Angola*, 74 D2
Luanda, *Angola, national capital*, 74 B1
Luangwa, *Africa*, 74 F2
Luanshya, *Zambia*, 74 E2
Lubango, *Angola*, 74 B2
Lubbock, *U.S.A.*, 26 F4
Lublin, *Poland*, 61 G6
Lubny, *Ukraine*, 58 C3
Lubumbashi, *Democratic Republic of Congo*, 72 E6
Lucena, *Philippines*, 47 H5
Lucerne, *Switzerland*, 64 D2
Lucira, *Angola*, 74 B2
Lucknow, *India*, 50 E5
Luderitz, *Namibia*, 74 C5
Ludhiana, *India*, 50 D4
Ludza, *Latvia*, 61 H4
Luena, *Angola*, 74 C2
Luganville, *Vanuatu*, 41 N3
Lugo, *Spain*, 63 C6
Luhansk, *Ukraine*, 58 D4
Luiana, *Angola*, 74 D3
Lukulu, *Zambia*, 74 D2
Lumbala Kaquengue, *Angola*, 74 D2
Lumbala Nguimbo, *Angola*, 74 D2
Lundazi, *Zambia*, 75 F2
Lupilichi, *Mozambique*, 75 G2
Lusaka, *Zambia, national capital*, 74 E3
Lutsk, *Ukraine*, 61 H6
Luxembourg, *Europe, country*, 62 F4
Luxembourg, *Luxembourg, national capital*, 62 F4
Luxor, *Egypt*, 69 H3
Luzhou, *China*, 48 G5
Luzon, *Philippines*, 47 H4
Luzon Strait, *Philippines*, 47 H4
Lviv, *Ukraine*, 61 H6
Lyon, *France*, 63 F5
Lysychansk, *Ukraine*, 58 D4

m

Maan, *Jordan*, 53 C5
Maastricht, *Netherlands*, 62 F4
Macae, *Brazil*, 34 K4
Macapa, *Brazil*, 33 H3
Macau, *China*, 49 H6
Macedonia, *Europe, country*, 65 G3

Maceio, *Brazil*, 33 L5
Machakos, *Kenya*, 73 G4
Machala, *Ecuador*, 32 C4
Machu Picchu, *Peru*, 32 D6
Mackay, *Australia*, 41 J4
Mackenzie, *Canada*, 24 G2
Mackenzie Bay, *Canada*, 24 F2
Mackenzie Mountains, *Canada*, 24 F2
Macon, *U.S.A.*, 27 K4
Madagascar, *Africa, country*, 75 J4
Madang, *Papua New Guinea*, 45 L5
Madeira, *Atlantic Ocean*, 70 B2
Madeira, *Brazil*, 32 F5
Madingou, *Congo*, 72 B4
Madison, *U.S.A., internal capital*, 27 J2
Madras, *India*, 51 E8
Madrid, *Spain, national capital*, 63 D6
Madurai, *India*, 51 D9
Maevatanana, *Madagascar*, 75 J3
Mafeteng, *Lesotho*, 74 E5
Mafia Island, *Tanzania*, 73 H5
Magadan, *Russia*, 55 H3
Magangue, *Colombia*, 32 D2
Magdalena, *Bolivia*, 34 F2
Magdeburg, *Germany*, 62 G3
Magellan, Strait of, *South America*, 35 E10
Magnitogorsk, *Russia*, 59 H3
Mahajanga, *Madagascar*, 75 J3
Mahalapye, *Botswana*, 74 E4
Mahilyow, *Belarus*, 61 J5
Mahon, *Spain*, 63 F7
Maiduguri, *Nigeria*, 68 D6
Mai-Ndombe, Lake, *Democratic Republic of Congo*, 72 C4
Maine, *U.S.A., internal admin. area*, 27 N1
Maine, Gulf of, *U.S.A.*, 27 N2
Maio, *Cape Verde*, 71 M11
Majorca, *Spain*, 63 E7
Majuro, *Marshall Islands, national capital*, 38 E4
Makarikari, *Botswana*, 74 D4
Makassar Strait, *Indonesia*, 45 E4
Makeni, *Sierra Leone*, 71 C7
Makgadikgadi Pans, *Botswana*, 74 D4
Makhachkala, *Russia*, 52 E3
Makkovik, *Canada*, 25 P3
Makokou, *Gabon*, 72 B3
Makumbako, *Tanzania*, 73 F5
Makurdi, *Nigeria*, 72 A2
Mala, *Peru*, 32 C6
Malabo, *Equatorial Guinea, national capital*, 72 A3
Maladzyechna, *Belarus*, 61 H5
Malaga, *Spain*, 63 C7
Malaimbandy, *Madagascar*, 75 J4
Malakal, *Sudan*, 73 F2
Malakula, *Vanuatu*, 41 N3
Malang, *Indonesia*, 44 D5
Malanje, *Angola*, 74 C1
Malar, Lake, *Sweden*, 60 F4
Malatya, *Turkey*, 52 C4
Malawi, *Africa, country*, 75 F2
Malawi, Lake, *Africa*, 73 F6
Malaysia, *Asia, country*, 44 B2
Maldives, *Asia, country*, 51 C9
Male, *Maldives, national capital*, 51 C10
Malegaon, *India*, 51 C6
Mali, *Africa, country*, 70 E5
Malindi, *Kenya*, 73 H4
Malmo, *Sweden*, 61 E5
Malpelo Island, *Colombia*, 32 B3
Malta, *Europe, country*, 64 E4
Mamoudzou, *Mayotte*, 75 J2
Mamuno, *Botswana*, 74 D4
Man, *Ivory Coast*, 71 D7
Manado, *Indonesia*, 45 F3
Managua, *Nicaragua, national capital*, 29 G5
Manakara, *Madagascar*, 75 J4
Manama, *Bahrain, national capital*, 53 F6
Manaus, *Brazil*, 33 G4
Manchester, *United Kingdom*, 62 D3
Manchuria, *China*, 49 K2
Mandalay, *Burma*, 46 C3
Mandera, *Kenya*, 73 H3

Mandritsara, *Madagascar*, 75 J3
Mandurah, *Australia*, 40 C6
Mangalore, *India*, 51 C8
Mania, *Madagascar*, 75 J3
Manicouagan Reservoir, *Canada*, 25 N3
Manila, *Philippines, national capital*, 47 H5
Manisa, *Turkey*, 65 H4
Man, Isle of, *Europe*, 62 C3
Manitoba, *Canada, internal admin. area*, 25 K3
Manitoba, Lake, *Canada*, 25 K3
Manizales, *Colombia*, 32 C2
Manja, *Madagascar*, 75 H4
Mannar, *Sri Lanka*, 51 E9
Mannar, Gulf of, *Asia*, 51 D9
Mannheim, *Germany*, 62 G4
Mansa, *Zambia*, 74 E2
Manta, *Ecuador*, 32 B4
Manzhouli, *China*, 55 F3
Mao, *Chad*, 68 E6
Maoke Range, *Indonesia*, 45 J4
Maputo, *Mozambique, national capital*, 75 F5
Maraba, *Brazil*, 33 J5
Maracaibo, *Venezuela*, 32 D1
Maracaibo, Lake, *Venezuela*, 32 D2
Maracay, *Venezuela*, 32 E1
Maradi, *Niger*, 68 C6
Maranon, *Peru*, 32 C4
Marathon, *Canada*, 25 L4
Mar del Plata, *Argentina*, 35 G7
Margarita Island, *Venezuela*, 32 F1
Margherita Peak, *Africa*, 72 E3
Marib, *Yemen*, 53 E8
Maribor, *Slovenia*, 64 E2
Marie Byrd Land, *Antarctica*, 79 Q3
Mariental, *Namibia*, 74 C4
Marijampole, *Lithuania*, 61 G5
Marilia, *Brazil*, 34 J4
Marimba, *Angola*, 74 C1
Mariupol, *Ukraine*, 58 D4
Marka, *Somalia*, 73 H3
Marmara, Sea of, *Turkey*, 65 J3
Maroantsetra, *Madagascar*, 75 J3
Maroua, *Cameroon*, 72 B1
Marquesas Islands, *French Polynesia*, 39 K5
Marrakech, *Morocco*, 70 D2
Marra, Mount, *Sudan*, 68 F6
Marsa Matruh, *Egypt*, 69 G2
Marseille, *France*, 63 F6
Marshall Islands, *Oceania, country*, 38 D3
Martapura, *Indonesia*, 44 D4
Martinique, *North America*, 28 M5
Mary, *Turkmenistan*, 52 H4
Maryland, *U.S.A., internal admin. area*, 27 L3
Masaka, *Uganda*, 73 F4
Masasi, *Tanzania*, 73 G6
Masbate, *Philippines*, 47 H5
Maseru, *Lesotho, national capital*, 74 E5
Mashhad, *Iran*, 52 G4
Masirah Island, *Oman*, 53 G7
Massachusetts, *U.S.A., internal admin. area*, 27 M2
Massangena, *Mozambique*, 75 F4
Massawa, *Eritrea*, 69 J5
Massif Central, *France*, 63 E5
Massinga, *Mozambique*, 75 G4
Masvingo, *Zimbabwe*, 74 F4
Matagalpa, *Nicaragua*, 29 G5
Matala, *Angola*, 74 B2
Matamoros, *Mexico*, 28 E2
Matanzas, *Cuba*, 29 H3
Mataram, *Indonesia*, 44 E5
Mataro, *Spain*, 63 E6
Matehuala, *Mexico*, 28 D3
Mato Grosso, Plateau of, *Brazil*, 33 G6
Matsuyama, *Japan*, 49 M4
Maturin, *Venezuela*, 32 F2
Maui, *U.S.A.*, 27 P7
Maun, *Botswana*, 74 D3
Mauritania, *Africa, country*, 70 C5
Mauritius, *Indian Ocean, country*, 75 L3
Mavinga, *Angola*, 74 D3

Mayotte, *Africa*, 75 J2
Mazar-e Sharif, *Afghanistan*, 50 B3
Mazatlan, *Mexico*, 28 C3
Mazyr, *Belarus*, 61 J5
Mbabane, *Swaziland, national capital*, 74 F5
Mbala, *Zambia*, 74 F1
Mbale, *Uganda*, 73 F3
Mbandaka, *Democratic Republic of Congo*, 72 C3
Mbarara, *Uganda*, 73 F4
Mbeya, *Tanzania*, 73 F5
Mbuji-Mayi, *Democratic Republic of Congo*, 72 D5
McClintock Channel, *Canada*, 24 J1
McClure Strait, *Canada*, 24 G1
McKinley, Mount, *U.S.A.*, 24 D2
Mead, Lake, *U.S.A.*, 26 D3
Mecca, *Saudi Arabia*, 53 C7
Mecula, *Mozambique*, 75 G2
Medan, *Indonesia*, 44 A3
Medellin, *Colombia*, 32 C2
Medford, *U.S.A.*, 26 B2
Medina, *Saudi Arabia*, 53 C7
Mediterranean Sea, *Africa/Europe*, 21
Medvezhyegorsk, *Russia*, 60 K3
Meerut, *India*, 50 D5
Meiktila, *Burma*, 46 C3
Meizhou, *China*, 49 J6
Mekele, *Ethiopia*, 73 G1
Meknes, *Morocco*, 70 D2
Mekong, *Asia*, 46 E5
Melaka, *Malaysia*, 44 B3
Melamo, Cape, *Mozambique*, 75 H2
Melanesia, *Oceania*, 38 D5
Melbourne, *Australia, internal capital*, 40 H7
Melekeok, *Palau, national capital*, 38 A4
Melilla, *Africa*, 63 D7
Melitopol, *Ukraine*, 58 D4
Melo, *Uruguay*, 34 H6
Melville Island, *Australia*, 40 F2
Melville Island, *Canada*, 24 H1
Melville Peninsula, *Canada*, 25 L2
Memphis, *U.S.A.*, 27 J3
Mendoza, *Argentina*, 34 E6
Menongue, *Angola*, 74 C2
Mentawai Islands, *Indonesia*, 44 A4
Menzel Bourguiba, *Tunisia*, 68 C1
Mergui, *Burma*, 46 C5
Mergui Archipelago, *Burma*, 46 C5
Merida, *Mexico*, 28 G3
Meridian, *U.S.A.*, 27 J4
Merlo, *Argentina*, 34 E6
Mersin, *Turkey*, 52 B4
Meru, *Kenya*, 73 G3
Messina, *Italy*, 64 E4
Messina, *South Africa*, 74 F4
Metz, *France*, 62 F4
Mexicali, *Mexico*, 28 A1
Mexico, *North America, country*, 28 D3
Mexico City, *Mexico, national capital*, 28 E4
Mexico, Gulf of, *North America*, 28 F3
Mexico, Plateau of, *Mexico*, 28 D2
Miami, *U.S.A.*, 27 K5
Michigan, *U.S.A., internal admin. area*, 27 J2
Michigan, Lake, *U.S.A.*, 27 J2
Michurinsk, *Russia*, 58 E3
Micronesia, *Oceania*, 38 C4
Micronesia, Federated States of, *Oceania, country*, 38 C4
Middlesbrough, *United Kingdom*, 62 D3
Midway Islands, *Pacific Ocean*, 38 F2
Mikkeli, *Finland*, 60 H3
Milan, *Italy*, 64 D2
Milange, *Mozambique*, 75 G3
Mildura, *Australia*, 40 H6
Milwaukee, *U.S.A.*, 27 J2
Minas, *Uruguay*, 34 G6
Mindanao, *Philippines*, 47 H6
Mindelo, *Cape Verde*, 71 M11
Mindoro, *Philippines*, 47 H5
Mingacevir, *Azerbaijan*, 52 E3
Minna, *Nigeria*, 71 G7

Nuqui, *Colombia,* 32 C2
Nuremberg, *Germany,* 62 G4
Nyala, *Sudan,* 68 F6
Nyasa, Lake, *Africa,* 73 F6
Nyeri, *Kenya,* 73 G4
Nykobing, *Denmark,* 61 D5
Nzerekore, *Guinea,* 71 D7
Nzwani, *Comoros,* 75 H2

O

Oahu, *U.S.A.,* 27 P7
Oaxaca, *Mexico,* 28 E4
Ob, *Russia,* 54 D2
Obi, *Indonesia,* 45 G4
Obninsk, *Russia,* 58 D2
Obo, *Central African Republic,* 72 E2
Odda, *Norway,* 60 C3
Odemis, *Turkey,* 65 J4
Odense, *Denmark,* 61 D5
Oder, *Europe,* 61 E5
Odesa, *Ukraine,* 58 C4
Odienne, *Ivory Coast,* 71 D7
Ogbomoso, *Nigeria,* 71 F7
Ogden, *U.S.A.,* 26 D2
Ohio, *U.S.A.,* 27 J3
Ohio, *U.S.A., internal admin. area,* 27 K2
Ojinaga, *Mexico,* 28 D2
Ojos del Salado, Mount, *South America,* 34 E5
Oka, *Russia,* 58 E2
Okahandja, *Namibia,* 74 C4
Okaukuejo, *Namibia,* 74 C3
Okavango, *Africa,* 74 D3
Okavango Swamp, *Botswana,* 74 D3
Okayama, *Japan,* 49 M4
Okeechobee, Lake, *U.S.A.,* 27 K5
Okhotsk, Sea of, *Asia,* 55 H3
Okinawa, *Japan,* 49 L5
Oklahoma, *U.S.A., internal admin. area,* 26 G4
Oklahoma City, *U.S.A., internal capital,* 26 G3
Oktyabrskiy, *Russia,* 59 G3
Oland, *Sweden,* 61 F4
Olavarria, *Argentina,* 35 F7
Olbia, *Italy,* 64 D3
Oleksandriya, *Ukraine,* 58 C4
Ollague, *Chile,* 34 E4
Olomouc, *Czech Republic,* 64 F1
Olongapo, *Philippines,* 47 H5
Olsztyn, *Poland,* 61 G5
Olympia, *U.S.A., internal capital,* 26 B1
Olympus, Mount, *Greece,* 65 G3
Omaha, *U.S.A.,* 27 G2
Oman, *Asia, country,* 53 G7
Oman, Gulf of, *Asia,* 53 G7
Omdurman, *Sudan,* 69 H5
Omsk, *Russia,* 54 D3
Ondangwa, *Namibia,* 74 C3
Onega, Lake, *Russia,* 60 K3
Onitsha, *Nigeria,* 71 G7
Ontario, *Canada, internal admin. area,* 25 L3
Ontario, Lake, *U.S.A.,* 27 L2
Opochka, *Russia,* 61 J4
Opole, *Poland,* 61 F6
Oporto, *Portugal,* 63 B6
Oppdal, *Norway,* 60 D3
Opuwo, *Namibia,* 74 B3
Oradea, *Romania,* 65 G2
Oral, *Kazakhstan,* 59 G3
Oran, *Algeria,* 70 E1
Orange, *Africa,* 74 C5
Orange, Cape, *Brazil,* 33 H3
Orapa, *Botswana,* 74 E4
Orebro, *Sweden,* 60 E4
Oregon, *U.S.A., internal admin. area,* 26 B2
Orel, *Russia,* 58 D3
Orenburg, *Russia,* 59 H3
Orense, *Spain,* 63 C6
Orinoco, *Venezuela,* 32 F2
Orinoco Delta, *Venezuela,* 32 F2
Oristano, *Italy,* 64 D4
Orizaba, *Mexico,* 28 E4

Orkney, *South Africa,* 74 E5
Orkney Islands, *United Kingdom,* 62 D2
Orlando, *U.S.A.,* 27 K5
Orleans, *France,* 62 E4
Orsha, *Belarus,* 61 J5
Orsk, *Russia,* 59 H3
Osaka, *Japan,* 49 N4
Osh, *Kyrgyzstan,* 50 C2
Osijek, *Croatia,* 65 F2
Oskarshamn, *Sweden,* 61 F4
Oslo, *Norway, national capital,* 60 D4
Osnabruck, *Germany,* 62 G3
Osorno, *Chile,* 35 D8
Ostersund, *Sweden,* 60 E3
Ostrava, *Czech Republic,* 65 F1
Otavi, *Namibia,* 74 C3
Otjiwarongo, *Namibia,* 74 C4
Ottawa, *Canada, national capital,* 25 M4
Ouadda, *Central African Republic,* 72 D2
Ouagadougou, *Burkina Faso, national capital,* 71 E6
Ouahigouya, *Burkina Faso,* 71 E6
Ouargla, *Algeria,* 70 G2
Ouarzazate, *Morocco,* 70 D2
Oudtshoorn, *South Africa,* 74 D6
Ouesso, *Congo,* 72 C3
Oujda, *Morocco,* 70 E2
Oulu, *Finland,* 60 H2
Oulu Lake, *Finland,* 60 H2
Ovalle, *Chile,* 34 D6
Oviedo, *Spain,* 63 C6
Owando, *Congo,* 72 C4
Owen Sound, *Canada,* 25 L4
Owo, *Nigeria,* 71 G7
Oxford, *United Kingdom,* 62 D4
Oyem, *Gabon,* 72 B3
Ozark Plateau, *U.S.A.,* 27 H3

P

Paarl, *South Africa,* 74 C6
Pacasmayo, *Peru,* 32 C5
Pacific Ocean, 20
Padang, *Indonesia,* 44 B4
Pafuri, *Mozambique,* 74 F4
Pagadian, *Philippines,* 47 H6
Paijanne Lake, *Finland,* 60 H3
Pakistan, *Asia, country,* 50 B5
Pakxe, *Laos,* 46 E4
Palangkaraya, *Indonesia,* 44 D4
Palau, *Oceania, country,* 38 A4
Palawan, *Philippines,* 47 G6
Palembang, *Indonesia,* 44 B4
Palencia, *Spain,* 63 C6
Palermo, *Italy,* 64 E4
Palikir, *Federated States of Micronesia, national capital,* 38 C4
Palk Strait, *Asia,* 51 D9
Palma, *Mozambique,* 75 H2
Palma, *Spain,* 63 E7
Palmas, Cape, *Africa,* 71 D8
Palmyra Atoll, *Oceania,* 38 G4
Palopo, *Indonesia,* 45 F4
Palu, *Indonesia,* 45 F4
Pampas, *Argentina,* 35 F7
Pamplona, *Colombia,* 32 D2
Pamplona, *Spain,* 63 D6
Panama, *North America, country,* 29 H6
Panama Canal, *Panama,* 29 J6
Panama City, *Panama, national capital,* 29 J6
Panama, Gulf of, *North America,* 29 J6
Panay, *Philippines,* 47 H5
Panevezys, *Lithuania,* 61 H5
Pangkalpinang, *Indonesia,* 44 C4
Panjgur, *Pakistan,* 50 A5
Pantelleria, *Italy,* 64 E4
Panzhihua, *China,* 48 F5
Papeete, *French Polynesia,* 39 J6
Papua, Gulf of, *Papua New Guinea,* 45 K5
Papua New Guinea, *Oceania, country,* 45 L5
Paracel Islands, *Asia,* 47 F4
Paraguaipoa, *Venezuela,* 32 D1

Paraguay, *South America,* 34 G4
Paraguay, *South America, country,* 34 F4
Parakou, *Benin,* 71 F7
Paramaribo, *Suriname, national capital,* 33 G2
Parana, *South America,* 34 G6
Paranagua, *Brazil,* 34 J5
Parepare, *Indonesia,* 45 E4
Paris, *France, national capital,* 62 E4
Parma, *Italy,* 64 D2
Parnaiba, *Brazil,* 33 K4
Parnu, *Estonia,* 60 H4
Parry Islands, *Canada,* 24 J1
Pasadena, *U.S.A.,* 26 C4
Passo Fundo, *Brazil,* 34 H5
Pasto, *Colombia,* 32 C3
Patagonia, *Argentina,* 35 E9
Pathein, *Burma,* 46 B4
Patna, *India,* 50 F5
Patos de Minas, *Brazil,* 34 J3
Patos Lagoon, *Brazil,* 34 H6
Patra, *Greece,* 65 G4
Pattaya, *Thailand,* 46 D5
Pau, *France,* 63 D6
Pavlodar, *Kazakhstan,* 54 D3
Paysandu, *Uruguay,* 34 G6
Peace River, *Canada,* 24 H3
Pecos, *U.S.A.,* 26 F4
Pecs, *Hungary,* 61 F7
Pedro Juan Caballero, *Paraguay,* 34 G4
Pegu, *Burma,* 46 C4
Peipus, Lake, *Europe,* 60 H4
Peiraias, *Greece,* 65 G4
Pekanbaru, *Indonesia,* 44 B3
Pelagian Islands, *Italy,* 64 E5
Peleng, *Indonesia,* 45 F4
Pelotas, *Brazil,* 34 H6
Pematangsiantar, *Indonesia,* 44 A3
Pemba, *Mozambique,* 75 H2
Pemba Island, *Tanzania,* 73 G5
Penang, *Malaysia,* 44 B2
Penas, Gulf of, *Chile,* 35 C9
Pennsylvania, *U.S.A., internal admin. area,* 27 L2
Pensacola, *U.S.A.,* 27 J4
Penza, *Russia,* 58 F3
Penzance, *United Kingdom,* 62 C4
Peoria, *U.S.A.,* 27 J2
Pereira, *Colombia,* 32 C3
Perm, *Russia,* 59 H2
Perpignan, *France,* 63 E6
Persepolis, *Iran,* 53 F6
Persian Gulf, *Asia,* 53 F6
Perth, *Australia, internal capital,* 40 C6
Peru, *South America, country,* 32 C5
Perugia, *Italy,* 64 E3
Pescara, *Italy,* 64 E3
Peshawar, *Pakistan,* 50 C4
Petauke, *Zambia,* 74 F2
Petra, *Jordan,* 53 C5
Petrolina, *Brazil,* 33 K5
Petropavlovsk-Kamchatskiy, *Russia,* 55 H3
Petrozavodsk, *Russia,* 60 K3
Philadelphia, *U.S.A.,* 27 L3
Philippines, *Asia, country,* 47 J5
Philippine Sea, *Asia,* 47 H5
Phitsanulok, *Thailand,* 46 D4
Phnom Penh, *Cambodia, national capital,* 46 D5
Phoenix, *U.S.A., internal capital,* 26 D4
Phongsali, *Laos,* 46 D3
Piatra Neamt, *Romania,* 65 H2
Pica, *Chile,* 34 E4
Pico, *Azores,* 70 K10
Pielis Lake, *Finland,* 60 J3
Pierre, *U.S.A., internal capital,* 26 F2
Pietermaritzburg, *South Africa,* 74 F5
Pietersburg, *South Africa,* 74 E4
Pihlaja Lake, *Finland,* 60 J3
Pik Pobedy, *Asia,* 50 E2
Pilcomayo, *South America,* 34 F4
Pilsen, *Czech Republic,* 64 E1
Pinar del Rio, *Cuba,* 29 H3
Pindus Mountains, *Greece,* 65 G4
Pingdingshan, *China,* 49 H4
Pinsk, *Belarus,* 61 H5

Pisa, *Italy,* 64 D3
Pitcairn Islands, *Oceania,* 39 L7
Pitesti, *Romania,* 65 H2
Pittsburgh, *U.S.A.,* 27 L2
Piura, *Peru,* 32 B5
Platte, *U.S.A.,* 26 F2
Pleven, *Bulgaria,* 65 H3
Plock, *Poland,* 61 F5
Ploiesti, *Romania,* 65 H2
Plovdiv, *Bulgaria,* 65 H3
Plumtree, *Zimbabwe,* 74 E4
Plymouth, *United Kingdom,* 62 C4
Po, *Italy,* 64 D2
Pocos de Caldas, *Brazil,* 34 J4
Podgorica, *Montenegro, national capital,* 65 F3
Podolsk, *Russia,* 58 D2
Pointe-Noire, *Congo,* 72 B4
Poitiers, *France,* 63 E5
Pokhara, *Nepal,* 50 E5
Poland, *Europe, country,* 61 F6
Polatsk, *Belarus,* 61 J5
Poltava, *Ukraine,* 58 C4
Polynesia, *Oceania,* 38 G5
Pompeii, *Italy,* 64 E3
Ponta Delgada, *Azores,* 70 K10
Ponta Pora, *Brazil,* 34 G4
Pontianak, *Indonesia,* 44 C3
Poole, *United Kingdom,* 62 D4
Poopo, Lake, *Bolivia,* 34 E3
Popayan, *Colombia,* 32 C3
Porbandar, *India,* 51 B6
Pori, *Finland,* 60 G3
Porlamar, *Venezuela,* 28 M5
Port-au-Prince, *Haiti, national capital,* 29 K4
Port Blair, *India,* 51 G8
Port Elizabeth, *South Africa,* 74 E6
Port-Gentil, *Gabon,* 72 A4
Port Harcourt, *Nigeria,* 71 G8
Port Hardy, *Canada,* 24 G3
Port Hedland, *Australia,* 40 C4
Portland, *Australia,* 40 H7
Portland, *Maine, U.S.A.,* 27 M2
Portland, *Oregon, U.S.A.,* 26 B1
Port Louis, *Mauritius, national capital,* 75 L4
Port Macquarie, *Australia,* 41 K6
Port McNeill, *Canada,* 24 G3
Port Moresby, *Papua New Guinea, national capital,* 45 K5
Porto Alegre, *Brazil,* 34 H5
Port-of-Spain, *Trinidad and Tobago, national capital,* 28 M5
Porto-Novo, *Benin, national capital,* 71 F7
Porto-Vecchio, *France,* 63 G6
Porto Velho, *Brazil,* 32 F5
Port Said, *Egypt,* 69 H2
Portsmouth, *United Kingdom,* 62 D4
Port Sudan, *Sudan,* 69 J5
Portugal, *Europe, country,* 63 B7
Port-Vila, *Vanuatu, national capital,* 41 N3
Porvenir, *Chile,* 35 D10
Posadas, *Argentina,* 34 G5
Poti, *Georgia,* 52 D3
Potiskum, *Nigeria,* 68 D6
Potosi, *Bolivia,* 34 E3
Potsdam, *Germany,* 62 H3
Poyang Lake, *China,* 49 J5
Poznan, *Poland,* 61 F5
Prachuap Khiri Khan, *Thailand,* 46 C5
Prague, *Czech Republic, national capital,* 64 E1
Praia, *Cape Verde, national capital,* 71 M12
Presidente Prudente, *Brazil,* 34 H4
Presov, *Slovakia,* 61 G6
Pretoria, *South Africa, national capital,* 74 E5
Preveza, *Greece,* 65 G4
Prieska, *South Africa,* 74 D5
Prilep, *Macedonia,* 65 G3
Prince Albert, *Canada,* 24 J3
Prince Edward Island, *Canada, internal admin. area,* 25 N4
Prince George, *Canada,* 24 G3

Prince of Wales Island, *Canada*, 25 K1
Prince Rupert, *Canada*, 24 F3
Principe, *Sao Tome and Principe*, 71 G8
Pripet, *Europe*, 61 J6
Pripet Marshes, *Europe*, 61 H5
Pristina, *Kosovo, national capital*, 65 G3
Providence, *Seychelles*, 75 K1
Providence, *U.S.A., internal capital*, 27 M2
Providence, Cape, *New Zealand*, 41 N9
Provo, *U.S.A.*, 26 D2
Prudhoe Bay, *U.S.A.*, 24 E1
Pskov, *Russia*, 61 J4
Pskov, Lake, *Europe*, 60 J4
Pucallpa, *Peru*, 32 D5
Puebla, *Mexico*, 28 E4
Pueblo, *U.S.A.*, 26 F3
Puerto Ayora, *Ecuador*, 32 N10
Puerto Cabezas, *Nicaragua*, 29 H5
Puerto Deseado, *Argentina*, 35 E9
Puerto Inirida, *Colombia*, 32 E3
Puerto Leguizamo, *Colombia*, 32 D4
Puerto Maldonado, *Peru*, 32 E6
Puerto Montt, *Chile*, 35 D8
Puerto Natales, *Chile*, 35 D10
Puerto Paez, *Venezuela*, 32 E2
Puerto Princesa, *Philippines*, 47 G6
Puerto Rico, *North America*, 28 L4
Puerto Suarez, *Bolivia*, 34 G3
Puerto Vallarta, *Mexico*, 28 C3
Pula, *Croatia*, 64 E2
Pulog, Mount, *Philippines*, 47 H4
Puncak Jaya, *Indonesia*, 45 J4
Pune, *India*, 51 C7
Puno, *Peru*, 32 D7
Punta Arenas, *Chile*, 35 D10
Puntarenas, *Costa Rica*, 29 H5
Purus, *Brazil*, 32 E5
Pusan, *South Korea*, 49 L3
Pushkin, *Russia*, 60 J4
Puula Lake, *Finland*, 60 H3
Pweto, *Democratic Republic of Congo*, 72 E5
Pya, Lake, *Russia*, 60 J2
Pye, *Burma*, 46 C4
Pyinmana, *Burma*, 46 C4
Pyongyang, *North Korea, national capital*, 49 L3
Pyramids of Giza, *Egypt*, 69 H3
Pyrenees, *Europe*, 63 D6
Pyrgos, *Greece*, 65 G4

q

Qaidam Basin, *China*, 50 G3
Qaraghandy, *Kazakhstan*, 54 D3
Qatar, *Asia, country*, 53 F6
Qattara Depression, *Egypt*, 69 G3
Qazvin, *Iran*, 52 E4
Qena, *Egypt*, 69 H3
Qingdao, *China*, 49 K3
Qinghai Lake, *China*, 48 F3
Qinhuangdao, *China*, 49 J3
Qiqihar, *China*, 49 K1
Qom, *Iran*, 52 F5
Qostanay, *Kazakhstan*, 59 J3
Quanzhou, *China*, 49 J6
Quebec, *Canada, internal admin. area*, 25 M3
Quebec, *Canada, internal capital*, 25 M4
Queen Charlotte Islands, *Canada*, 24 F3
Queen Elizabeth Islands, *Canada*, 24 H1
Queen Maud Land, *Antarctica*, 79 C3
Queensland, *Australia, internal admin. area*, 40 H4
Quelimane, *Mozambique*, 75 G3
Quellon, *Chile*, 35 D8
Quetta, *Pakistan*, 50 B4
Quevedo, *Ecuador*, 32 C4
Quezaltenango, *Guatemala*, 28 F4
Quezon City, *Philippines*, 47 H5
Quibdo, *Colombia*, 32 C2
Quimper, *France*, 62 C5
Quincy, *U.S.A.*, 27 H3
Qui Nhon, *Vietnam*, 46 E5
Quirima, *Angola*, 74 C2

Quito, *Ecuador, national capital*, 32 C4
Qurghonteppa, *Tajikistan*, 50 B3
Qyzylorda, *Kazakhstan*, 52 J3

r

Raahe, *Finland*, 60 H2
Rabat, *Morocco, national capital*, 70 D2
Rabaul, *Papua New Guinea*, 45 M4
Rabnita, *Moldova*, 65 J2
Radisson, *Canada*, 25 M3
Radom, *Poland*, 61 G6
Ragusa, *Italy*, 64 E4
Rahimyar Khan, *Pakistan*, 50 C5
Rainier, Mount, *U.S.A.*, 26 B1
Raipur, *India*, 51 E6
Rajahmundry, *India*, 51 E7
Rajkot, *India*, 51 C6
Rajshahi, *Bangladesh*, 51 F6
Rakops, *Botswana*, 74 D4
Raleigh, *U.S.A., internal capital*, 27 L3
Ralik Islands, *Marshall Islands*, 38 D3
Ramnicu Valcea, *Romania*, 65 H2
Rancagua, *Chile*, 34 D6
Ranchi, *India*, 51 F6
Randers, *Denmark*, 61 D4
Rangoon, *Burma, national capital*, 46 C4
Rangpur, *Bangladesh*, 50 F5
Rapid City, *U.S.A.*, 26 F2
Ras Dashen, *Ethiopia*, 73 G1
Rasht, *Iran*, 52 E4
Ratak Islands, *Marshall Islands*, 38 E3
Rat Islands, *U.S.A.*, 25 A3
Rauma, *Finland*, 60 G3
Ravenna, *Italy*, 64 E2
Rawson, *Argentina*, 35 E8
Rechytsa, *Belarus*, 61 J5
Recife, *Brazil*, 33 M5
Reconquista, *Argentina*, 34 G5
Red, *Asia*, 48 F6
Red, *U.S.A.*, 27 G4
Red Deer, *Canada*, 24 H3
Redding, *U.S.A.*, 26 B2
Red Sea, *Africa/Asia*, 69 J4
Regensburg, *Germany*, 62 H4
Regina, *Canada, internal capital*, 24 J3
Regina, *French Guiana*, 33 H3
Rehoboth, *Namibia*, 74 C4
Reims, *France*, 62 F4
Reindeer Lake, *Canada*, 24 J3
Rennell Island, *Solomon Islands*, 41 M2
Rennes, *France*, 62 D4
Reno, *U.S.A.*, 26 C3
Reunion, *Indian Ocean*, 75 L4
Revelstoke, *Canada*, 24 H3
Revillagigedo Islands, *Mexico*, 28 B4
Reykjavik, *Iceland, national capital*, 60 N2
Rhine, *Europe*, 62 F4
Rhode Island, *U.S.A., internal admin. area*, 27 M2
Rhodes, *Greece*, 65 J4
Rhone, *Europe*, 63 F5
Riau Islands, *Indonesia*, 44 B3
Ribeirao Preto, *Brazil*, 34 J4
Riberalta, *Bolivia*, 34 E2
Richards Bay, *South Africa*, 74 F5
Richmond, *U.S.A., internal capital*, 27 L3
Riga, *Latvia, national capital*, 61 H4
Riga, Gulf of, *Europe*, 61 G4
Rijeka, *Croatia*, 64 E2
Rimini, *Italy*, 64 E2
Rio Branco, *Brazil*, 32 E5
Rio Cuarto, *Argentina*, 34 F6
Rio de Janeiro, *Brazil*, 34 K4
Rio Gallegos, *Argentina*, 35 E10
Rio Grande, *Argentina*, 35 E10
Rio Grande, *Brazil*, 34 H6
Rio Grande, *U.S.A.*, 26 F5
Riohacha, *Colombia*, 32 D1
Rivas, *Nicaragua*, 29 G5
Rivera, *Uruguay*, 34 G6
Riverside, *U.S.A.*, 26 C4
Rivne, *Ukraine*, 61 H6
Riyadh, *Saudi Arabia, national capital*, 53 E7
Roanoke, *U.S.A.*, 27 L3
Robson, Mount, *Canada*, 24 H3

Rochester, *U.S.A.*, 27 L2
Rockford, *U.S.A.*, 27 J2
Rockhampton, *Australia*, 41 K4
Rocky Mountains, *U.S.A.*, 26 D1
Romania, *Europe, country*, 65 G2
Rome, *Italy, national capital*, 64 E3
Rondonopolis, *Brazil*, 34 H3
Ronne, *Denmark*, 61 E5
Ronne Ice Shelf, *Antarctica*, 79 S3
Roraima, Mount, *South America*, 32 F2
Rosario, *Argentina*, 34 F6
Roseau, *Dominica, national capital*, 28 M4
Roslavl, *Russia*, 61 K5
Ross Ice Shelf, *Antarctica*, 79 M4
Rosso, *Mauritania*, 71 B5
Rostock, *Germany*, 62 H3
Rostov, *Russia*, 58 D4
Roti, *Indonesia*, 45 F6
Rotorua, *Australia*, 41 Q7
Rotterdam, *Netherlands*, 62 F4
Rouen, *France*, 62 E4
Rovaniemi, *Finland*, 60 H2
Roxas, *Philippines*, 47 H5
Rub al Khali, *Asia*, 53 E8
Rudnyy, *Kazakhstan*, 59 J3
Rufino, *Argentina*, 34 F6
Rufunsa, *Zambia*, 74 E3
Rukwa, Lake, *Tanzania*, 73 F5
Rundu, *Namibia*, 74 C3
Rurrenabaque, *Bolivia*, 34 E2
Ruse, *Bulgaria*, 65 H3
Russia, *Asia/Europe, country*, 54 E3
Ruvuma, *Africa*, 73 G6
Rwanda, *Africa, country*, 72 E4
Ryazan, *Russia*, 58 D3
Rybinsk, *Russia*, 58 D2
Rybinsk Reservoir, *Russia*, 58 D2
Rybnik, *Poland*, 61 F6
Ryukyu Islands, *Japan*, 49 L5
Rzeszow, *Poland*, 61 G6
Rzhev, *Russia*, 58 C2

s

Saarbrucken, *Germany*, 62 F4
Saarijarvi, *Finland*, 60 H3
Sabha, *Libya*, 68 D3
Sabzevar, *Iran*, 52 G4
Sacramento, *U.S.A., internal capital*, 26 B3
Sadah, *Yemen*, 53 E8
Safi, *Morocco*, 70 D2
Sahara, *Africa*, 68 C5
Saharanpur, *India*, 50 D5
Sahel, *Africa*, 68 C6
Sahiwal, *Pakistan*, 50 C4
Saida, *Algeria*, 70 F2
Saigon, *Vietnam*, 46 E5
Saimaa Lake, *Finland*, 60 H3
St. Andrew, Cape, *Madagascar*, 75 H3
St. Denis, *Reunion*, 75 L4
St. Etienne, *France*, 63 F5
St. Francis, Cape, *South Africa*, 74 D6
St. George, *U.S.A.*, 26 D3
St. George's, *Grenada, national capital*, 28 M5
St. Helier, *Channel Islands*, 62 D4
Saint John, *Canada*, 25 N4
St. John's, *Antigua and Barbuda, national capital*, 28 M4
St. John's, *Canada, internal capital*, 25 P4
St. Kitts and Nevis, *North America, country*, 28 M4
St. Lawrence, *Canada*, 25 M4
St. Lawrence, Gulf of, *Canada*, 25 N4
St. Lawrence Island, *U.S.A.*, 24 B2
St. Louis, *Senegal*, 71 B5
St. Louis, *U.S.A.*, 27 H3
St. Lucia, *North America, country*, 28 M5
St. Lucia, Cape, *South Africa*, 75 F5
St. Malo, *France*, 62 D4
St. Martha, Cape, *Angola*, 74 B2
St. Martin, *North America*, 28 M4
St. Mary, Cape, *Madagascar*, 75 J5
St. Paul, *U.S.A., internal capital*, 27 H1

St. Petersburg, *Russia*, 60 J4
St. Petersburg, *U.S.A.*, 27 K5
St. Pierre, *Seychelles*, 75 J1
St. Pierre and Miquelon, *North America*, 25 P4
St. Polten, *Austria*, 64 E1
St. Vincent, Cape, *Portugal*, 63 B7
St. Vincent and the Grenadines, *North America, country*, 28 M5
Sakhalin, *Russia*, 55 H3
Saki, *Azerbaijan*, 52 E3
Saki, *Nigeria*, 71 F7
Sakishima Islands, *Japan*, 49 K6
Sal, *Cape Verde*, 71 M11
Salado, *Argentina*, 34 F5
Salalah, *Oman*, 53 F8
Salamanca, *Spain*, 63 C6
Salem, *India*, 51 D8
Salem, *U.S.A., internal capital*, 26 B1
Salerno, *Italy*, 64 E3
Salihorsk, *Belarus*, 61 H5
Salinas, *U.S.A.*, 26 B3
Salta, *Argentina*, 34 E4
Saltillo, *Mexico*, 28 D2
Salt Lake City, *U.S.A., internal capital*, 26 D2
Salto, *Uruguay*, 34 G6
Salton Sea, *U.S.A.*, 26 C4
Salvador, *Brazil*, 33 L6
Salween, *Asia*, 46 C4
Salzburg, *Austria*, 64 E2
Samar, *Philippines*, 47 J5
Samara, *Russia*, 59 G3
Samarinda, *Indonesia*, 44 E4
Samarqand, *Uzbekistan*, 50 B3
Sambalpur, *India*, 51 E6
Samoa, *Oceania, country*, 38 F6
Sampwe, *Democratic Republic of Congo*, 72 E5
Sam Rayburn Reservoir, *U.S.A.*, 27 H4
Samsun, *Turkey*, 52 C3
San, *Mali*, 71 E6
Sana, *Yemen, national capital*, 53 D8
Sanandaj, *Iran*, 52 E4
San Andres Island, *Colombia*, 29 H5
San Antonio, *U.S.A.*, 26 G5
San Antonio, Cape, *Argentina*, 35 G7
San Antonio Oeste, *Argentina*, 35 F8
San Cristobal, *Ecuador*, 32 P10
San Cristobal, *Venezuela*, 32 D2
Sandakan, *Malaysia*, 45 E2
San Diego, *U.S.A.*, 26 C4
Sandoway, *Burma*, 46 B4
San Fernando, *Chile*, 34 D6
San Fernando de Apure, *Venezuela*, 32 E2
San Francisco, *Argentina*, 34 F6
San Francisco, *U.S.A.*, 26 B3
San Francisco, Cape, *Ecuador*, 32 B3
Sangihe Islands, *Indonesia*, 45 G3
San Jorge, Gulf of, *Argentina*, 35 E9
San Jose, *Costa Rica, national capital*, 29 H6
San Jose, *U.S.A.*, 26 B3
San Jose de Chiquitos, *Bolivia*, 34 F3
San Jose del Guaviare, *Colombia*, 32 D3
San Juan, *Argentina*, 34 E6
San Juan, *Puerto Rico*, 28 L4
San Julian, *Argentina*, 35 E9
Sanliurfa, *Turkey*, 52 C4
San Lucas, Cape, *Mexico*, 28 B3
San Luis, *Argentina*, 34 E6
San Luis Obispo, *U.S.A.*, 26 B3
San Luis Potosi, *Mexico*, 28 D3
San Marino, *Europe, country*, 64 E3
San Matias, Gulf of, *Argentina*, 35 F8
San Miguel de Tucuman, *Argentina*, 34 E5
San Nicolas de los Arroyos, *Argentina*, 34 F6
San Pedro, *Ivory Coast*, 71 D8
San Pedro de Atacama, *Chile*, 34 E4
San Rafael, *Argentina*, 34 E6
San Remo, *Italy*, 64 C3
San Salvador, *Ecuador*, 32 N10
San Salvador, *El Salvador, national capital*, 28 G5

San Salvador de Jujuy, *Argentina*, 34 E4
San Sebastian, *Spain*, 63 D6
Santa Clara, *Cuba*, 29 H3
Santa Cruz, *Bolivia*, 34 F2
Santa Cruz, *Ecuador*, 32 N10
Santa Cruz Islands, *Solomon Islands*, 41 N2
Santa Elena, *Venezuela*, 32 F3
Santa Fe, *Argentina*, 34 F6
Santa Fe, *U.S.A., internal capital*, 26 E3
Santa Maria, *Brazil*, 34 H5
Santa Marta, *Colombia*, 32 D1
Santander, *Spain*, 63 D6
Santarem, *Brazil*, 33 H4
Santa Rosa, *Argentina*, 35 F7
Santiago, *Chile, national capital*, 34 D6
Santiago, *Dominican Republic*, 29 K4
Santiago, *Panama*, 29 H6
Santiago de Compostela, *Spain*, 63 B6
Santiago de Cuba, *Cuba*, 29 J3
Santiago del Estero, *Argentina*, 34 F5
Santo Antao, *Cape Verde*, 71 L11
Santo Domingo, *Dominican Republic*, 29 L4
Santo Domingo de los Colorados, *Ecuador*, 32 C4
San Valentin, Mount, *Chile*, 35 D9
Sanya, *China*, 48 G7
Sao Francisco, *Brazil*, 33 L5
Sao Jose do Rio Preto, *Brazil*, 34 J4
Sao Luis, *Brazil*, 33 K4
Sao Miguel, *Azores*, 70 K10
Sao Nicolau, *Cape Verde*, 71 M11
Sao Paulo, *Brazil*, 34 J4
Sao Roque, Cape, *Brazil*, 33 L4
Sao Tiago, *Cape Verde*, 71 M11
Sao Tome, *Sao Tome and Principe, national capital*, 71 G8
Sao Tome and Principe, *Africa, country*, 71 G8
Sapporo, *Japan*, 49 P2
Saqqara, *Egypt*, 69 H3
Sarajevo, *Bosnia and Herzegovina, national capital*, 65 F3
Saransk, *Russia*, 58 F3
Sarapul, *Russia*, 59 G2
Saratov, *Russia*, 59 F3
Saratov Reservoir, *Russia*, 59 F3
Sardinia, *Italy*, 64 D3
Sargodha, *Pakistan*, 50 C4
Sarh, *Chad*, 72 C2
Sarremaa, *Estonia*, 60 G4
Saskatchewan, *Canada, internal admin. area*, 24 J3
Saskatoon, *Canada*, 24 J3
Sassari, *Italy*, 64 D3
Satu Mare, *Romania*, 65 G2
Saudi Arabia, *Asia, country*, 53 E7
Sault Ste. Marie, *Canada*, 25 L4
Saurimo, *Angola*, 74 D1
Savannah, *U.S.A.*, 27 K4
Savannakhet, *Laos*, 46 D4
Sawu, *Indonesia*, 45 F6
Sawu Sea, *Indonesia*, 45 F5
Schwerin, *Germany*, 62 G3
Scotland, *United Kingdom, internal admin. area*, 62 C2
Seattle, *U.S.A.*, 26 B1
Seeheim, *Namibia*, 74 C5
Sefadu, *Sierra Leone*, 71 C7
Seg, Lake, *Russia*, 60 K3
Segou, *Mali*, 71 D6
Seine, *France*, 62 E4
Sekondi-Takoradi, *Ghana*, 71 E8
Selebi-Phikwe, *Botswana*, 74 E4
Selibabi, *Mauritania*, 71 C5
Selvas, *Brazil*, 32 E5
Semarang, *Indonesia*, 44 D5
Semenov, *Russia*, 58 E2
Semiozernoe, *Kazakhstan*, 59 J3
Sendai, *Japan*, 49 P3
Senegal, *Africa*, 71 C5
Senegal, *Africa, country*, 71 B6
Seoul, *South Korea, national capital*, 49 L3
Serang, *Indonesia*, 44 C5

Serbia, *Europe, country*, 65 G2
Seremban, *Malaysia*, 44 B3
Sergiyev Posad, *Russia*, 58 D2
Serov, *Russia*, 54 F2
Serowe, *Botswana*, 74 E4
Serpukhov, *Russia*, 58 D3
Serres, *Greece*, 65 G3
Sesheke, *Zambia*, 74 D3
Setif, *Algeria*, 70 G1
Setubal, *Portugal*, 63 B7
Sevastopol, *Ukraine*, 65 K2
Severn, *United Kingdom*, 62 D3
Severnaya Zemlya, *Russia*, 55 F2
Severomorsk, *Russia*, 60 K1
Sevettijarvi, *Finland*, 60 J1
Seville, *Spain*, 63 C7
Seward, *U.S.A.*, 24 E2
Seward Peninsula, *U.S.A.*, 24 C2
Seychelles, *Indian Ocean, country*, 75 J1
Seydhisfjordhur, *Iceland*, 60 Q2
Sfax, *Tunisia*, 68 D2
Shalqar, *Kazakhstan*, 52 G2
Shanghai, *China*, 49 K4
Shannon, *Ireland*, 62 C3
Shantou, *China*, 49 J6
Shaoguan, *China*, 49 H6
Sharjah, *United Arab Emirates*, 53 G6
Sharm el Sheikh, *Egypt*, 69 H3
Shasta, Mount, *U.S.A.*, 26 B2
Sheffield, *United Kingdom*, 62 D3
Shenyang, *China*, 49 K2
Shepetivka, *Ukraine*, 61 H6
Shetland Islands, *United Kingdom*, 62 D1
Shieli, *Kazakhstan*, 52 J3
Shihezi, *China*, 50 F2
Shijiazhuang, *China*, 49 H3
Shikoku, *Japan*, 49 M4
Shillong, *India*, 50 G5
Shiraz, *Iran*, 53 F6
Shishaldin Volcano, *U.S.A.*, 25 C3
Shiyan, *China*, 48 H4
Shizuoka, *Japan*, 49 N3
Shkoder, *Albania*, 65 F3
Shreveport, *U.S.A.*, 27 H4
Shumen, *Bulgaria*, 65 H3
Shymkent, *Kazakhstan*, 50 B2
Sialkot, *Pakistan*, 50 C4
Siauliai, *Lithuania*, 61 G5
Sibiti, *Congo*, 72 B4
Sibiu, *Romania*, 65 H2
Sibolga, *Indonesia*, 44 A3
Sibu, *Malaysia*, 44 D3
Sicily, *Italy*, 64 E4
Sicuani, *Peru*, 32 D6
Sidi-Bel-Abbes, *Algeria*, 70 E1
Sidon, *Lebanon*, 52 C5
Sidra, Gulf of, *Africa*, 68 E2
Sierra Leone, *Africa, country*, 71 C7
Sierra Morena, *Spain*, 63 C7
Sierra Nevada, *Spain*, 63 D7
Sierra Nevada, *U.S.A.*, 26 B3
Siglufjordhur, *Iceland*, 60 P2
Siguiri, *Guinea*, 71 D6
Sikasso, *Mali*, 71 D6
Sikhote Alin Range, *Russia*, 49 N1
Siling Lake, *China*, 50 F4
Simao, *China*, 48 F6
Simeulue, *Indonesia*, 44 A3
Simferopol, *Ukraine*, 65 K2
Simpson Desert, *Australia*, 40 G4
Sinai, *Egypt*, 69 H3
Sinai, Mount, *Egypt*, 69 H3
Sincelejo, *Colombia*, 32 C2
Sines, *Portugal*, 63 B7
Sinnamary, *French Guiana*, 33 H2
Sinuiju, *North Korea*, 49 K2
Sioux City, *U.S.A.*, 27 G2
Sioux Falls, *U.S.A.*, 27 G2
Sirjan, *Iran*, 53 G6
Sittwe, *Burma*, 46 B3
Sivas, *Turkey*, 52 C4
Skagen, *Denmark*, 61 D4
Skagerrak, *Europe*, 61 C4

Skelleftea, *Sweden*, 60 G2
Skikda, *Algeria*, 70 G1
Skopje, *Macedonia, national capital*, 65 G3
Skyros, *Greece*, 65 H4
Slavonski Brod, *Croatia*, 64 F2
Sligo, *Ireland*, 62 B3
Sliven, *Bulgaria*, 65 H3
Slovakia, *Europe, country*, 61 F6
Slovenia, *Europe, country*, 64 E2
Slovyansk, *Ukraine*, 58 D4
Slupsk, *Poland*, 61 F5
Slutsk, *Belarus*, 61 H5
Smallwood Reservoir, *Canada*, 25 N3
Smola, *Norway*, 60 C3
Smolensk, *Russia*, 61 J5
Sobradinho Reservoir, *Brazil*, 33 K6
Sobral, *Brazil*, 33 K4
Sochi, *Russia*, 52 C3
Society Islands, *French Polynesia*, 39 J6
Socotra, *Yemen*, 53 F9
Sodankyla, *Finland*, 60 H2
Sodertalje, *Sweden*, 60 F4
Sofia, *Bulgaria, national capital*, 65 G3
Sohag, *Egypt*, 69 H3
Sokhumi, *Georgia*, 52 D3
Sokode, *Togo*, 71 F7
Sokoto, *Nigeria*, 71 G6
Solapur, *India*, 51 D7
Solikamsk, *Russia*, 59 H2
Solomon Islands, *Oceania, country*, 38 D5
Solomon Sea, *Papua New Guinea*, 45 M5
Solwezi, *Zambia*, 74 E2
Somalia, *Africa, country*, 73 J2
Somerset Island, *Canada*, 25 K1
Songea, *Tanzania*, 73 G6
Songo, *Mozambique*, 75 F3
Son La, *Vietnam*, 46 D3
Sorong, *Indonesia*, 45 H4
Soroti, *Uganda*, 73 G3
Soroya, *Norway*, 60 G1
Sotra, *Norway*, 60 C3
Souk Ahras, *Algeria*, 64 C4
Sousse, *Tunisia*, 68 D1
South Africa, *Africa, country*, 74 D6
South America, 20
Southampton, *United Kingdom*, 62 D4
Southampton Island, *Canada*, 25 L2
South Australia, *Australia, internal admin. area*, 40 F5
South Bend, *U.S.A.*, 27 J2
South Carolina, *U.S.A., internal admin. area*, 27 K4
South China Sea, *Asia*, 47 F5
South Dakota, *U.S.A., internal admin. area*, 26 F2
South East Cape, *Australia*, 40 J8
Southend-on-Sea, *United Kingdom*, 62 E4
Southern Ocean, 20
Southern Sierra Madre, *Mexico*, 28 D4
South Georgia, *Atlantic Ocean*, 35 L10
South Island, *New Zealand*, 41 N8
South Korea, *Asia, country*, 49 L3
South Orkney Islands, *Atlantic Ocean*, 35 J12
South Sandwich Islands, *Atlantic Ocean*, 35 N10
South Shetland Islands, *Atlantic Ocean*, 35 G12
South West Cape, *New Zealand*, 41 N9
Spain, *Europe, country*, 63 D7
Split, *Croatia*, 64 F3
Spokane, *U.S.A.*, 26 C1
Spratly Islands, *Asia*, 47 F5
Springfield, *Illinois, U.S.A., internal capital*, 27 J3
Springfield, *Massachusetts, U.S.A.*, 27 M2
Springfield, *Missouri, U.S.A.*, 27 H3
Springs, *South Africa*, 74 E5
Sri Jayewardenepura Kotte, *Sri Lanka, national capital*, 51 E9
Sri Lanka, *Asia, country*, 51 E9
Srinagar, *India*, 50 C4
Standerton, *South Africa*, 74 E5
Stanley, *Falkland Islands*, 35 G10
Stara Zagora, *Bulgaria*, 65 H3

Staryy Oskol, *Russia*, 58 D3
Stavanger, *Norway*, 60 C4
Stavropol, *Russia*, 52 D2
Steinkjer, *Norway*, 60 D2
Stellenbosch, *South Africa*, 74 C6
Sterlitamak, *Russia*, 59 H3
Stewart Island, *New Zealand*, 41 N9
Stockholm, *Sweden, national capital*, 60 F4
Stoeng Treng, *Cambodia*, 46 E5
Stoke-on-Trent, *United Kingdom*, 62 D3
Stora Lule Lake, *Sweden*, 60 F2
Storavan Lake, *Sweden*, 60 F2
Stor Lake, *Sweden*, 60 E3
Stornoway, *United Kingdom*, 62 C2
Stranraer, *United Kingdom*, 62 C3
Strasbourg, *France*, 62 F4
Sturt Stony Desert, *Australia*, 40 G5
Stuttgart, *Germany*, 62 G4
Subotica, *Serbia*, 65 F2
Suceava, *Romania*, 65 H2
Sucre, *Bolivia, national capital*, 34 E3
Sudan, *Africa, country*, 69 G5
Sudbury, *Canada*, 25 L4
Suez, *Egypt*, 69 H3
Suez Canal, *Egypt*, 69 H2
Suhar, *Oman*, 53 G7
Sukkur, *Pakistan*, 50 B5
Sukses, *Namibia*, 74 C4
Sula, *Norway*, 60 C3
Sula Islands, *Indonesia*, 45 G4
Sullana, *Peru*, 32 B4
Sulu Archipelago, *Philippines*, 47 H6
Sulu Sea, *Asia*, 47 G6
Sumatra, *Indonesia*, 44 B3
Sumba, *Indonesia*, 45 E5
Sumbawa, *Indonesia*, 44 E5
Sumqayit, *Azerbaijan*, 52 E3
Sumy, *Ukraine*, 58 C3
Sunderland, *United Kingdom*, 62 D3
Sundsvall, *Sweden*, 60 F3
Superior, Lake, *U.S.A.*, 27 J1
Sur, *Oman*, 53 G7
Surabaya, *Indonesia*, 44 D5
Surakarta, *Indonesia*, 44 D5
Surat, *India*, 51 C6
Surgut, *Russia*, 54 D2
Surigao, *Philippines*, 47 J6
Suriname, *South America, country*, 33 G3
Surt, *Libya*, 68 E2
Sutherland Falls, *New Zealand*, 41 N8
Suva, *Fiji, national capital*, 41 Q3
Suwalki, *Poland*, 61 G5
Suwon, *South Korea*, 49 L3
Svalbard, *Norway*, 54 A2
Svetlahorsk, *Belarus*, 61 J5
Svolvaer, *Norway*, 60 E1
Swakopmund, *Namibia*, 74 B4
Swan Islands, *Honduras*, 29 H4
Swansea, *United Kingdom*, 62 D4
Swaziland, *Africa, country*, 74 F5
Sweden, *Europe, country*, 60 E3
Swift Current, *Canada*, 24 J3
Swindon, *United Kingdom*, 62 D4
Switzerland, *Europe, country*, 64 C2
Sydney, *Australia, internal capital*, 41 K6
Sydney, *Canada*, 25 N4
Syktyvkar, *Russia*, 59 G1
Sylhet, *Bangladesh*, 51 G6
Syracuse, *Italy*, 64 E4
Syracuse, *U.S.A.*, 27 L2
Syr Darya, *Asia*, 52 H2
Syria, *Asia, country*, 52 C4
Syrian Desert, *Asia*, 53 C5
Syzran, *Russia*, 59 F3
Szczecin, *Poland*, 61 E5
Szeged, *Hungary*, 61 G7
Szekesfehervar, *Hungary*, 61 F7
Szombathely, *Hungary*, 61 F7

t

Tabora, *Tanzania*, 73 F5
Tabriz, *Iran*, 52 E4
Tabuk, *Saudi Arabia*, 53 C6
Tacloban, *Philippines*, 47 J5
Tacna, *Peru*, 32 D7

Tacoma, *U.S.A.*, 26 B1
Tacuarembo, *Uruguay*, 34 G6
Tademait Plateau, *Algeria*, 70 F3
Tadmur, *Syria*, 52 C5
Taegu, *South Korea*, 49 L3
Taejon, *South Korea*, 49 L3
Tagus, *Europe*, 63 B7
Tahat, Mount, *Algeria*, 70 G4
Tahiti, *French Polynesia*, 39 J6
Tahoua, *Niger*, 68 C6
Taian, *China*, 49 J3
Taichung, *China*, 49 K6
Tai Lake, *China*, 49 J4
Taimyr Peninsula, *Russia*, 55 F2
Tainan, *China*, 49 K6
Taipei, *China*, 49 K5
Taiping, *Malaysia*, 44 B3
Taiwan, *China*, 49 K6
Taiwan Strait, *Asia*, 49 J6
Taiyuan, *China*, 48 H3
Taizz, *Yemen*, 53 D9
Tajikistan, *Asia, country*, 50 B3
Taj Mahal, *India*, 50 D5
Tajumulco, *Mexico*, 28 F4
Taklimakan Desert, *China*, 50 E3
Talara, *Peru*, 32 B4
Talaud Islands, *Indonesia*, 45 G3
Talca, *Chile*, 35 D7
Taldyqorghan, *Kazakhstan*, 50 D1
Tallahassee, *U.S.A., internal capital*, 27 K4
Tallinn, *Estonia, national capital*, 60 H4
Taltal, *Chile*, 34 D5
Tamale, *Ghana*, 71 E7
Tamanrasset, *Algeria*, 70 G4
Tambacounda, *Senegal*, 71 C6
Tambov, *Russia*, 58 E3
Tampa, *U.S.A.*, 27 K5
Tampere, *Finland*, 60 G3
Tampico, *Mexico*, 28 E3
Tana, Lake, *Ethiopia*, 73 G1
Tandil, *Argentina*, 35 G7
Tanga, *Tanzania*, 73 G5
Tanganyika, Lake, *Africa*, 72 E5
Tangier, *Morocco*, 70 D1
Tangshan, *China*, 49 J3
Tanimbar Islands, *Indonesia*, 45 H5
Tanjungkarang-Telukbetung, *Indonesia*, 44 C5
Tanjungredeb, *Indonesia*, 44 E3
Tanta, *Egypt*, 69 H2
Tan-Tan, *Morocco*, 70 C3
Tanzania, *Africa, country*, 73 F5
Tapachula, *Mexico*, 28 F5
Tapajos, *Brazil*, 33 G5
Tarakan, *Indonesia*, 44 E3
Taranto, *Italy*, 64 F3
Taraz, *Kazakhstan*, 50 C2
Targu Mures, *Romania*, 65 H2
Tarija, *Bolivia*, 34 F4
Tarim Basin, *China*, 50 E3
Tarkwa, *Ghana*, 71 E7
Tarnow, *Poland*, 61 G6
Tarragona, *Spain*, 63 E6
Tartagal, *Argentina*, 34 F4
Tartu, *Estonia*, 60 H4
Tartus, *Syria*, 52 C5
Tashkent, *Uzbekistan, national capital*, 50 B2
Tasmania, *Australia, internal admin. area*, 41 J8
Tasman Sea, *Australasia*, 41 L7
Tataouine, *Tunisia*, 68 D2
Taunggyi, *Burma*, 46 C3
Taupo, Lake, *New Zealand*, 41 Q7
Taurus Mountains, *Turkey*, 65 J4
Tavoy, *Burma*, 46 C5
Tawau, *Malaysia*, 45 E3
Taytay, *Philippines*, 47 G5
Taza, *Morocco*, 70 E2
Tbilisi, *Georgia, national capital*, 52 D3
Tchibanga, *Gabon*, 72 B4
Tebessa, *Algeria*, 70 G1
Tegal, *Indonesia*, 44 C5
Tegucigalpa, *Honduras, national capital*, 29 G5
Tehran, *Iran, national capital*, 52 F4

Tehuacan, *Mexico*, 28 E4
Tehuantepec, Gulf of, *Mexico*, 28 E4
Tehuantepec, Isthmus of, *Mexico*, 28 E4
Tekirdag, *Turkey*, 65 H3
Tel Aviv-Yafo, *Israel*, 53 B5
Teller, *U.S.A.*, 24 C2
Temuco, *Chile*, 35 D7
Ten Degree Channel, *India*, 51 G9
Tenerife, *Canary Islands*, 70 B3
Tenkodogo, *Burkina Faso*, 71 E6
Tennessee, *U.S.A.*, 27 J3
Tennessee, *U.S.A., internal admin. area*, 27 J3
Teofilo Otoni, *Brazil*, 34 K3
Teotihuacan, *Mexico*, 28 E4
Terceira, *Azores*, 70 K10
Teresina, *Brazil*, 33 K4
Ternate, *Indonesia*, 45 G3
Terni, *Italy*, 64 E3
Ternopil, *Ukraine*, 61 H6
Terracotta Army, *China*, 48 G4
Terra Firma, *South Africa*, 74 D5
Teseney, *Eritrea*, 69 J5
Tete, *Mozambique*, 75 F3
Tetouan, *Morocco*, 70 D1
Tetovo, *Macedonia*, 65 G3
Texarkana, *U.S.A.*, 27 H4
Texas, *U.S.A., internal admin. area*, 26 G4
Thailand, *Asia, country*, 46 D4
Thailand, Gulf of, *Asia*, 46 D6
Thai Nguyen, *Vietnam*, 46 E3
Thames, *United Kingdom*, 62 D4
Thanh Hoa, *Vietnam*, 46 E4
Thar Desert, *Asia*, 50 B5
Thasos, *Greece*, 65 H3
Thaton, *Burma*, 46 C4
Thessaloniki, *Greece*, 65 G3
Thies, *Senegal*, 71 B6
Thika, *Kenya*, 73 G4
Thimphu, *Bhutan, national capital*, 50 F5
Thompson, *Canada*, 25 K3
Three Points, Cape, *Africa*, 71 E8
Thunder Bay, *Canada*, 25 L4
Tianjin, *China*, 49 J3
Tibesti Mountains, *Africa*, 68 E4
Tibet, *China*, 50 F4
Tibet, Plateau of, *China*, 50 F4
Tidjikja, *Mauritania*, 70 C5
Tien Shan, *Asia*, 50 D2
Tierra del Fuego, *South America*, 35 E10
Tighina, *Moldova*, 65 J2
Tigris, *Asia*, 52 D4
Tijuana, *Mexico*, 28 A1
Tikal, *Guatemala*, 28 G4
Tikhvin, *Russia*, 60 K4
Tillaberi, *Niger*, 71 F6
Timbuktu, *Mali*, 71 E5
Timisoara, *Romania*, 65 G2
Timor, *Asia*, 45 F5
Timor Leste, *see East Timor*
Timor Sea, *Asia/Australasia*, 45 G6
Tindouf, *Algeria*, 70 D3
Tirana, *Albania, national capital*, 65 F3
Tiraspol, *Moldova*, 65 J2
Tiruchchirappalli, *India*, 51 D8
Titicaca, Lake, *South America*, 32 E7
Tlemcen, *Algeria*, 70 E2
Toamasina, *Madagascar*, 75 J3
Tobago, *Trinidad and Tobabo*, 28 M5
Toba, Lake, *Indonesia*, 44 A3
Tobol, *Asia*, 59 K2
Tobolsk, *Russia*, 59 K2
Tobyl, *Kazakhstan*, 59 J3
Tocantins, *Brazil*, 33 J4
Togo, *Africa, country*, 71 F7
Tokelau, *Oceania*, 38 G5
Tokyo, *Japan, national capital*, 49 N3
Tolanaro, *Madagascar*, 75 J5
Toledo, *Spain*, 63 D7
Toledo, *U.S.A.*, 27 K2
Toledo Bend Reservoir, *U.S.A.*, 27 H4
Toliara, *Madagascar*, 75 H4
Tolyatti, *Russia*, 59 G3
Tolybay, *Kazakhstan*, 59 J3

Tomakomai, *Japan*, 49 P2
Tombouctou, *Mali*, 71 E5
Tomsk, *Russia*, 54 E3
Tonga, *Oceania, country*, 38 F6
Tonkin, Gulf of, *Asia*, 46 E4
Tongliao, *China*, 49 K2
Tonle Sap, *Cambodia*, 46 D5
Toowoomba, *Australia*, 41 K5
Topeka, *U.S.A., internal capital*, 27 G3
Top, Lake, *Russia*, 60 K2
Topoli, *Kazakhstan*, 59 G4
Torghay, *Kazakhstan*, 59 J4
Tornio, *Finland*, 60 H2
Toronto, *Canada, internal capital*, 25 M4
Torrens, Lake, *Australia*, 40 G6
Torreon, *Mexico*, 28 D2
Torres Strait, *Australasia*, 40 H2
Tortuga Island, *Venezuela*, 32 E1
Toubkal, *Morocco*, 70 D2
Tougan, *Burkina Faso*, 71 E6
Touggourt, *Algeria*, 70 G2
Toulon, *France*, 63 F6
Toulouse, *France*, 63 E6
Tours, *France*, 62 E5
Townsville, *Australia*, 40 J3
Toyama, *Japan*, 49 N3
Tozeur, *Tunisia*, 68 C2
Trabzon, *Turkey*, 52 C3
Tralee, *Ireland*, 62 B3
Transantarctic Mountains, *Antarctica*, 79 S4
Transylvanian Alps, *Romania*, 65 G2
Trapani, *Italy*, 64 E4
Trento, *Italy*, 64 D2
Trenton, *U.S.A., internal capital*, 27 M2
Tres Arroyos, *Argentina*, 35 F7
Tres Marias Reservoir, *Brazil*, 34 J3
Tres Puntas, Cape, *Argentina*, 35 E9
Trieste, *Italy*, 64 E2
Trincomalee, *Sri Lanka*, 51 E9
Trinidad, *Bolivia*, 34 F2
Trinidad, *Trinidad and Tobago*, 28 M5
Trinidad and Tobago, *North America, country*, 28 M5
Tripoli, *Lebanon*, 52 C5
Tripoli, *Libya, national capital*, 68 D2
Trivandrum, *India*, 51 D9
Trnava, *Slovakia*, 61 F6
Trois-Rivieres, *Canada*, 25 M4
Tromso, *Norway*, 60 F1
Trondheim, *Norway*, 60 D3
Troyes, *France*, 62 F4
Trujillo, *Peru*, 32 C5
Tsau, *Botswana*, 74 D4
Tses, *Namibia*, 74 C5
Tshabong, *Botswana*, 74 D5
Tshane, *Botswana*, 74 D4
Tshikapa, *Democratic Republic of Congo*, 72 D5
Tshwane, *Botswana*, 74 D4
Tsimlyansk Reservoir, *Russia*, 58 E4
Tsiroanomandidy, *Madagascar*, 75 J3
Tsumeb, *Namibia*, 74 C3
Tuamotu Archipelago, *French Polynesia*, 39 K6
Tubmanburg, *Liberia*, 71 C7
Tubruq, *Libya*, 68 F2
Tubuai Islands, *French Polynesia*, 39 J7
Tucson, *U.S.A.*, 26 D4
Tucupita, *Venezuela*, 32 F2
Tucurui Reservoir, *Brazil*, 33 J4
Tugela Falls, *South Africa*, 74 E5
Tuguegarao, *Philippines*, 47 H4
Tula, *Russia*, 58 D3
Tulcea, *Romania*, 65 J2
Tulsa, *U.S.A.*, 27 G3
Tumaco, *Colombia*, 32 C3
Tumbes, *Peru*, 32 B4
Tunduma, *Tanzania*, 73 F5
Tunduru, *Tanzania*, 73 G6
Tunis, *Tunisia, national capital*, 68 D1
Tunisia, *Africa, country*, 68 C2
Tunja, *Colombia*, 32 D2
Tupelo, *U.S.A.*, 27 J4
Tupiza, *Bolivia*, 34 E4
Turbat, *Pakistan*, 53 H6

Turbo, *Colombia*, 32 C2
Turin, *Italy*, 64 C2
Turkana, Lake, *Africa*, 73 G3
Turkey, *Asia, country*, 52 C4
Turkistan, *Kazakhstan*, 50 B2
Turkmenabat, *Turkmenistan*, 52 H4
Turkmenbasy, *Turkmenistan*, 52 F3
Turkmenistan, *Asia, country*, 52 G4
Turks and Caicos Islands, *North America*, 29 K3
Turku, *Finland*, 60 G3
Turpan, *China*, 50 F2
Turpan Depression, *China*, 50 G2
Tuscaloosa, *U.S.A.*, 27 J4
Tuvalu, *Oceania, country*, 38 E5
Tuxtla Gutierrez, *Mexico*, 28 F4
Tuzla, *Bosnia and Herzegovina*, 65 F2
Tuz, Lake, *Turkey*, 65 K4
Tver, *Russia*, 58 D2
Twin Falls, *U.S.A.*, 26 D2
Tynda, *Russia*, 55 G3
Tyrrhenian Sea, *Europe*, 64 D3
Tyumen, *Russia*, 59 K2

U

Ubangi, *Africa*, 72 C3
Uberaba, *Brazil*, 34 J3
Uberlandia, *Brazil*, 34 J3
Ubon Ratchathani, *Thailand*, 46 D4
Ucayali, *Peru*, 32 D5
Udaipur, *India*, 51 C6
Uddevalla, *Sweden*, 60 D4
Udon Thani, *Thailand*, 46 D4
Uele, *Democratic Republic of Congo*, 72 D3
Ufa, *Russia*, 59 H3
Uganda, *Africa, country*, 73 F3
Uitenhage, *South Africa*, 74 E6
Ujung Pandang, *Indonesia*, 45 E5
Ukhta, *Russia*, 54 C2
Ukraine, *Europe, country*, 58 C4
Ulan Bator, *Mongolia, national capital*, 48 G1
Ulanhot, *China*, 49 K1
Ulan Ude, *Russia*, 55 F3
Ulm, *Germany*, 62 D6
Uluru, *Australia*, 40 F5
Ulyanovsk, *Russia*, 59 F3
Uman, *Ukraine*, 61 J6
Ume, *Sweden*, 60 F2
Umea, *Sweden*, 60 G3
Umnak Island, *U.S.A.*, 25 C3
Umtata, *South Africa*, 74 E6
Unalaska Island, *U.S.A.*, 25 C3
Ungava Bay, *Canada*, 25 N3
Ungava Peninsula, *Canada*, 25 M2
Unimak Island, *U.S.A.*, 25 C3
United Arab Emirates, *Asia, country*, 53 F7
United Kingdom, *Europe, country*, 62 D3
United States of America, *North America, country*, 26 F3
Upington, *South Africa*, 74 D5
Uppsala, *Sweden*, 60 F4
Ural, *Asia*, 59 G4
Ural Mountains, *Russia*, 59 H2
Uray, *Russia*, 59 J1
Urganch, *Uzbekistan*, 50 A2
Urmia, *Iran*, 52 E4
Uruapan, *Mexico*, 28 D4
Urucui, *Brazil*, 33 K5
Uruguaiana, *Brazil*, 34 G5
Uruguay, *South America, country*, 34 G6
Urumqi, *China*, 50 F2
Usak, *Turkey*, 65 J4
Ushuaia, *Argentina*, 35 E10
Uskemen, *Kazakhstan*, 54 E3
Utah, *U.S.A., internal admin. area*, 26 D3
Utsjoki, *Finland*, 60 H1
Utsunomiya, *Japan*, 49 N3
Uy, *Asia*, 59 J3
Uyuni, *Bolivia*, 34 E4
Uzbekistan, *Asia, country*, 54 D3
Uzhhorod, *Ukraine*, 61 G6

GENERAL INDEX

Acknowledgements

Cover design by Hannah Ahmed   Managing editor: Gillian Doherty   Managing designer: Mary Cartwright

Every effort has been made to trace the copyright holders of the material in this book. If any rights have been omitted, the publishers offer to rectify this in any subsequent edition, following notification. The publishers are grateful to the following organizations and individuals for their contributions and permission to reproduce material (t=top, m=middle, b=bottom, l=left, r=right, bg = background):

© **Agripicture** 57br (Peter Dean). © **Air Photographics, Inc., CNOVS-969-20** 4tr. © Courtesy **CIA** 84-97. © **Craig Asquith** 11 projections, 14b, 15, 82.
© **Corbis** 6tr (Dan Guravich), 7tr (W. Perry Conway), 10 (Christopher Cormack), 12–13(Raymond Gehman), 12tr (Owen Franken), 13tr (Adam Woolfitt),
14tr (Bill Ross), 22bl (Richard Cummins), 23br (W. Perry Conway), 30b (Galen Rowell), 31tr (Eye Ubiquitous), 37br (Bates Littlehales),
42–43b (Michael S. Yamashita), 43br (Keren Su), 66–67b (Tom Brakefield), 67br (Gallo Images), 76bl (Galen Rowell), 78b (Wolfgang Kaehler).
© **Digital Vision** 1, 2–3, 4bl, 8–9bg, 16bg, 18–21bg, 24–29bg, 32–35bg, 38–41bg, 44–55bg, 56–57bg, 58–65bg, 68–75bg, 76br, 80–81bg, 84–97bg.
© **European Map Graphics Ltd** 5t, bm & br, 7bl, 16–21, 22–23 map, 24–29, 30–31 map, 32–35, 36–37 map, 38–41, 42–43 map, 44–55, 56–57 map,
58–65, 66–67 map, 68–75, 77, 79. © **Stephen Moncrieff** 4ml simple map, 6bl globes, 11 globes. © **NERC Satellite Station,** University of Dundee
www.sat.dundee.ac.html 9tl. © **PHOTO ESA** 8mr. © **Science Photo Library** 9br (European Space Agency), 76tr (Worldsat International), 78mr (NASA).
© **Still Pictures** 36–37t (Pascal Kobeh). © **UN/Mark Garten** 97b.